Entrepreneurship

JOHN R BESSANT

JOE TIDD

T0337932

WILEY

VP AND EDITORIAL DIRECTOR	Michael McDonald
EXECUTIVE EDITOR	Lise Johnson
SENIOR EDITORIAL MANAGER	Leah Michael
EDITORIAL ASSISTANT	Alden Farrar
CONTENT MANAGEMENT DIRECTOR	Lisa Wojcik
CONTENT MANAGER	Nichole Urban
SENIOR CONTENT SPECIALIST	Nicole Repasky
PRODUCTION EDITOR	Rajeshkumar Nallusamy
COVER PHOTO CREDIT	©Digital Vision./Getty Images

This book was set in 9.5/12.5 pt Source Sans Pro by SPi Global and printed and bound by Quad/Graphics.

Founded in 1807, John Wiley & Sons, Inc. has been a valued source of knowledge and understanding for more than 200 years, helping people around the world meet their needs and fulfill their aspirations. Our company is built on a foundation of principles that include responsibility to the communities we serve and where we live and work. In 2008, we launched a Corporate Citizenship Initiative, a global effort to address the environmental, social, economic, and ethical challenges we face in our business. Among the issues we are addressing are carbon impact, paper specifications and procurement, ethical conduct within our business and among our vendors, and community and charitable support. For more information, please visit our website: www.wiley.com/go/citizenship.

Copyright 2018 John Wiley & Sons, Inc. All rights reserved. No part of this publication may be reproduced, stored in a retrieval system, or transmitted in any form or by any means, electronic, mechanical, photocopying, recording, scanning or otherwise, except as permitted under Sections 107 or 108 of the 1976 United States Copyright Act, without either the prior written permission of the Publisher, or authorization through payment of the appropriate per-copy fee to the Copyright Clearance Center, Inc., 222 Rosewood Drive, Danvers, MA 01923 (Web site: www.copyright.com). Requests to the Publisher for permission should be addressed to the Permissions Department, John Wiley & Sons, Inc., 111 River Street, Hoboken, NJ 07030-5774, (201) 748-6011, fax (201) 748-6008, or online at: www.wiley.com/go/permissions.

Evaluation copies are provided to qualified academics and professionals for review purposes only, for use in their courses during the next academic year. These copies are licensed and may not be sold or transferred to a third party. Upon completion of the review period, please return the evaluation copy to Wiley. Return instructions and a free of charge return shipping label are available at: www.wiley.com/go/returnlabel. If you have chosen to adopt this textbook for use in your course, please accept this book as your complimentary desk copy. Outside of the United States, please contact your local sales representative.

ISBN: 978-1-119-22186-9 (PBK)
ISBN: 978-1-119-47849-2 (EVALC)

Library of Congress Cataloging in Publication Data:

SKY10050896_071123

LCCN: 2018007233

The inside back cover will contain printing identification and country of origin if omitted from this page. In addition, if the ISBN on the back cover differs from the ISBN on this page, the one on the back cover is correct.

Contents

13 Learning to Manage Entrepreneurship 187

Preface

New ventures that innovate are much more likely to create value, both private and social, but few new ventures are successful, and fewer manage to grow and prosper. Part of the challenge lies in the way we bridge the gap between a great idea and realizing its value, whether commercial or social. We now have a great deal of research understanding about the process of entrepreneurship, and this resource is an attempt to integrate that in a practical fashion for a wide audience. It is targeted at the needs of a growing body of students enrolled in degree programs around entrepreneurship and innovation, but is of interest to a wider group of people concerned with taking ideas forward, whether as start-ups or as part of new ventures within established organizations.

We draw upon the latest theories, research, and practice of entrepreneurship, including business model canvas, lean start-ups, and entrepreneurial effectuation, and propose tools and exercises to support understanding, training, and practice. We build upon the success of our Wiley portfolio: *Managing Innovation* (6th edition, 2018); *Innovation & Entrepreneurship* (3rd edition, 2015); *Strategic Innovation Management* (1st edition, 2015); and the associated web resource on the innovation portal (www.innovation-portal.info).

This resource is conceived as a hybrid, interactive ebook and printed student workbook with a practical "how to" focus, including online exercises, cases, and videos. To structure the material, we have adapted our popular process model, which we developed for *Innovation & Entrepreneurship* over three editions, but with less focus on innovation and more on mainstream entrepreneurship.

The resource covers:

Entrepreneurial Goals and Context

1. The entrepreneurial imperative
2. Social entrepreneurship
3. Globalization, development, and emerging markets
4. Sustainability

Recognising the Opportunity

5. Entrepreneurial creativity
6. Sources of inspiration
7. Identifying & assessing opportunities

Finding the Resources

8. Building the business case
9. Raising finance and resources
10. Developing the team
11. Exploiting networks

Developing the Venture

12. Developing new products & services
13. Creating a new venture
14. Growing the enterprise

Creating Value

15. Exploiting knowledge & intellectual property
16. Evolving the business model
17. Harvesting the benefits and value

Our growing experience with using the online portal is that it opens up many possibilities for additional and complementary material to build a platform around the text. Therefore, we have drawn from our extensive library of cases, media, tools, and activities to support this publication and to enable easier access to these via embedded resources. We have also developed a supporting Lecturer guide to help make full use of the resource in constructing a variety of courses and learning experiences, with activities aimed at different class sizes and modes of interaction, including support for assessment.

We welcome your feedback and invite you to share your experiences.

JOHN BESSANT AND JOE TIDD
March 2018

PROFESSOR JOHN BESSANT, BSC., PHD. Originally a chemical engineer, John Bessant has been active in the field of research and consultancy in technology and innovation management for over 35 years. He currently holds the Chair in Innovation and Entrepreneurship at the University of Exeter and has visiting appointments at the universities of Erlangen-Nuremburg and Queensland University of Technology. In 2003, he was elected a Fellow of the British Academy of Management and, in 2016, a Fellow of the International Society for Professional Innovation Management (ISPIM). He has acted as advisor to various national governments, international bodies (including the United Nations, World Bank, and OECD), and to many public and private sector organizations. He is the author of 30 books and many articles on the topic and has lectured and consulted widely around the world.

See www.johnbessant.org for more details.

PROFESSOR JOE TIDD, BSC, MSC, MBA, DPHIL Joe Tidd is a physicist with subsequent degrees in technology policy and business administration. He is professor of technology and innovation management at SPRU, visiting Professor at University College London, and previously at Cass Business School, Copenhagen Business School, and Rotterdam School of Management. Dr. Tidd was previously Deputy Director of SPRU, as well as Head of the Innovation Group and Director of the Executive MBA Program at Imperial College.

He has worked as policy adviser to the CBI (Confederation of British Industry), presented expert evidence to three Select Committee Enquiries held by the House of Commons and House of Lords, and was the only academic member of the UK Government Innovation Review. He is a founding partner of Management Masters, LLP.

He was a researcher for the five-year International Motor Vehicle Program of the Massachusetts Institute of Technology (MIT), which identified Lean Production, and has worked on technology and innovation management projects for consultants Arthur D. Little, CAP Gemini, and McKinsey; numerous technology-based firms, including American Express Technology, Applied Materials, ASML, BOC Edwards, BT, Marconi, National Power, NKT, Nortel Networks, and Petrobras; and international agencies, such as UNESCO in Africa. He is the winner of the Price Waterhouse Urwick Medal for contribution to management teaching and research, and the Epton Prize from the R&D Society.

He has written nine books and more than sixty papers on the management of technology and innovation, with **17,000** research citations. He is Managing Editor of the *International Journal of Innovation Management*, the official journal of International Society of Professional Innovation Management. He hosts the Innovation Masters YouTube channel, and is part of the Intrapreneurship Hub, a collaborative venture between Sussex, Bocconi, and Renmin business schools.

Acknowledgments

We would like to thank all those colleagues and students at SPRU, Exeter, CENTRIM, Imperial College, and elsewhere who have provided feedback on our work over many years. We are also grateful for the more formal reviews by various anonymous reviewers whose comments and suggestions helped develop this new resource.

Thanks are also due to Dave Francis, Howard Rush, Stefan Kohn, Girish Prabhu, Richard Philpott, David Simoes-Brown, Alastair Ross, Suzana Moreira, Michael Bartl, Roy Sandbach, Lynne Maher, Philip Cullimore, Helle-Vibeke Carstensen, Helen King, Patrick McLaughlin, Melissa Clark-Reynolds, Boyi Li, Simon Tucker, Ana Sena, Victor Cui, Emma Taylor, Armin Rau, Francisco Pinheiro, David Overton, Michelle Lowe, Gerard Harkin, Dorothea Seebode, Fabian Schlage, Catherina van Delden, John Thesmer, Tim Craft, Bettina von Stamm, Mike Pitts, and Kathrin Moeslein for their help in creating case studies and podcast/video material for the text and website. Particular thanks are due to Anna Trifilova and Emily Bessant for their help in background research and assembling many of the web-based cases.

As always we're really grateful for the help and support of the extended team at Wiley, especially Steve Hardman and Deb Egleton, with whom we worked on the early ideas and Leah Michael, Jenny Ng, and Courtney Luzzi, who subsequently picked up the ball and ran with it.

Introduction to Entrepreneurship

LEARNING OBJECTIVES

By the end of this chapter you will be able to understand:

1. the idea of entrepreneurship as creating value from ideas

2. the idea that innovation is enabled by entrepreneurs

3. the motivations behind being an entrepreneur

4. the characteristics associated with being an entrepreneur

5. the process through which entrepreneurs make innovation happen

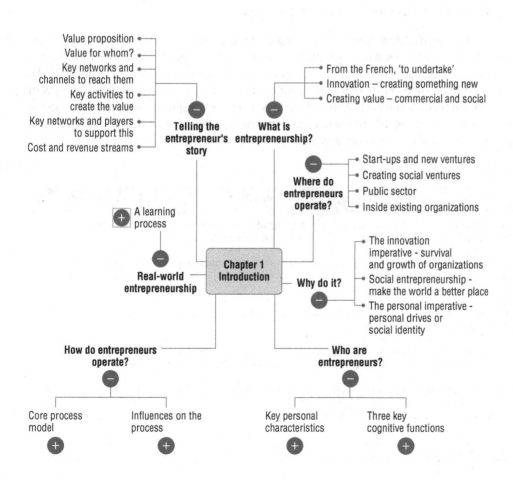

- Value proposition
- Value for whom?
- Key networks and channels to reach them
- Key activities to create the value
- Key networks and players to support this
- Cost and revenue streams

Telling the entrepreneur's story

What is entrepreneurship?
- From the French, 'to undertake'
- Innovation – creating something new
- Creating value – commercial and social

Where do entrepreneurs operate?
- Start-ups and new ventures
- Creating social ventures
- Public sector
- Inside existing organizations

A learning process

Real-world entrepreneurship

Chapter 1 Introduction

Why do it?
- The innovation imperative - survival and growth of organizations
- Social entrepreneurship - make the world a better place
- The personal imperative - personal drives or social identity

How do entrepreneurs operate?
- Core process model
- Influences on the process

Who are entrepreneurs?
- Key personal characteristics
- Three key cognitive functions

1.0 | What is Entrepreneurship?

These days, you'd have to be deaf and blind not to notice the "I" word – innovation. It's everywhere! It leaps out at you from a thousand mission statements and strategy documents, each stressing how important innovation is to "our customers/our shareholders/our business/our future," and most often, "our survival and growth." Innovation shouts at you from advertisements for products ranging from hairspray to hospital care. It nestles deep in the heart of our history books, pointing out how far and for how long it has shaped our lives. And it is on the lips of every politician, recognizing that our lifestyles are constantly shaped and reshaped by the process of innovation.

But innovation doesn't just magically appear. Change requires someone to make it happen, and that someone is an entrepreneur. The word comes from the French, "*entreprendre*" which means "to undertake," and typical dictionary definitions see an entrepreneur as:

> "*a person who organizes and manages any enterprise, especially a business, usually with considerable initiative and risk.*"

(Dictonary.com)

But it's not just about running a business; there's an element of creating something *new*. That's where innovation comes in. Innovation is all about changing what we offer the world and the ways in which we create and deliver that offering, and there's plenty of scope for entrepreneurs to find new or improved ways of meeting that challenge.

As the famous management writer Peter Drucker put it:

> "*Innovation is the specific tool of entrepreneurs, the means by which they exploit change as an opportunity for a different business or service*"[1]

In other words, "*innovation is what entrepreneurs do,*" and we can think of many examples, like the Steve Jobs/Steve Wozniak Apple team, Stelios Haji-Iannou of EasyJet, Mark Zuckerberg of Facebook, or Sergey Brin and Larry Page of Google. This isn't a new thing; entrepreneurs like Thomas Edison and Henry Ford played an important role in shaping the twentieth century with their innovations. And it isn't always about making money; major social innovations like the Open University in the UK are the work of entrepreneurs like Michael Young. **Table 1.1** gives some examples of entrepreneurs and the innovations they are associated with.

TABLE 1.1 Examples of Entrepreneurs

Entrepreneur	Innovation
Muhamed Younis	Concerned about the difficulties people on low incomes in Bangladesh were having in raising loans, he developed the concept of "microfinance" and established the Grameen Bank as a vehicle for supporting them.
James Dyson	An engineer and long-standing inventor, he combined insight and perseverance to reinvent a whole range of domestic appliances including vacuum cleaners, fans, and drying systems. His start-up business is now worth several billion, and operates on the international stage.
Amancio Ortega	From early days pedaling his bicycle around northeastern Spain to deliver his products, he grew a global textile empire (Inditex) with major brands including Zara.
Govindappa Venkataswamy	A retired eye surgeon who wanted to bring safe, reliable, low-cost care to low-income villagers in India, he developed the Aravind Eye Care System which has restored eyesight for millions of the world's poor.
Neil Tomlinson	Concerned with one of the big humanitarian problems, he founded Aquapax to bring clean water to disaster areas.
Jon Buscemi and Ryan Babenzien	Two entrepreneurs who saw an opportunity for a start-up competing in the high brand-value footwear space – Greats
Megan Grassell	Annoyed at the difficulties in finding suitable clothes for her early teenage sister, she started Yellowberry to meet this need.
Alex and Robbie Georgiou	Long-standing interest in sustainability led this pair to establish Espresso Mushroom – a start-up based on environmentally friendly fertilizer.

1.1   Where do Entrepreneurs Operate?

We often think of the start-up as the typical model of entrepreneurs in action, but there are many other situations where we can see entrepreneurship. It's the same basic process but played out in all sorts of different places. Sometimes that will involve creating a new venture from zero, but it's also the mechanism through which established organizations renew themselves. Coming up with new ideas for projects – new products and services, new processes – is a key part of business life, and that's something which is driven by internal entrepreneurs.

And it's not just in the business world; entrepreneurs are also involved in new ventures which create social value and make the world a better place. They may be start-ups created by passionate individuals, or they may be changes brought about by people working in large public-sector organizations, trying to improve public services. We can find them in the charity sector, in aid agencies, in voluntary advice centers, in soup kitchens, and in community shops.

Local organizations in which people spend some of their "spare" time are also prime sites for new projects – coming up with a plan for a community hall, or a new gym for the school are typical examples. And they don't magically appear; they involve raising the money, twisting people's arms to help with time, skills, and labor, and managing the project from gleam in the eye to the final day when everyone can celebrate the new arrival on the local scene. That's a classic example of entrepreneurship in action. In fact, the more we think about it, the more we realize there are entrepreneurs operating anywhere that change is happening.

This idea of entrepreneurship driving innovation to create value – social and commercial – across the life cycle of organizations is central to this book. **Table 1.2** gives some examples.

And it's rarely a complete solo act – entrepreneurship is usually more of a multiplayer game. There may be someone at the center with the vision and passion, but behind them, there's often a team helping to realize the vision and make the great idea actually happen. And as the idea grows, so does the network of players linked to making it become real.

Entrepreneurship is a hot topic, but what is it actually about, and how might we make it happen? That's the purpose of this book, and in this chapter, we'll try and lay some foundations about what it is and how it works. In particular, we're interested in both the character – the entrepreneur – and the process they go through to create value through something new.

TABLE 1.2   Entrepreneurship and Innovation

Stage in life cycle of an organization	Start-up	Growth	Sustain/scale	Renew
Creating commercial value	Individual entrepreneur exploiting new technology or market opportunity	Growing the business through adding new products/ services or moving into new markets	Building a portfolio of incremental and radical innovation to sustain the business and/or spread its influence into new markets	Returning to the radical frame-breaking kind of innovation which began the business and enables it to move forward as something very different
Creating social value	Social entrepreneur, passionately concerned with improving or changing something in their immediate environment	Developing the ideas and engaging others in a network for change – perhaps in a region or around a key issue	Spreading the idea widely, diffusing it to other communities of social entrepreneurs, engaging links with mainstream players like public sector agencies	Changing the system – and then acting as an agent for the next wave of change

1.3 | Why do It?

What motivates someone to be an entrepreneur? As we'll see, it takes a lot of time, energy, passion, and sheer hard work. So why would anyone want to do it? Research suggests that it's a mixture of external forces – threats and opportunities driving change – and internal factors. Let's take a look at each of these, starting with the outside perspective.

Innovation makes a huge difference to organizations of all shapes and sizes. The logic is simple: if we don't change what we offer the world (products and services) and how we create and deliver them, we risk being overtaken by others who do. At the limit, it's about survival, and history is very clear on this point: survival is not compulsory! Those enterprises which survive do so because they are capable of regular and focused change.

VIDEO: Tim Jones, of Innovation Leaders & Future Agenda, on Identifying Effective Innovations

Tim Jones has insight about the link between successful innovating organizations and how they invest at https://www.youtube.com/watch?v=YZDDr8JUxIw. Link included with permission of ISPIM.

On the plus side, innovation is also strongly associated with *growth*. New business is created by new ideas, by the process of creating competitive advantage in what a firm can offer. Economists have argued for decades over the exact nature of the relationship but they are generally agreed that innovation accounts for a sizeable proportion of economic growth.

Innovation in Action: Joseph Schumpeter

One of the most significant figures in this area of economic theory was Joseph Schumpeter, who wrote extensively on the subject. He had a distinguished career as an economist and served as Minister for Finance in the Austrian government. His argument was simple: entrepreneurs will seek to use technological innovation – a new product/service or a new process for making it – to get strategic advantage. For a while, this may be the only example of the innovation so the entrepreneur can expect to make a lot of money – what Schumpeter calls "monopoly profits." But of course, other entrepreneurs will see what he has done and try to imitate it, with the result that other innovations emerge, and the resulting "swarm" of new ideas chips away at the monopoly profits until an equilibrium is reached. At this point, the cycle repeats itself – our original entrepreneur (or someone else) looks for the next innovation which will rewrite the rules of the game, and off we go again. Schumpeter talks of a process of "creative destruction" in which there is a constant search to create something new which simultaneously destroys the old rules and establishes new ones – all driven by the search for new sources of profits.

In his view "[What counts is] competition from the new commodity, the new technology, the new source of supply, the new type of organization. . . competition which. . . strikes not at the margins of the profits and the outputs of the existing firms but at their foundations and their very lives."[2]

Survival and growth pose a problem for established players, but a huge opportunity for newcomers to rewrite the rules of the game. One person's problem is another's opportunity, and the nature of innovation is that it is fundamentally about *entrepreneurship*. The skill to spot opportunities and create new ways to exploit them is at the heart of the innovation process. Entrepreneurs are risk-takers, but they calculate the costs of taking a bright idea forward against the potential gains if they succeed in doing something different – especially if that involves upstaging the players already in the game.

Of course, it's not just about making money. There are many areas in which this "innovation imperative" is about creating social value. For example, in the wake of humanitarian crises like natural or man-made disasters, innovation really can be a matter of life and death. Look at the example of the Aravind Eye Care System,† a response by a "silver entrepreneur," Dr. Venkataswamy,

†Case study also available on the book companion website

who decided that his post-retirement project was to bring safe, reliable eye surgery to millions of people in the poorest villages in India. His experience as an eye surgeon helped, but he had to demonstrate real entrepreneurial skills to bring the costs of a cataract operation down from $300 in the big Indian cities to around $30 if his project was to succeed. He managed it, and thirty years later, the model he developed has meant that millions of people around the world who would otherwise be blind are now able to see.

Everyday innovation in social and community activities – healthcare, education, transportation, housing and shelter – depends on a continuous stream of improvements to make better, more customized services available at costs which are sustainable. The challenge of living on one planet with finite resources opens up another huge arena for innovation, much of it driven by a desire to make more sustainable living a viable prospect. And the wide world of arts and culture is another sphere in which individual ideas carried forward with passion can create wonderful new opportunities and experiences. All involve innovation driven by entrepreneurship. (We'll look in more detail at "social entrepreneurship" in the next chapter).

And for the sake of completeness, we shouldn't forget the criminal fraternity. Not all innovation is positive in terms of the value it creates, and the dark world of crime is driven by a continuing stream of innovation, not least in the murky world of cybercrime.

But entrepreneurs are not machines; they are human beings, and their inner makeup plays an important role in answering the question "Why be an entrepreneur?" Research suggests that there are often powerful internal drives, for example, to achieve recognition or obtain a sense of self-worth, or to demonstrate the ability to "make a mark on the world." Entrepreneurs are often characterized by a high level of what psychologists call "need for achievement" (nAch).

It's not just internal identity. We are social creatures, and another key psychological theme is that our sense of who we are comes from our interactions with others. "Social identity" theory suggests that entrepreneurs create a sense of positive identity through engaging in innovation, which helps fulfill themselves, but which also connects to a wider community that respects and values them for this contribution.

We'll come back to some of these internal psychological themes in Chapter 7.

1.4   Who are Entrepreneurs?

Close your eyes and imagine an entrepreneur. Chances are you are picturing someone like Mark Zuckerberg, Beyonce Knowles, Steve Jobs, or Richard Branson. You'd be right in that these are all good examples, but the risk in picking cases like these is that they tend to reinforce the idea that entrepreneurs are somehow different, a breed apart.

One good way to remind ourselves that they have feet of clay is to look at some of the early pictures of them, looking decidedly less confident and assured! And it's worth remembering that many of them only succeeded after several early failures and false starts.

This "hero/heroine" model of entrepreneurs is at odds with the reality that everyone could become an entrepreneur. There is nothing specific in the genetic makeup. Entrepreneurs are made, not born.

That's not to say it is easy; much of the research on entrepreneurs suggests that they practice hard at the craft. They learn and develop skills, rehearsing and improving them to the point where they are able to turn their hand to many different ventures using the same capabilities.

Coming up with good ideas is what human beings are good at. We have this facility already fitted as standard equipment in our brains! But taking those ideas forward is not quite so simple, and most new ideas fail. It takes a particular mix of energy, insight, belief, and determination to push against these odds; it also requires the judgment to know when to stop banging against the brick wall and move on to something else.

It's important here to remember a key point: new ventures often fail, but it is the ventures, rather than the people, which do so. Successful entrepreneurs recognize that failure is an intrinsic part of the process. They learn from mistakes, understanding where and when timing, market conditions, technological uncertainties, etc., mean that even a great idea isn't going to work. They also recognize that, while the idea itself may have had its weaknesses, they have not personally failed. Instead, they learned some useful insights to carry over to their next venture.

Entrepreneurs in Action: Failure breeds success

Thomas Edison was a pretty successful entrepreneur with over 1,000 patents to his name and the reputation for bringing many key technologies into widespread use, including the phonograph, the electric telegraph, and the light bulb; he also founded the General Electric Company, which is still a major player today. He is famous for his attitude towards failure, typified by his search for the right material to make the filament for his incandescent light bulb, for which he explored over 1,000 different options. He is reported as having said that the process did not involve failure so much as "the elimination of a design that didn't work, so we must be getting close."

We've learned a lot through research about the nature of entrepreneurs and the process they engage in to create innovation. Sometimes it's a solo act, but very often it's about networks of resources, mobilized and orchestrated to help achieve a clear vision. Entrepreneurs are multiskilled, able to see things, build clear focused visions, engage others in those visions, organize and network to achieve them, and manage the process of convincing others along the way, clearing the path to successful implementation. In particular, research suggests that successful entrepreneurs share three cognitive functions:

- perception, the ability to see things differently from others and embrace novelty;
- fear response, the ability to cope with fear of uncertainty and of failure;
- social intelligence, the ability to communicate and socialize a new idea.

Question:

What do you think are typical characteristics associated with entrepreneurs?

When we see them in action we recognize entrepreneurs by characteristic behaviors like:

Challenging – breaking the frame, opening up existing situations to new perceptions

Creating – finding new patterns, new constructions to put on a set of elements in a situation

Tolerating ambiguity – being able to hold several ideas at the same time

(Calculated) risk-taking – Experimenting and learning through trying out ideas, even if the prototypes fail

Articulating a vision – elaborating and 'coloring in' the picture to make it real to others

Selling – being good at convincing others of their point of view;

Networking – being able to connect with a wide range of people.

That's an extensive list and there are plenty more we could add. In fact, if we were writing a job description for an entrepreneur, the advertisement might read like this:

Wanted!

Visionary, creative individual with energy and passion, able to communicate ideas fluently who can engage others in the excitement of bringing innovative projects into being. You will be comfortable with uncertainty, ambiguity and risk taking – but not a gambler. Able to see the bigger picture you know how to respond to problems as challenges. An experienced team player you can create effective team dynamics and foster creative ideas while managing and resolving creative conflicts. While you can tolerate failure as an essential avenue to learning you don't repeat mistakes and are willing if necessary, to break the rules.

This may sound like a pretty demanding job description, but the good news is that we now know a lot about how to develop these skills. They have been extensively studied and researched, and we can model and practice them to build up our capabilities as entrepreneurs. In the book, we'll look at them in more detail and give you an opportunity to explore and develop them. But before we do that, we'll finish this chapter by looking at one more important question: *How* do entrepreneurs transform ideas into value?

1.5   How do Entrepreneurs Operate?

One of the most important things successful entrepreneurs recognize is that innovation isn't like the cartoons, where a light bulb flashes on above someone's head, and suddenly, there you have an innovation.

The reality is that the original bright idea needs shaping, developing, and building into something which creates value – personal, social, or commercial. And this process involves a journey through a number of stages, from initial gleam in the eye to successfully applied idea. Understanding the steps on the way and navigating past the roadblocks and obstacles are a key part of the entrepreneur's skill set.

Typically, the journey has the following stations:

- Finding/ recognizing an opportunity – coming up with the idea
- Mobilizing resources – articulating and sharing the vision, building a network of support, convincing others
- Making the idea happen – managing the change project, dealing with the uncertainties and surprises
- Capturing value – adoption and diffusion, securing the benefits, capturing the learning for next time

Whether we are looking at an individual entrepreneur bringing her idea into action or a team within a multimillion-dollar corporation launching the latest in a stream of new products, the same basic framework applies.

Creating the Context for Success

It's all very well putting a basic process for turning ideas into reality into place. But it doesn't take place in a vacuum; it is subject to a range of internal and external influences which shape what is possible and what actually emerges. This process is shaped and influenced by a variety of factors. In particular, innovation needs:

- *Clear strategic leadership and direction*, plus the commitment of resources to make this happen. Innovation is about taking risks, and going into new and sometimes completely unexplored spaces. We don't want to gamble, simply changing things for their own sake or because the fancy takes us. No organization has resources to waste in that scattergun fashion; innovation needs a strategy. But equally, we need to have a degree of courage and leadership, steering the organization away from what everyone else is doing or what we've always done and into new spaces.

  In the case of the individual entrepreneur, this challenge translates into one in which a clear personal vision can be shared in ways which engage and motivate others to "buy in" and contribute their time, energy, money, etc., to help make it happen. Without a compelling vision, it is unlikely that the venture will get off the ground.

- *An innovative organization* in which the structure and climate enable people to deploy their creativity and share their knowledge to bring about change. It's easy to find prescriptions for innovative organizations which highlight the need to eliminate stifling bureaucracy, unhelpful structures, brick walls blocking communication, and other factors stopping good ideas from getting through. But we must be careful not to fall into the chaos trap; not all innovation works in organic, loose, informal environments or "skunk works," and these types of organization can sometimes act against the interests of successful innovation. We need to determine appropriate organization, that is, the most suitable organization given the operating contingencies. Too little order and structure may be as bad as too much.

  This is one area where start-ups often have a major advantage; by definition, they are small organizations (often one-person ventures) with a high degree of communication and cohesion. They are bound together by a shared vision, and they have high levels of cooperation and trust, giving them enormous flexibility. But the downside of being small is a lack of resources, and so successful start-ups are often those which can build a network around them through which to tap into needed key resources. Building and managing such networks are key factors in creating an extended form of organization.

- *Pro-active links* across boundaries inside the organization and to the many external agencies who can play a part in the innovation process: suppliers, customers, sources of finance, and skilled resources, and of knowledge, etc. Twenty-first century innovation is most certainly not a solo act, but a multiplayer game across boundaries inside the organization and to the many external agencies who can play a part in the innovation process. These days, it's about a global game, one in which connections and the ability to find, form, and deploy creative relationships is of the essence. Once again, this idea of successful lone entrepreneurs and small-scale start-ups as network builders is critical. It's not necessary to know or have everything in hand, as long as you know where and how to get it!

1.6 | Real-World Entrepreneurship

The process model build (see Section 1.5) gives us a helpful map, and this is certainly useful for planning a journey. But how does the journey actually happen? What elements do we need to consider as we go through this journey? Who are the players? How do they interact? What challenges do they face, and how do they overcome them? The reality is, of course, that the journey is never as simple as the map suggests.

What we've learned about the process is that it involves a lot of "probe and learn," trying things out, and (if they don't work) revising our ideas and trying again. Many of the powerful methods now available – ideas like the "lean start-up" (which we'll look at in more detail later) – are based on the principle of fast cycles of learning, failing, pivoting, and gradually moving forward.[3, 4]

Instead of seeing the model as a series of stages, we might see it as a sequence of divergence – exploring possibilities, trying things out, experimenting – and then convergence, closing in on key options and moving on to the next stage. This "explore/focus" approach (see **Figure 1.1**) is very much a part of the "agile" approach to innovation which emphasizes learning and experimentation.

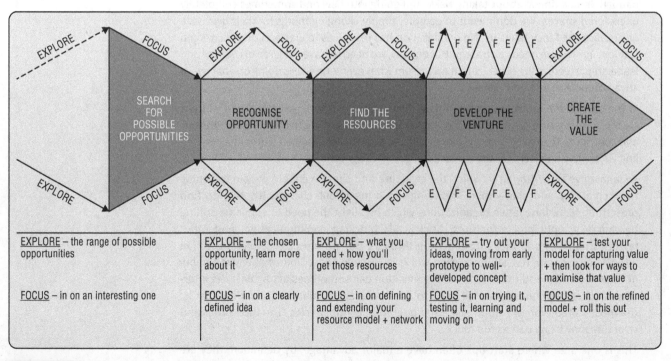

FIGURE 1.1 The "Explore/Focus" Approach

And successful entrepreneurs reach their goals less through following a detailed plan than in being flexible, adapting to the lessons they learn along the way and mobilizing the resources they can muster in creative ways to deal with the challenges. Again this "effectuation" model is one which we'll look at in more detail as we go through the book.[5]

DEEPER DIVE: Effectuation and Bricolage

Read the Deeper Dive: Effectuation and Bricolage document in the ebook or from the book companion site.

This doesn't mean that the process model build outlined earlier in Section 1.5 is useless – far from it. But we should recognize it as a map of the journey and make sure we have done some thinking about how the journey might actually take place. One way we can do this is to imagine telling a story of the journey and gradually elaborating on and adding to that story as we make the journey – an approach we'll look at briefly in this final section.

1.7 | Telling the Entrepreneur's Story

Any new venture is a story. It starts with an idea – something which will be valued by somebody. Maybe it's a new thing, maybe a new service, but it has to mean something to somebody; otherwise, it's just a lonely idea.

As soon as you start thinking about who it is for, you have your first characters in the story. Think about them, who they are, what they do, why they will value your new thing. Paint the picture, make the sketch, bring them to life.

And as you think about them, go back to your idea and make that a little more detailed. How can it be made attractive to your new characters? Bring it to life not just as your dream but as something which they might find valuable.

And, unless your idea is for something the world has never seen before, why is your idea better than someone else's? Why will your characters choose it rather than something else? Think about them and how it fits with their lifestyle, why it would matter to them. Most importantly, why would they pay for it and how much?

Answering that question means you need to think about the value they would place on it once again. If it is a well-made, nicely served cup of coffee, why would they pay you more than they pay for the coffee they can get next door? If it is a handmade chair, beautifully crafted out of old polished wood, why would they pay twice the price of a simple chair they can buy from IKEA?

As your story develops, you can think about how can you reach them. Where do they meet you and your idea? Do they come to the market square and find you and your idea at a stall? Do they go online and find it via the internet? Do they learn about it from friends and come knocking at your door? Do you have a shop? What does it look like? Bring the different ways to life; develop the sketches of how they encounter you and your idea.

Of course, you are interested in more than one person taking up your idea, so repeat the above, adding more characters to your story. Maybe they are all versions of the same person, maybe there are different characters who find you through different channels.

Now step back for a moment and look at what you've been doing. You've begun to tell a story; it looks like an early sketch or draft of a film script or a piece of theatre, or maybe the outline of a novel. Try telling it as a story out loud, or even better, to someone else. And as you tell it, go back and fill in more detail.

We need to add some more to this simple tale. The idea doesn't just happen. It is created by someone (maybe you, maybe you and others).

What's involved in making your idea real so that your user can value it and buy it? What things have to happen to bring it to life? Think of this as a subplot in your story. Maybe it is about buying the wood, cutting the pieces, assembling them into a beautiful chair, and polishing and finishing it with care and pride. Where is the workshop, what does it look like? What tools are you using, and where did they come from? Where do you get your wood, and how do you choose it, where do you store it? Flesh out the story about how your chair comes into being, and who's involved in that process. Add more characters into the story.

Or maybe it is about buying the ingredients and then making the perfect cup of fresh steaming coffee. What does the china look like? Where did you buy it? What about the coffee machinery – a simple kettle and cafetiere, or a complex silver Italian super machine? Once again, bring the story to life: the coffee doesn't just appear, it comes about as a result of different activities.

And think about the "who" in all of this. You have some new characters to add to your story, some of them walk-on parts, people who come and go but don't play much of a role. But there may be others who feature regularly and are a key part of what you do. Maybe your wood supplier is important because he delivers great quality and on time so you are never waiting for what you need to make great chairs. Maybe you have a friend who helps you in the café dealing with the early morning rush of people wanting their fresh coffee on the way to work.

The story is beginning to take shape. You now have a cast of characters and a core story about creating and delivering value through your idea. Try telling it again as a chronological sequence; what has to happen in order for the next thing to happen, and the next? How does the story develop? Maybe it's a linear process from developing the idea and then trying it out on your market. Or maybe it's two parallel streams: one about creating the idea while the other is simultaneously exploring the market side.

Now let's add some more detail. If this thing is going to work, it needs resources – time, energy, money. Think of them as characters of a different sort, and position them first of all on the left-hand side, waiting in the wings to come on stage. Try and develop the detail again – how much time, what kinds of materials, how much money?

Think about when you would need them, what has to be there from the start, what comes into play as you start to develop the idea? How do the resources flow to support the creation and delivery of the idea?

Unless you have a wealthy benefactor or an indulgent parent, you are going to need to get those resources from somewhere. Where do the revenues (the resources flowing in) come from? If you have read them right, then your market will pay for your idea, and you'll have their money flowing back in. Where else might revenues come from? Maybe loans, or maybe you can sell the idea to someone else as a license or franchise. Create a cast of characters on this side of the story.

And, just as before, try and work out the timing of the revenue flows.

Tell the story again, this time focusing on trying to keep the balance between the income and the outflow of resources. If this flow doesn't at least balance, you're in trouble; your idea is going to cost more than it brings in, and pretty soon, you'll run out of resources. How can you increase the number of characters or their timing to keep this balance? Could you reduce some of the costs?

You've now got the very basic outline of a story – a storyboard, a picture of how the themes will develop, and the movement of different characters and scenery. Now start to run the story as if it were a movie, looking for the flow and watching what happens over time as it develops. Imagine (on your own and then telling it to and with others) how it plays out. What happens?

A key part of this imagining is to think about what happens when external things come into the picture, things you hadn't originally thought about. What if there is a new competitor who comes along and copies your idea? How could you tell the story to make sure that doesn't spoil your happy ending? Can you protect your idea in some way? Or can you make your relationships with your customers so personal that someone else trying to muscle in isn't trusted?

Or what if the costs of some of your materials go up suddenly? Or a key resource or person disappears from the story? Try and imagine a whole set of "what ifs" and think about how you would change the story to make sure they didn't spoil the happy ending. Of course, it's not just bad things that can happen "out there"; there are also positive things. What if a large company comes along and likes your product so much they ask to buy it from you, or to license it from you?

What if you get an unsolicited rave review on a website from a celebrity talking about your product? What if your service gets featured in an influential business newspaper as an example of an exciting new start-up? What if an old college friend (a marketing expert) offers to help you with some important introductions to key networks and customers?

Like any story, it can develop in many ways. It makes sense early on to sketch it out as a draft and run it a few times, finding out where it needs strengthening, where it isn't clear. The happy ending is when you are able to use your idea to create value, and enough revenues flow to help you maintain and develop, maybe building on the idea, maybe launching a new one.

The whole idea of the storyboard is to make explicit and visual your thoughts about how your idea could create value. The more detailed the imagined picture, the less you will be surprised, and the more prepared you will be. And in creating it in this visual storytelling form, you make it possible for other people to share your vision. Sure, they may challenge and question it, but that could be very useful; they may see something which you don't. At some stage, you may well need to "pitch" your story to someone else to get their support – maybe an investor, maybe a key partner. By telling them a well-developed story and inviting them to add to it, tell it in their way, you are bringing them on board or at least around the table, perhaps giving you some sharp advice, perhaps asking you a key question which you have missed.

Throughout the book, we'll be exploring different aspects of being an entrepreneur and developing an innovative venture. We'll use the storyboard as a framework to hang these ideas on, giving you more questions to ask and themes to look at as you build you own venture. And we'll provide with you a wide variety of tools to help you explore and answer those questions.

Chapter Summary

- Innovation is about growth, about recognizing opportunities for doing something new and implementing those ideas to create some kind of value. It could be business growth; it could be social change. But at its heart is the creative human spirit, the urge to make change in our environment.

- Innovation is also a survival imperative. If an organization doesn't change what it offers the world and the ways in which it creates and delivers its offerings, it may well be in trouble. And innovation contributes to competitive success in many different ways: it's a *strategic* resource to getting the organization where it is trying to go, be it delivering shareholder value for private sector firms, providing better public services, or enabling the start-up and growth of new enterprises.

- Innovation doesn't just happen. It is driven by *entrepreneurship*. This powerful mixture of energy, vision, passion, commitment, judgment, and risk-taking provides the motive power behind the innovation process. It's the same whether we are talking about a solo start-up venture or a key group within an established organization trying to renew its products or services.

- Innovation doesn't happen simply because we hope it will. It's a complex process which carries risks and needs careful and systematic *management*. Innovation isn't a single event, like the light bulb going off above a cartoon character's head. It's an

extended process of picking up on ideas for change and turning them through into effective reality. The core entrepreneurial process involves four steps:

  ○ recognizing opportunities
  ○ finding resources
  ○ developing the venture
  ○ capturing value

The challenge comes in doing this in an organized fashion and being able to repeat the trick.

- This core process doesn't take place in a vacuum. We also know that it is strongly influenced by many factors. In particular, innovation needs:

  ○ clear strategic leadership and direction, plus the commitment of resources to make this happen

  ○ an innovative organization in which the structure and climate enable people to deploy their creativity and share their knowledge to bring about change

  ○ proactive links across boundaries inside the organization and to the many external agencies who can play a part in the innovation process (suppliers, customers, sources of finance, skilled resources and of knowledge, etc.).

Key Terms

Effectuation theory of entrepreneurship which suggests that rather than work with simple causal models, entrepreneurs manage the innovation process through building on the resources which they have.

Entrepreneurship the powerful mixture of energy, vision, passion, commitment, judgement and risk-taking, which provides the motive power behind the innovation process.

Incremental innovation small improvements to existing products, services or processes - 'doing what we do, but better'.

Innovation the process of translating ideas into value: social or commercial.

Invention coming up with a new idea

Lean start-up an approach to managing the entrepreneurship process which stressed the use of multiple short experimentation and learning cycles, rather than a single 'master' plan

nAch need for achievement, a psychological theory which suggests that entrepreneurs are motivated by their desire to make a mark upon the world

Radical innovation significantly different changes to products, services or processes – 'doing something completely different'.

Social innovation, social entrepreneurship creating new ventures where the primary goal is social change (making the world a better place), rather than commercial advantage

System innovation (sometimes called Architectural innovation) changes in the whole system, for example moving from that computer design to a completely different way of processing information

References

[1] Drucker, P. (1985). *Innovation and entrepreneurship*. New York: Harper and Row.

[2] Schumpeter, J. (2006). *Capitalism, socialism and democracy*. 6th ed. London: Routledge.

[3] Ries, E. (2011). *The Lean Startup: How Today's Entrepreneurs Use Continuous Innovation to Create Radically Successful Businesses*. New York: Crown.

[4] Blank, S. (2013). Why the Lean Start-Up Changes Everything. *Harvard Business Review*, 91(5), p. 63-72.

[5] Sarasvathy, S. (2008). *Effectuation: Elements of entrepreneurial expertise*. Cheltenham: Edward Elgar.

CHAPTER 2

Social and Sustainable Entrepreneurship

LEARNING OBJECTIVES

By the end of this chapter, you will be able to understand:

1. Social entrepreneurship and social innovation

2. Sustainability as a key area for innovation

3. Social entrepreneurship as an organized and disciplined process rather than well-meaning but unfocused intervention

4. The difficulties in managing what is just as much an uncertain and risky process as "conventional" economically motivated innovation

5. The key themes in thinking about how to manage this process effectively

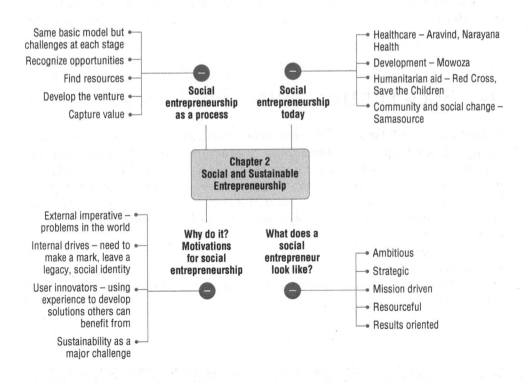

2.0 So You Want to Change the World?

In this book, we're looking at the challenge of *change* – and how individuals and groups of entrepreneurs, working alone or inside organizations, try and bring this about. We've seen that innovation is not a simple flash of inspiration but an extended and organized process of turning bright ideas into successful reality.

Above all, we've seen that getting innovation to happen depends on a focused and determined drive – a passion to change things which we call "entrepreneurship." Essentially, this is about being prepared to challenge and change, to take (calculated) risks, and put energy and enthusiasm into the venture, picking up and enthusing other supporters along the way. If we think about successful entrepreneurs, they are typically ambitious, mission-driven, passionate, strategic (not just impulsive), resourceful, and results-oriented. And we can think of plenty of names to fit this frame: Bill Gates (Microsoft), Cher Wang (co-founder of HTC), Anita Roddick (The Body Shop), Richard Branson (Virgin), James Dyson (Dyson), Beyoncé Knowles (entertainer), Larry Page and Sergey Brin (Google), or Jeff Bezos (Amazon) and Sarah Blakely (founder of Spanx and the youngest self-made female billionaire in America).

But we could also apply these terms to describe people whose motivation was to change the world, to make it a better place. These are "social entrepreneurs," and there is a long tradition of this kind of innovation. People like Florence Nightingale, Elizabeth Fry, and Albert Schweitzer are famous examples from the past, but we can also find plenty of individuals whose work today is along the same lines.

Their work often leaves a significant mark on the world. For example, in the 19th century in the UK, the strong Quaker values held by key entrepreneurial figures like George Cadbury led to innovations in social housing, community development, and education as well as in the factories which they organized and managed.

Major social innovations include the kindergarten, the co-operative movement, first aid, and the fair-trade movement, all of which began with social entrepreneurs and spread internationally.

2.1 Social Entrepreneurship Today

We don't have to look far in today's world to find examples of social entrepreneurs. For example, Dr. Devi Shetty is sometimes called "the Henry Ford of heart surgery" in India, referring to his entrepreneurial approach to healthcare provision which has brought the costs of even major procedures down to a fraction of those in mainstream hospitals in India. His work extends to health insurance and telemedicine, bringing healthcare education, support, and treatment to isolated rural communities, as well as meeting the needs of the poor in major cities.

Or Jane Chen, also working in India, whose idea for a low-cost baby incubator has saved the lives of many newborn infants.

(Jane Chen (2009) has a TED talk on her work at https://www.ted.com/talks/jane_chen_a_warm_embrace_that_saves_lives.)

CASE STUDY: Samasource

Read the Case Study_Samasource document in the ebook or from the book companion site regarding Leila Janah's use of advanced communications across mobile phone platforms to bring employment and income to refugees living in the huge camps springing up around war zones.

2.2 | So, What Does a Social Entrepreneur Look Like?

Social entrepreneurs share a number of characteristics which we can summarize as:

- **Ambitious:** they tackle major social issues – poverty, healthcare, equal opportunities, etc. – with a passion to make a change. They may work alone or from within a wide range of existing organizations including those which mix elements of non-profit and for-profit activity.
- **Mission-driven:** their primary concern is generating social value rather than wealth. Like business entrepreneurs, social entrepreneurs are intensely focused in their pursuit of a social vision.
- **Strategic:** they see and act upon what others miss– opportunities to improve systems, create solutions, and invent new approaches that create social value.
- **Resourceful:** social entrepreneurs often operate in situations where they have limited access to resources. They are highly skilled at improvising solutions, mobilizing resources, and using networks.
- **Results-oriented:** they are motivated by a desire to see things change and to produce measurable returns. Just as business entrepreneurs use measures of success like the amount of wealth they can create or the size of business they establish, so social entrepreneurs look for measurable impact in terms of "making the world a better place," for example, through improving quality of life, access to basic resources, supporting disadvantaged groups, etc.

Of course, it is often the case that these characteristics emerge among a team of people committed to the goals of *social entrepreneurship*. You can see this coming through in the case of Lifeline Energy, in which several key individuals helped make this important social venture happen over an extended period. In different ways, they were all driven by the goal of improving access to communication (especially by children) in developing countries.

CASE STUDY: Lifeline Energy

Read the Case Study_Lifeline Energy document in the ebook or from the book companion site.

And you can also see the same motivations in the Red Button team who shared a passion for helping with one of the enduring problems in development –providing clean drinking water.

CASE STUDY: Red Button Design

Read the Case Study_Red Button Design document in the ebook or from the book companion site.

2.3 | Why Do It?

Do we need social innovation? That might sound like a stupid question, but in terms of our model of entrepreneurship, it's worth looking for a moment at the "recognize opportunity" stage. Just as a business entrepreneur can explore in many directions to find innovation space, so there is enormous scope for social entrepreneurs to act. There is certainly an "innovation imperative" in this field; there is no shortage of global problems, but there are also opportunities at a local level.

For example, the humanitarian sector faces enormous challenges linked to natural and man-made disasters. We often hear people say that innovation is about survival, but in the world in which organizations like the Red Cross or Save the Children operate, that is literally true. Without innovative solutions (often improvised under severe resource constraints), things could be much worse. And their activity depends on entrepreneurs, but also on an organized process capable of repeating the innovation trick and scaling and spreading solutions.*

CASE STUDY: Cash-Based Programming

Read the Case Study_Cash-Based Programming document in the ebook or from the book companion site.

Why Do Individuals Do It?

It's worth pausing for a moment to reflect on the underlying motivation for social innovation, whether we are talking about passionate individuals, enlightened corporations, public sector institutions, or "third sector" organizations.

Just as mountaineers climb peaks simply *because they are there,* sometimes the motivation for innovating comes because of a desire to make a difference. Psychological studies of entrepreneurs suggest they often have high need for achievement (nAch), which is a measure of how far they want to make their mark on the world. [1] High nAch requires some evidence that a mark has been made, but this doesn't have to be in terms of profit or loss on a balance sheet. As we saw earlier, many people find entrepreneurial satisfaction through social value creation, and even those with a long track record of building successful businesses may find themselves drawn into this territory.

Back in the early 17th century, Thomas Coram, a successful businessman who had made his fortune in transatlantic trade, was so concerned with infant mortality in London that he set up the Foundling Hospital, pestering his friends and colleagues to raise the funding to support the project.

More recent examples are Bill Gates who withdrew from Microsoft to concentrate on the Bill and Melinda Gates Foundation, the largest fund in the world (worth around $55billion) dedicated to social innovation. Or Mark Zuckerberg, the Facebook founder, who has pledged 18 million shares in the company to a fund for social innovation.

Entrepreneurship in Action: Different types of entrepreneurs

In a recent award-winning paper, Emmanuelle Fauchart and Marc Gruber studied the motivations and underlying psychological drivers among entrepreneurial founders of businesses in the sports equipment sector. Their study used social identity theory to explore the underlying self-perceptions and aspirations and found three distinct types of role identity among their sample. "Darwinians" were primarily concerned with competing and creating business success, whereas "Communitarians" were much more concerned with social identities which related to participating in and contributing to a community. "Missionaries" had a strong inner vision and desire to change the world, and their entrepreneurial activity was an expression of this. [2]

---

*You can find links to some examples of humanitarian innovations on the book companion website.

> ### CASE STUDY: Eastville Community Shop
>
> Read the Case Study_Eastville Community Shop document in the ebook or from the book companion site about establishing a local community resource which looks at different motivations of the players involved.

User Innovators

Another important area in which individuals have been a powerful source of social innovation comes from the world of "user-innovators." Typically, these people have a high incentive to innovate (they really want something changed), and they are tolerant of imperfection; they'll work with prototypes and beta versions which get the job done, and then they will work to improve it. Farmers are a good example of such improvising innovators, and improvising innovators are also a strong contributor in the world of medical innovation.[3]

Recent studies by the UK think tank NESTA suggest as many as 10% of UK citizens engage in such "do-it-yourself" innovation around products and services which they want, and 15% do it to improve the processes they work with. These figures are almost certainly an underestimate; frustrated users are an important source of innovation.[4]

This class of innovator is increasingly important and has often been at the heart of major social change. Experiencing problems first-hand can often provide the trigger for change, for example, in healthcare. Patients and their caregivers can be remarkably resourceful and inventive in coming up with innovations to help them and others with their condition. For example, the way in which diabetes sufferers inject themselves was transformed by an innovation introduced by the giant Novo Nordisk company – the Novopen. Instead of a syringe and vial, the user has a device like a simple pen. It is discreet, reliable, and practical, and insulin pens like this are used by over 90% of diabetics in Europe and Asia. The original idea came not from the company's R&D labs, but from a young schoolgirl who experimented herself with the idea before the company read about it and put their resources behind its development and commercialization.[†]

Sustainability as Social Innovation

One field in which there is plenty of scope for entrepreneurship, and which combines commercial and social innovation, is that of sustainability. The challenge is easy enough to see: we are fast running out of planet! A challenging report by the WWF suggests that lifestyles in the developed world at present require the resources of around 2 planets, and if emerging economies follow the same trajectory, this will rise to 2.5 by 2050.[5] Many key energy and raw material resources are close to passing their "peak" of availability and will become increasingly scarce.[6]

At the same time, the dangers of global warming have moved to center stage, and climate change – and how to deal with it – is an urgent political, as well as economic, issue. This translates to increasingly strong legislation forcing organizations to change their products and processes to reduce carbon footprint, greenhouse gas emission, and energy consumption. Behind this is the growing challenge of environmental pollution and the concern not only to stop the increasing damage being done to the natural environment, but also to reverse the impacts of earlier practices.[7]

But it's not all doom and gloom. There are also immense opportunities for entrepreneurs to move into this space. For example, a PWC report suggests that providing "green" goods and services could represent a market size of 3% of global GDP. As the writer C. K. Prahalad put it:

> "... sustainability is a mother lode of organizational and technological innovations
> that yield both bottom-line and top-line returns. Becoming environment-friendly lowers

---

[†]You can find some examples of user-led innovation in healthcare on the book companion website.

costs because companies end up reducing the inputs they use. In addition, the process generates additional revenues from better products or enables companies to create new businesses. In fact, because [growing the top and bottom lines] are the goals of corporate innovation, we find that smart companies now treat sustainability as innovation's new frontier."[8]

Entrepreneurship in Action: Ray Anderson and Interface

One of the success stories in *sustainability-led innovation* has been the growth of flooring business Interface, which has made radical changes to its business and operating model and secured significant business growth. Interface has cut greenhouse gas emissions by 82%, fossil fuel consumption by 60%, waste by 66%, water use by 75%, and increased sales by 66%, doubled earnings, and raised profit margins. To quote Ray Anderson, founder and chairman," As we climb Mount Sustainability with the four sustainability principles on top, we are doing better than ever on bottom-line business. This is not at the cost of social or ecological systems, but at the cost of our competitors who still haven't got it."

VIDEO: Ray Anderson, Founder of Interface

Ray Anderson (2009), founder of Interface, speaks about the sustainability space in his TED talk at https://www.ted.com/talks/ray_anderson_on_the_business_logic_of_sustainability?language=en.

The following table provides examples of opportunities in the sustainability space.

We can see the "journey" toward full sustainability as involving three dimensions which underpin a change in the overall approach from treating the symptoms of a problem to eventually working with the system in which the problem originates (See **Figure 2.1**).

In particular, we can think of three stages in the evolution of SLI, from simple compliance and "doing what we do better" innovation to more radical exploration of new business opportunities. The third stage is all about system change, where significant effects can be achieved, but which rely on cooperation and co-evolution of innovative solutions across a group of stakeholders (**Table 2.1**).

TABLE 2.1   **Examples of Sustainability-Led Innovation**

Innovation Target	Examples
Product/Service offering	"Green" products, design for greener manufacture and recycling, service models replacing consumption/ownership models
Process innovation	Improved and novel manufacturing processes, lean systems inside the organization and across supply chain, green logistics
Position innovation	Rebranding the organization as "green," meeting needs of underserved communities – that is, bottom of pyramid
	Read the Case Study_Natura document in the ebook or from the book companion site regarding Natura, a Brazilian cosmetics company which has built a large market on the basis of sustainability values.
"Paradigm" innovation – changing business models	System-level change, multi-organization innovation, servitization (moving from manufacturing to service emphasis)

DEEPER DIVE: Sustainability-Led Innovation

Read the Deeper Dive: Sustainability-Led Innovation document in the ebook or from the book companion site.

FIGURE 2.1   The Journey Towards Sustainability-Led Innovation[9]

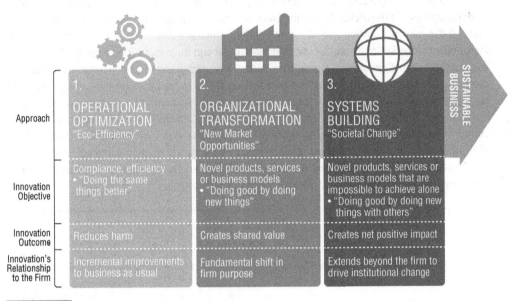

FIGURE 2.2   A Model for Sustainability-Led Innovation[10]

Making the journey involves moving from optimization to full-scale system change, as **Figure 2.2** shows.

There are many opportunities in this space for entrepreneurs. For example, Elon Musk is placing a big bet with his commitment to electric cars and, perhaps more importantly, the battery and energy storage technology behind them. Venture capital investments in renewable energy technology in 2014 ran at a level of $15billion with similar growth in other sustainability-linked sectors.

But moving to system-level change is not without its problems, as the case of Better Place indicates. A persuasive entrepreneur, Shen Agassi, managed to raise $200 million (the fifth biggest start-up in history) for his new venture based on electric mobility. Despite considerable promise and the backing of powerful players in industry and the political sphere, the venture failed and closed with losses of around $800 million.

CASE STUDY: Better Place

Read the Case Study_Better Place document in the ebook or from the book companion site.

2.4   Social Entrepreneurship as a Process

We saw in the last chapter that innovation isn't like the cartoons, a bright idea which suddenly appears and creates value. Instead, it involves a journey with some recognizable key stages. So how does this play out in the case of social entrepreneurs? The same process is involved, but there are some particular challenges.

Challenges in Social Entrepreneurship

While changing the world with social innovation is possible, it isn't easy! Just because there is no direct profit motive doesn't take the commercial challenges out of the equation. If anything, it becomes harder to be an entrepreneur when the challenge is not only to convince people that it can be done (and use all the tricks of the entrepreneur's trade to do so), but also to do so in a form that makes it commercially sustainable. Bringing a radio within reach of rural poor across Africa is a great idea, but someone still must pay for raw materials, build and run a factory, arrange for distribution, and collect the small amount of money from sales. None of this comes cheap, and setting up such a venture faces economic, political, and business obstacles every bit as hard as a bright start-up company in medical devices or computer software working in a developed country environment.

Take a look at the earlier case study of Lifeline Energy, a social innovation based on bringing communication and its accompanying benefits to children in the developing world. It describes the difficulties in moving from an important good idea to building a sustainable and scalable venture.

There are plenty of challenges in putting a venture like this together, and in sustaining it to create value. **Table 2.2** summarizes some of the key challenges.

Question:

What do you think are the challenges which a social entrepreneur might face when trying to get their venture off the ground and successfully create value?

TABLE 2.2   **Challenges in Social Innovation**

Problem area	Challenges
Resources	Not easily available and may need to cast the net widely to secure funding and other support. For example, LifeStraw (a product to enable easy access to clean drinking water) built a funding model around carbon credits available to poor countries to offset emission problems in wealthier nations.
Conflicts	While the overall goal may be to meet a social need, there may be conflicts in how this can be balanced against the need to generate revenue. For example, Lifeline Energy wanted to provide simple communication devices for the developing world, but it also wanted to provide employment to disabled people. The costs of the latter made the former difficult to achieve competitively and set up a major conflict for the management of the enterprise. Similar problems faced the producers of PlumpyNut, a nutritional aid for malnourished children.
Voluntary nature	Many people involved in social innovation are there because of core values and beliefs and contribute their time and energy in a voluntary way. This means that "traditional" forms of organization and motivation may not be available, posing a significant human resource management challenge.
"Lumpy" funding	Unlike commercial businesses where a stream of revenue can be used to fund innovation in a consistent fashion, many *social enterprises* rely on grants, donations, and other sources which are intermittent and unpredictable.
Scale of the challenge	The sheer size of many of the issues being addressed – how to provide clean drinking water, how to deliver reliable low-cost healthcare, combating illiteracy – means that having a clear focus is essential. Without a targeted innovation strategy, social enterprises risk dissipating their efforts.

2.5 Let's do it. . .

So, how could we develop a social enterprise? A good place to start would be to use our framework model – the Entrepreneur's Storyboard – and apply it to our challenge. In the accompanying workbook, there is an activity about asking key questions to build a rich picture of the venture and how it could create sustainable social value.

Who Could Help Me Explore This Further?

Social innovation is seen as having a major role in improving living standards, so it has attracted growing attention from a variety of agencies aiming to support and stimulate it. For example, there are investment vehicles(like the Big Society Capital fund in the UK and specialist venture funds like Acumen in the United States) which provide an alternative source of capital. Additionally, there are coordinating agencies (like the Young Foundation in the UK) which provide further support for the mobilization and institutionalization of social innovation.

Another increasingly significant development is that established organizations and successful business entrepreneurs are setting up charitable foundations whose aim is explicitly to enable social entrepreneurship, and the scaling of ideas with potential benefits. Examples include the Nike Foundation, Schwab Foundation, Skoll Foundation (established by Jeffrey Skoll, founder of eBay), and the Gates Foundation (established by Microsoft founder Bill Gates and which increasingly receives support from financier Warren Buffett).

Chapter Summary

- Innovation is about creating value, and one important dimension of this is making change happen in a socially valuable direction.
- "Social entrepreneurs"– individuals and organizations – recognize a social problem and organize an innovation process to enable social change.
- Just because there is no direct profit motive doesn't take the commercial challenges out of the equation. If anything, it becomes harder to be an entrepreneur when the challenge is not only to convince people that it can be done (and use all the tricks of the entrepreneur's trade to do so) but also to do so in a form that makes it commercially sustainable.
- Social entrepreneurship of this kind is also an increasingly important component of "big business," as large organizations realize that they only secure a license to operate if they can demonstrate some concern for the wider communities in which they are located.
- There are also benefits which emerge through aligning corporate values with those of employees within organizations.
- And there are significant learning opportunities through experiments in social innovation which may have impact on mainstream innovation.
- Making social entrepreneurship happen will require learning and absorbing a new set of skills to sit alongside our current ways of thinking about and managing innovation. How do we find opportunities which deliver social as well as economic benefits? How do we identify and engage a wide range of stakeholders, and understand and meet their very diverse expectations? How do we mobilize resources across networks; how do we build coalitions of support for socially valuable ideas?

Key Terms

Social enterprise   an organization that tries to pursue a double bottom line or a triple bottom line

Social entrepreneurship   applying entrepreneurship to achieve social goals rather than (but not excluding) financial reward

Sustainability-led innovation   using innovation to make progress towards sustainability goals like resource utilization pollution and environmental damage limitation, etc.

References

1 McClelland, D.(1965). *The achieving society*. New York: Van Nostrand Rheinhold.

2 Gruber, M. and Fauchart,E.(2011). Darwinians, communitarians and missionaries: the role of founder identity in entrepreneurship. *Academy of Management Journal*, 54(5).

3 Von Hippel, E.(2005).*The democratization of innovation*. Cambridge, MA: MIT Press.

4 NESTA.(2007). *Hidden innovation*. NESTA: London.

5 WWF.(2010). *Living planet report 2010: biodiversity, biocapacity and development*. Gland, Switzerland:WWF International.

6 Brown, L.(2011).*World on the edge: how to prevent environmental and economic collapse*. New York: Norton.

7 Heinberg, R.(2007). *Peak everything: waking up to the century of decline in earth's resources*. London: Clairview.

8 Nidumolu, R., Prahalad,C. and Rangaswami,M.(2009). Why sustainability is not the key driver of innovation. *Harvard Business Review*, (September2009), pp. 57-61.

9 Adams, R., et al. (2012). Innovating for sustainability: a guide for executives. [online] *Network for Business Sustainability*. Available at: http://www.nbs.net/knowledge.

10 Adams, R., et al.(2012). Innovating for sustainability: a guide for executives.[online] *Network for Business Sustainability*. Available at: http://www.nbs.net/knowledge.

CHAPTER 3

Entrepreneurial Creativity

LEARNING OBJECTIVES

By the end of this chapter you will be able to:

1. *Understand the role creativity plays in entrepreneurship throughout the journey from opportunity recognition right through to capturing value*

2. *Understand the way in which the creative process plays out*

3. *Acquire and practice some key thinking tools to help take a more creative approach to individual and group problem solving*

4. *Understand some of the key contextual influences on creativity*

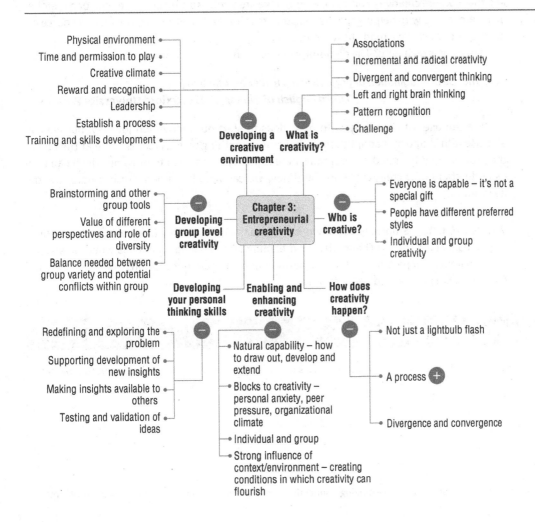

3.0 | What is Creativity?

"Seek and ye shall find." Well maybe, but part of being an entrepreneur is seeing opportunities that others don't. And, having seen them, another part of the role is about finding novel ways to pull together the key resources needed to start the new venture. It doesn't stop there: entrepreneurs also must reckon with things not going according to plan.They need to be flexible and agile, able to think their way around the inevitable problems which arise in trying to develop the venture.

All those activities need a certain mindset, a flexible way of thinking which can find or combine solutions in novel ways.(One theory about entrepreneurship is that it involves improvising, finding solutions, and reframing the problem as the story plays out.[1] And sometimes this involves "creating something out of nothing"as a way of dealing with resource constraints.[2] We explored these ideas of *effectuation* and entrepreneurial *bricolage* in Chapter 1.)That's where *creativity* comes to the fore; in entrepreneurship, developing the skills to see things in new ways or recombine existing elements into something new is a key part of the process. In this chapter, we'll explore a little more around these skills and how you can develop them.

For our ancestors, the creativity thing was a matter of survival.If we couldn't think our way out of a problem (like an approaching predator), then we wouldn't be around for long! Dealing with the daily struggle to survive required us to be innovative, and the key to that was the ability to imagine and explore different possibilities.

These days, we're more concerned with creating value, whether in a commercial or social sense, but the core skill remains one of finding, exploring, and solving problems and puzzles, and that's where creativity comes in. Whether we are a solo start-up entrepreneur, or a member of a team tasked with helping the organization to think "outside the box,"the main resource we need is one which we already have – creativity.

So, what is creativity? The dictionary defines it as:

"the use of imagination or original ideas to create something"
(*Oxford English Dictionary*, 2016, Oxford University Press)

We can use it to come up with new ideas to start our innovation journey, but we can also use it to shape and adapt them to become something which creates value at the end of the process. And the good news is that there is plenty of research to draw on which can help us understand how creativity works and how we can help it happen. For example, creativity is about:

Associations   Studies have shown it involves the brain making links, often between hitherto unconnected things. That's why daydreaming or coming up with ideas while we sleep is often an important part of the story; these are times when our unconscious brain can relax and forge new and unexpected connections.

Entrepreneurship in Action: The Innovator's DNA

Research at Harvard Business School [3] looking at the behavior of 3,000 executives over a six-year period found five important "discovery" skills for innovators:

- associating
- questioning
- observing
- experimenting
- networking

The most powerful overall driver of innovation was associating—making connections across "seemingly unrelated questions, problems, or ideas."

But it isn't just wild ideas and apparently random connections. Creativity is the ability to produce work that is both novel and *useful*. It's a purposive activity, one with a target in mind. The journey to get there may require playfulness, but there is a serious goal at the end.

Incremental and Radical

Creativity is about breaking through to radical new ideas, new ways of framing the problem, and new direction for solving it. But it's also about the hard work of polishing and refining those breakthrough ideas, debugging, and problem solving to get them to work. The pattern of innovation is one of occasional flashes of inspiration followed by long periods of incremental improvement around those breakthrough ideas. Creativity matters throughout this process.

Divergent and Convergent Thinking

Many studies of creative thinking have looked at two different modes of thinking – convergent and divergent. Convergent thinking is about focus, homing in on a single "best" answer, while divergent thinking is about making *associations*, often exploring round the edges of a problem. While there are some examples of problems which have a single "right" answer and need a convergent approach, most require a mixture of the two thinking skills. We need divergent thinking to open them up, explore their dimensions, create new associations, and we need convergent thinking to focus, refine, and improve the most useful solution for a particular context.

Left and Right Brain Thinking

Another key part of the puzzle lies in the way our brains operate. The brain is made up of two connected hemispheres and for a long-time neuro-scientists have known that different parts of brain function relate to these different areas. Work originally carried out by Nobel Prize winner Roger Sperry and colleagues back in the 1960s (and confirmed by more recent neuro-imaging techniques) shows that the left hemisphere is particularly associated with activities like language and calculation.[4] While our "left brain" seems linked to what we might call "logical" processing, the role of the "right" brain was, for a long time, much less well understood. Gradually, it became clear that the right brain is involved in associations, patterns, and emotional links; people with damage to the right hemisphere are often incapable of understanding humor or feeling moved by painting or music. Our ability to think in metaphors and to visualize and imagine in novel ways is strongly linked to activity on this side of the brain.

It's not a case of "creativity = right brain thinking," but rather that we need to recognize that both hemispheres (and within them many different regions of the brain) are involved, and they play different roles. This has important implications for developing the skills of creative thinking, as we'll see later, because we need to find ways to enable these interconnections.

Pattern Recognition

Creativity is particularly about patterns and our ability to see them. In its simplest form, if we see a pattern which we recognize, we have access to solutions which worked in the past and which we can apply again. But sometimes, it is a case of recognizing a similarity between a new problem and something like it which we have seen before. For example, Johannes Gutenberg saw the connection between the way winepresses worked and his idea for the printing press. Alastair Pilkington saw a link between the way fat floated on the surface of water and the way his company might make glass, eventually leading to the revolutionary "float glass" process with which most of the world's windows are now made. And James Dyson applied ideas about the large-scale industrial cyclones used to capture factory emissions to the world of domestic vacuum cleaners.

Challenge

Another key theme in creativity is that it sometimes involves breaking rules, changing perspectives, and seeing things differently. And this can set up tensions between the person coming up with this new way of seeing and the rest of the world who still have the old view.

Innovation in action: Sticky success

It was during a flight in 1967 that Wolfgang Dierichs, a scientist working for the German company Henkel, had a flash of creative insight. The company made a wide range of stationery products, and one area in which he worked was in adhesives. As he sat waiting for the plane to take off, he noticed the woman next to him applying lipstick. His insight was to see the potential of the lipstick tube as a new way to deliver glue. Put some solid glue in a tube, twist the cap, and apply it to any surface.

The company launched the "Pritt Stick" in 1969, and within two years, it was available in 38 countries around the world. Today, around 130 million Pritt Sticks are sold each year in 120 countries, and the product has sold over 2.5 billion units since its invention.

That's not always a comfortable position, because it can involve going head-to-head with an established view of the world. Those who hold it are likely to defend their view strongly. Creative people aren't always popular, especially when they stick to their guns and defend their crazy idea in the face of others trying to get them to conform. When Galileo the astronomer proposed a different view for the way the sun and planets operated, he was imprisoned and threatened with death by the Inquisition. In a version of this which was not quite so life-threatening, when Bob Dylan performed his new electric music at the Newport festival, he was booed off the stage. Steve Jobs was portrayed in the movie of the same name as another "difficult" visionary, and James Dyson chose an apt title for his autobiography, *Against the Odds*!

This isn't to say that entrepreneurs have to go out of their way to be "difficult" people, but rather that we need to recognize and manage the conflicts which can emerge, and to make sure we can bring people along with us, getting them to share in our vision rather than fighting against it.

3.1 | Who is Creative?

Close your eyes and imagine someone being creative. What do you see? Chances are you have begun to picture an artist, a musical composer, or perhaps a sculptor or poet wrestling with his or her imagination. Maybe you have a mad scientist in mind, a crazy white-haired professor who has questionable dress sense but a brilliant mind and is working out solutions to the problems of the universe.

These are common pictures which remind us that we tend to think of creativity as something rather special, very important in the worlds of art and science, but somehow the province of exceptional and rare individuals working on their own. The reality is different; what we know about creativity is that everyone is capable of it, and it can be developed and deployed in a wide variety of ways. It's at the heart of being human, something we have evolved over a long period of time. Watch any group of children in a playground to be reminded of this wonderful facility which is fitted as standard equipment! The question is not whether people are creative, but how to unlock what is already there and then hone and develop the skill.

But while we are all capable of creativity, we differ in how comfortable we feel about playing with new ideas or loosening up our minds to allow new thought patterns. We have a mental "comfort zone" within which we can be creative, and we can occasionally push the boundaries and explore something significantly novel. But few of us would want to spend all our time wrestling with the pain of trying to create something radically new.

As we saw earlier, a lot of creativity research has focused on *convergent and divergent thinking*. Studies suggest that people differ in their approaches; some are more comfortable in divergent thinking than others. Attempts have been made to map these to personality types and characteristics like introversion and extraversion. But the emerging conclusion is that people need both sets of skills for effective creativity, and those skills can be trained and developed.

Entrepreneurship in Action: The Kirton Adaptor/Innovator model

Everyone is creative, but we all have different preferred "styles" of behavior – how we like to express it and what we feel comfortable with. The UK psychologist Michael Kirton carried out extensive work and developed an instrument to measure these differences.[5] He defined two points on a scale running from "innovators" who were open to considerable flexibility in their creative thinking to "adaptors" who were more comfortable with incremental creativity.

We discuss the Kirton model in more detail in Chapter 7.

Another personal dimension of creativity is linked to experience and expertise. Creative people are often highly experienced in a field and thus able to see patterns and identify variations on a core theme which others won't see. Dorothy Leonard calls these "deep smarts," and many studies in psychology have shown the importance of such deep knowledge as a part of creativity.[6] But this raises the idea of "domain specificity"; people who may be highly creative in one field may not be so in another.

What all of this means is that if we want to mobilize and enhance creativity, then we need to find multiple ways of doing so. It's not simply a matter of finding an "on/off" switch, but rather building the context in which people can deliver their skills. Much of what we have learned about managing creativity is about configuring tools and resources to enable different people to feel comfortable and supported in the process. For some, this may be a very loose unstructured environment where crazy ideas fly around the room and bounce off each other in wild flights of fancy. For others, it may be more structured and systematic, supporting people in a guided process in which they can find and solve problems in incremental fashion.

The Power of the Group

So far, we have been talking about individual creativity, but it is also important to recognize the power of interaction with others. We are all different in personality, experience, and approach, and these differences mean that we see problems and solutions from different perspectives. Combining our approaches, sparking ideas off each other, building on shared insights are all powerful ways of amplifying creativity. The old proverb that "two heads are better than one"is often true; think about creative partnerships in the musical world like Lennon and McCartney, Rogers and Hammerstein, Rice and Lloyd Webber, the Gershwin brothers. Look at the world of theater and film and see how much success is the product of not a lone genius, but a team of co-creators, front and backstage, who help make it happen. Look at business ventures and very often you'll find a team: Eric Schmidt and Sergei Brin (Google), Bill Gates and Paul Allen (Microsoft), Andy Grove and Gordon Moore (Intel), Steve Jobs and Steve Wozniak (Apple), Anita and Gordon Roddick (The Body Shop), Jack Ma with Lucy Peng and several others (Alibaba).

Entrepreneurship in Action: The power of groups

Take any group of people and ask them to think of different uses for an everyday item – a cup, a brick, a ball, etc. Working alone, they will usually develop an extensive list. But then ask them to share the ideas they have generated. The resulting list will not only be much longer but will also contain much greater diversity in possible classes of solution to the problem. For example, uses for a cup might include using it as a container (vase, pencil holder, drinking vessel, etc.), a mold (for sandcastles, cakes, etc.), a musical instrument, a measure, a template around which one can draw, a device for eavesdropping (when pressed against a wall) and even, when thrown, a weapon!

The psychologist J.P. Guilford classed these two traits as "*fluency*" (the ability to produce ideas) and "flexibility" (the ability to come up with different types of idea). The above experiment will quickly show that working as a group, people are usually much more fluent and flexible than any single individual. When working together, people spark each other off, jump on and develop each other's ideas, encourage and support each other through positive emotional mechanisms like laughter and agreement, and in a variety of ways, stimulate a high level of shared creativity.[7]

3.2 How Does Creativity Happen?

It's easy to see creativity as that wonderful moment when we have a flash of inspiration. The light bulb goes on, and all suddenly becomes clear. But research has shown that it is not as simple as this; there is an underlying *process* which starts a long way before that light bulb moment.[8]

It begins with us recognizing that we have a puzzle or a problem to solve. If it is something we have seen before, we can often switch straight to applying a solution. But if it is something trickier, we need to explore it further. This can be frustrating; we may wrestle with it for some time without coming up with any insight about possible solutions. Or we may try various ideas out and realize they don't or won't work. Importantly, what's going on here is a process of recognizing and preparing the problem.

We might give up on the struggle and switch off our attention, but the reality is we don't let the problem go. Our brain continues to process and explore, trying out different connections, playing with different options. When we walk away from the problem, or decide to sleep on it, we are not leaving it behind, but rather passing the work of trying to solve it to our unconscious minds. This *incubation* stage is important; as the name suggests, we are allowing something to develop and grow.

At some stage, there is a moment, and the insight is born. It may be that we wake up with a fresh idea in our head, or we suddenly get that flash of inspiration. The "aha!" moment is often accompanied by feelings of certainty; even if we can't explain why, we just *know* this is the right solution. There's a flow of energy and a sense of direction to our thinking. The idea may still need a lot of work elaborating and developing it, but the underlying breakthrough has been made.

This pattern can be seen in many accounts of creativity in which people talk about how they came up with apparently radical new solutions. And it's a key resource for us in thinking about how we can build creativity. If it's a process, then we can map the stages, understand what's going on, and provide some resources to help.

Sometimes this process takes place almost instantaneously; we recognize the problem and can retrieve a solution almost instantaneously. But sometimes we need to work through the process in a more systematic fashion, allowing time for each stage. We mentioned divergent and convergent thinking a little earlier, and one way of seeing the creativity process is as a mixture of divergent and convergent cycles.

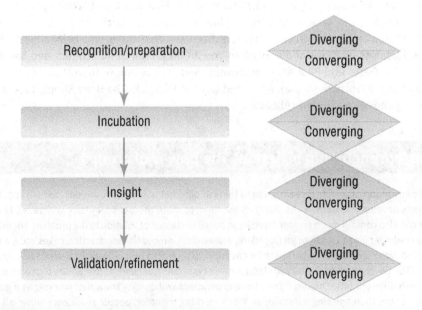

FIGURE 3.1 Cycles of Divergence and Convergence in Creativity

Source: Bessant, J. and Tidd, J. (2015). *Innovation and entrepreneurship*. Hoboken, NJ: Wiley.[9]

Entrepreneurship in Action: Snakes on a bus

The 19th century chemist Friedrich August Kekule is credited with having unraveled one of the keys to the development of organic chemistry, the structure of the benzene ring. This arrangement of atoms is central to understanding how to make a whole range of chemicals, from fertilizers to medicines and explosives, and its discovery enabled rapid acceleration of growth in the field. Having wrestled for a long period with the problem, he eventually had a flash of inspiration on waking from a dream in which he had seen the atoms dance. And then, the snake like atom chain began eating its own tail. This weird dream picture nudged him towards the key insight that benzene atoms are arranged in a ring.

He later reported another dream which he had while dozing on a London bus, in which atoms were dancing in different formations; this dream gave him further insight into the key components of chemical structure.

3.3 | Enabling and Enhancing Creativity

As we've seen, everyone is already capable of creativity; it's not a case of injecting them with some magic new ingredient. Instead, we need to look for ways in which this natural capability can be drawn out, developed, and extended. It's useful to start by thinking about what blocks this natural ability.

VIDEO: Sir Ken Robinson, education and creativity expert

Sir Ken Robinson (2006) speaks about creativity and how we block it out at https://www.ted.com/talks/ken_robinson_says_schools_kill_creativity?language=en.

It doesn't take long to see that there are all sorts of pressures, inside and outside our minds, which can block creativity. **Figure 3.2** summarizes some of these.

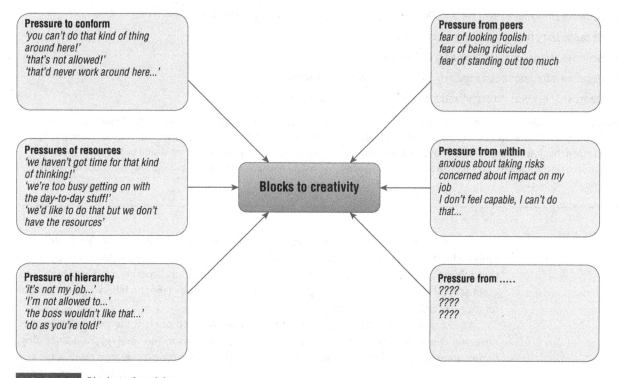

FIGURE 3.2 Blocks to Creativity

Source: Bessant, J. and Tidd, J.(2015). *Innovation and entrepreneurship*. Hoboken, NJ: Wiley.[10]

So, if we are going to enable creativity, then we need to provide ways of tackling these different areas and developing skills and resources to deal with them. We could use the metaphor of a "mental gym" in which there are various pieces of equipment to help us develop the muscles and techniques for creativity. There's no single solution, but our overall aim is improving fitness across the board.

In the following section, we'll look at three areas in which we might do this:

1. Developing individual thinking skills
2. Developing group level skills
3. Developing the environment

3.4 Developing Your Personal Thinking Skills

Look back and familiarize yourself again with **Figure 3.1**, our simple model of the creative process. Let's now look at ways in which we could help support the thinking processes at each stage. The good news is that there are plenty of tools available to help develop skills at each stage of the process.* For example, if we want to work on the "front end" of recognizing the problem and structuring it to generate some solutions, then we could try simple tools like the "Five Whys and a How" approach (see the following box for more on this).

Creativity in Action: Five whys and a how

This simple but powerful tool can help strip away the apparent problem to get through to the root problem, which is the one we need to solve. For example, waiting times and delays are a big problem in UK hospitals now, putting pressure on already scarce resources. Here's how one hospital applied the tool.

The apparent problem was that a patient arrived late in the operating theater, causing a delay.

- Why? – Because they had to wait for a trolley to take them from the ward to the theater.
- Why? – Because they had to find a replacement trolley.
- Why? – Because the original trolley had a defect; the safety rail had broken.
- Why? – Because it had not been regularly checked for wear and tear.
- Why? – Because there was no organized system of checking and maintenance.

Arriving at this root cause (the real problem is in the lack of systematic maintenance) gives plenty of clues about the "how," the potential solutions to the problem. Setting up a simple maintenance schedule could ensure that all trolleys are regularly checked and available for use. This would mean that future delays would be avoided, flow would improve, and overall system efficiency would be better. Importantly, if we had just focused on the apparent problem – a single broken trolley – we would have solved that by repairing the trolley, but the underlying problem would happen again.

On the book companion website, you can find other examples of such problem exploring tools including fishbone diagrams, levels of abstraction, SCAMPER, how-to statements, pattern recognition, and rich pictures. There are also some "heavy duty" methodologies which integrate several tools, for example, the popular TRIZ methodology (see the following box/sidebar for more) or Soft Systems Analysis.

It's the same story for generating solutions: if we want to open some new solution avenues, we could use approaches like attribute listing, metaphor and analogy, mindmapping, *brainstorming*, and *lateral thinking*. And once again, there are some integrated methodologies

*See the Further Resources section for this chapter on the book companion website.

The development of TRIZ

TRIZ was originally developed in 1946 by a Russian engineer, Genrich Altschuller. He was working in the "Inventions Inspection" department of the Caspian Sea flotilla of the Soviet Navy, where his job involved reviewing thousands of patent applications. He noticed that despite the patents covering widely different fields, they shared some underlying patterns, and he focused on the ways in which inventive solutions seemed to emerge when there was some kind of "unresolved contradiction." An example might be between the weight and cost of a car engine and the power it is able to deliver. What we might call a trade-off between these elements could be resolved if we think creatively about a new solution which resolves the apparent tension.

Over the following ten years, he analyzed thousands of inventions and noticed repeated patterns in the way solutions were presented even though they covered widely different fields. He suggested that all problems can be reduced to versions of a basic set of core themes ("principles of invention"); he identified forty and developed a matrix approach to help generate solutions based on reapplying solutions which shared a common problem root.

which bring together several tools, for example, the Creative Problem-Solving(CPS) model or design thinking.

At the "insight" stage of the process,there is the challenge of making your insight clear and available to others.There are tools for this as well, such as storytelling and visualization.

And the final stage involves trying out and improving the solution you have generated; tools to help with this include prototyping and value analysis.

The good news is that we have plenty of such tools and techniques to help develop our creative skills.[†] But creativity is also about motivation and communication; we need to feel comfortable about taking the risk of trying something new out, or trusting our intuition. For a few people, creativity is their way of life, they are constantly challenging and questioning;but for most people, there is an element of self-imposed limitation to it. Am I allowed to think this way? What if my idea is wrong? Will I be look/sound foolish for suggesting this? Can I trust my instincts which are leading me to think in this way?

Building confidence in our own ideas and then developing skills in communicating them and handling the feedback we get on them is another area where we can develop our creative capabilities. Successful entrepreneurs are not just able to come up with creative insights; they are also resilient in the face of feedback, using this to help shape and adapt their ideas. They have a strong sense of vision and can communicate and engage others in sharing that insight. And they are skilled at "pitching," communicating the core idea to others in ways which get past their critical comments and engage their interest (and hopefully their resource support).

VIDEO: David Kelley, designer and educator

David Kelley (2012) speaks about creative confidence in his TED talk at https://www.ted.com/talks/david_kelley_how_to_build_your_creative_confidence.

One key point is to understand the nature of the creative process as we have described it, and to recognize that it isn't entirely rational;emotions, intuitions, and odd insights are a valuable part of it, and ideas which emerge can be useful stepping stones or valuable in their own right. *"If it's worth thinking, it's worth saying,"* is a useful motto. But understanding the process also reminds us of different kinds of thinking associated with different stages, from divergent activities opening our minds to new connections to convergent thinking helping us focus in and whittle many wild ideas down to the ones with real potential value. We need to develop *flexibility* in our thinking, and as we'll see in the following section, in the thinking we do with other people, to deal with these different stages in creativity.

[†]See the Further Resources section for this chapter on the instructor book companion website.

Edward de Bono offers a very practical approach to help with this. His "*six thinking hats*" model uses the metaphor of wearing different hats when we undertake different kinds of thinking.[11] For example, a green hat is all about a freewheeling, anything goes kind of thinking, which is essentially opening up and allowing ideas to emerge. By contrast, a black hat is about judgment, evaluating, and criticizing ideas to winnow out the less valuable and focus in on the core. He suggests we need six different modes of thinking and offers helpful tools to develop the ability to recognize when they are needed, and the flexibility to move between them.

Six Thinking Hats

Explore the Six Thinking Hats document in the ebook or from the book companion site.

3.5 | Developing Group Level Creativity

Creativity is something we are all capable of; we can all come up with novel and useful ideas on our own. But working together with others can amplify that process, leading to more ideas, and more different insights which can lead to novel solutions. People differ in their experience, their personality, and their perspectives on the world, and this diversity is a rich resource for helping creativity to happen.

So, there's a lot to be said for working with others, and there's plenty of research to support the potential of doing so. But it's not as easy as it looks, and there are also many downsides to working in a group. Social pressures can act as a damper on individual sparks of ideas. Diversity can lead to conflict about the "right" solutions. Groups can quickly become political. As we'll see in Chapter 7, simply throwing people together does not make them a team, and the wrong mix can easily lead to the whole performing much less well than the sum of the parts.

Question:

What do you think are the main advantages and disadvantages of working in a group to deliver creative outcomes?

The following table gives some ideas based on various research studies of group dynamics

---

So, we need to look for ways in which we can amplify the positive aspects and minimize the negative, and there are various tools which can help in this process.

Brainstorming is one of the most widely used approaches and has its origins in this space. Originally developed in the 1950s by an advertising executive, Alex Osborn, brainstorming is basically an approach to group idea generation.[12] It recognizes that we tend to judge ideas quickly and in a group setting this can be negative; without meaning to, we can quickly pour cold water on the sparks. This may come from a simple reaction to the idea itself: "*that's stupid,*"

TABLE 3.1 Advantages and Disadvantages of Group-Level Creativity

Advantages	Disadvantages
Diversity – more different ideas	"Groupthink" - social pressures to conform
Volume of ideas – "many hands make light work"	Lack of focus – "too many cooks spoil the broth"
Elaboration – multiple resources to explore the problem	Group dynamics and hierarchy
Rich variety of prior experience	Political behavior, people following different agendas

"*that won't work,*" etc. Or it can come from hierarchy effects: "*junior employees should be seen and not heard,*" "*the best ideas come from the senior people,*" "*listen to the experts, they have the experience to solve this,*" etc. Or it can come from politics and interpersonal rivalries. For whatever reasons, judging ideas as they surface can quickly kill them off.

Given what we know about the creative process, sometimes those ideas might be half-formed. We don't quite know what we're suggesting; we haven't thought it through. They are newborn insights. So, they are at high risk surfacing in this group context. Brainstorming provides a simple set of rules to protect them mainly based on postponing judgment. Instead of reacting to ideas, people are encouraged to share them and build on them, exploring and adding to them. Only later does the group move into a judgment phase, winnowing out the novel and useful ideas from the many others which have been suggested.

The power of brainstorming (which is available in many different forms) is that it counters some of the negative effects of working in a group and builds on the positives like diversity. It enables practices like improvisation around a theme, acceptance, and building on whatever comes up; a core principle is that "quantity breeds quality," so generating many possible ideas statistically allows for the emergence of more good ones.

Entrepreneurship in Action: Improving the climate for creativity

The consultancy firm? Whatif! specializes in creative problem-solving for and with clients. They make use of many techniques linked to brainstorming, and they have a simple framework using the metaphor of helping nurture early shoots of ideas.[13]

They need plenty of SUN:

S = support, encourage

U = understand, listen to the ideas

N = nurture, help them to grow

And avoid too much RAIN:

R = react, respond directly, and judge the ideas rather than listen to them

A = assume, bringing your preconceptions and your interpretation too quickly

I = insist on your viewpoint, be closed in your mind to other ways of seeing the problem

N = negative, closing down and shutting out possible new directions, saying "no" to the idea in its early undeveloped form

---

Beyond brainstorming, many of the tools which we explored in the section on developing thinking skills can be deployed in a group setting and the diversity can amplify the effect. Within a session, the process leader may well throw in such techniques as a way of "stirring the pot" to trigger a new direction for thinking or move the group into new search space.

Variations on A Theme

It's important to not see the group as the solution to everything. While there are positive effects arising from interaction with others, there is also value in individual creativity. Many creativity workshops make use of both options, for example, encouraging people to work individually on a problem and write down their ideas before sharing those with a group and allowing for creative exploration of them. "Nominal group" approaches try to build in the complementary advantages of individual and group creativity. Approaches like these help balance out the tendency within groups for some people to dominate while others remain in the background.

Using Online Groups and Communities

One powerful new resource is internet forums and communities which allow many people to form together as a virtual group or community. This can capture some of the positive effects like diversity without some of the negative social effects in a face-to-face context. The downside is that such groups don't get the non-verbal or emotional charge, so it's a case of a complementary approach rather than a replacement.

CASE STUDY: Liberty Global

Read the Case Study_Liberty Global document in the ebook or from the book companion site regarding their Spark program.

Limits of Brainstorming

Brainstorming has its limits. It's not always effective, and sometimes the benefits in a group "wear out" over time. Think again of the examples of creative partnerships we explored earlier. Many of these have a short creative phase but then fall apart, with the members often acknowledging that they need to move on and find new combinations. Even in a simple brainstorming session, there is a phase where ideas come thick and fast, but this gradually dries up as the effects of group stimulation and interaction tail off. Under these conditions, it's often valuable for the session process leader to inject some new stimuli, perhaps bringing in some of the lateral thinking or metaphor techniques described earlier.

Another important feature is the approach to conflict. The "rules" of brainstorming say that ideas shouldn't be attacked or criticized, and that judgment should be suspended. But in many creative situations, arguments and debate are powerful features for moving things forward – think of a theater or a music group for example. It's the differences and debate which help create the edge and provide the spark that makes the difference. Research suggests that a degree of creative conflict is valuable; the secret is not to attack the person but to challenge the idea, and this often depends on having someone to moderate and guide the debate.

Studies of creativity in groups suggest there is an inverted U- shape to their effectiveness. As **Figure 3.3** shows, too little time together and they don't deliver much because they are lacking in trust and experience of each other; too long together, and a degree of groupthink sets in, and the ideas become stale. Similarly, too little conflict, and everyone agrees and the frontiers of thinking do not get pushed; too much conflict, and ideas get killed off too readily [14].

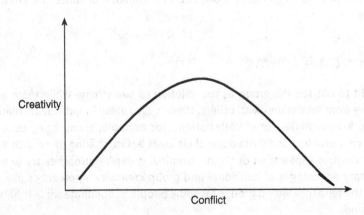

FIGURE 3.3 Conflict vs Creativity in Group Work

3.6 Developing a Creative Environment

For new start-ups, the tools and techniques we've been looking at may be sufficient. But there are many situations in which entrepreneurs are trying to work in larger organizations, for example, shop floor staff trying to improve their working processes, product and service developers trying to promote new concepts, change agents trying to challenge the way the organization works. These are situations in which we certainly need to develop creativity, and while individual and group level skills play a key role, we can also work with the wider environment to help support creativity.

For example, we can work with the physical environment to build spaces in which ideas can bump into each other using some of the principles like Tom Allen's findings on the importance of interaction (see the following box).

Creativity in Action: Managing the flow of ideas

During the 1970s, Tom Allen, a professor at MIT, was interested in how ideas emerged during large, complex, technical projects. He began studying organizations involved in the innovation challenges surrounding the US space program, finding ways to deliver on Kennedy's original goal of putting a man on the moon and bringing him home again safely.

He studied how people shared ideas and how they moved around and across organizations and laid the foundations for what we now call "social network analysis" as a way of mapping these interactions. He found, for example, the importance of key individuals (technological gatekeepers) through whom ideas travelled and were disseminated to relevant people. His book, *Managing the Flow of Technology*, contains a wealth of insights which are of continuing importance in designing today's network-based innovation processes.[15]

One project he undertook explored how the distance between engineers' offices coincided with the level of regular technical communication between them. His research results, now known as the Allen curve, revealed a distinct correlation between distance and frequency of communication (i.e., the more distance there is between people — 50 meters or more to be exact — the less they will communicate). This principle has been incorporated into forward-thinking commercial design ever since, in, for example, New York's Decker Engineering Building, Michigan's Steelcase Corporate Development Center, and Germany's BMW Research and Innovation Centre.

We also need to remember that creativity is about long periods of incubation and exploration, punctuated by flashes of insight. That's not a process that lends itself to being switched on and off to order, and organizations are increasingly realizing that if they want creativity to happen, they must make space for it. 3M is a business with a long tradition of breakthrough innovation: think about Post It notes, Scotch tape, industrial masking tape, and a host of other products we now take for granted. They came out of an organization which has recognized that it needs its employees to be curious, to play and explore, to make odd connections. And to do so, they need time allowed for this and permission to play within that time.

Not all organizations can afford the luxury of giving employees the freedom to take their own time. Toyota, for example, is driven by the huge commitment of keeping its production lines running, and interrupting them is costly and disruptive. But they, too, have their version of allowing time and space for creativity; every team spends fifteen minutes each day before and after its shift in group problem-solving, identifying issues to be worked on and coming up with new ideas to try out during the day. This constant, high-frequency, short-burst approach to creativity is called "kaizen," and it is central to their success as the world's most productive car maker. Process innovation keeps happening, driven by the creativity of thousands of employees; it's estimated that the company receives, on average, one useful idea per worker per week, and has done so since the 1960s when they began this approach to continuous improvement.

And creativity doesn't happen in a vacuum. Being able to come up with different new ideas is a process influenced by a whole series of external pressures which can act as a barrier, pushing our creative ideas back into the bottle. So, the organizational climate (the pattern of beliefs which people have about creativity) will also be important.

Entrepreneurship in Action: Killer phrases

One of the problems in creativity is that people react quickly to new things with reasons why they won't work. Such "killer phrases" are part of the aural landscape. We hear them wherever we go in organizations. They have the same basic structure: "that's a great idea, but. . ." Here are some typical examples, and you can almost certainly add your own to the list:

> We've never tried that before. . .
>
> We've always done it this way. . .
>
> The boss won't like it. . .
>
> We don't have the time for that. . .
>
> It's too expensive. . .
>
> You can't do that here. . .
>
> We're not that kind of organization. . .
>
> That's a brave suggestion,
>
> Etc.

In a recent study of a wide range of UK organizations in which employees at all levels were regularly contributing creative ideas, Julian Birkinshaw and Lisa Duke identified four key sets of enabling factors:[16]

- Time Out—to give employees the space in their working day for creative thought
- Expansive Roles—to help employees move beyond the confines of their assigned job
- Competitions—to stimulate action and to get the creative juices flowing
- Open Forums—to give employees a sense of direction and to foster collaboration.

If we want to enable creativity, we can do a lot by working with these levers to create a physical and mental environment which is supportive.

The following **Table 3.2** summarizes some of the key approaches.

TABLE 3.2 **Building a creative environment**

Environmental barrier	Ways of dealing with this	Examples
Physical environment Read Deeper Dive_ Physical Environment document in the ebook or from the book companion site.	Make the workplace stimulating Allow for interaction and bumping into new ideas Make ideas visible Get outside the work environment and experience the problem from a different perspective Build a virtual environment – an ICT platform	Pixar *Read Case Study_Pixar Animations document in the ebook or from the book companion site.* The UK Met Office is another example of using physical space, seen in this video at https://www.youtube.com/watch?v=-hyT6_GXPRk&feature=youtu.be. The Lufthansa Systems[§] case gives another example (like Liberty Global, mentioned earlier) where using an online platform can help stimulate ideas and collaboration
Time and permission to play Read Deeper Dive_Time, Space and Permission to Play document in the ebook or from the book companion site.	Allow (and even require) employees time to explore and be curious, to enable incubation.	3M offers a famous case of creating conditions which support innovation by allowing employees to spend up to 15% of their time working on their own ideas, curiosity-driven projects, etc. *Read Case Study_3M document in the ebook or from the book companion site.* It's an idea which has been widely copied; for example, Google's engineers are encouraged to spend 20% of their time playing with novel ideas of their own.

TABLE 3.2   Building a creative environment (*continued*)

Environmental barrier	Ways of dealing with this	Examples
Climate Read Deeper Dive_ Creative Climate document in the ebook or from the book companion site.	Create the supporting "rules of the game." Articulate and promote core values – for example, that everyone can contribute. Build a "no blame"culture – encourage experimentation. Promote "intelligent failure" –recognize that mistakes can offer learning opportunities.	Creative climate has been used to build up organizations like Redgate Software, Innocent Drinks, Denso (a large automotive component maker) and Veeder Root (a small supplier of measurement equipment).

*Case study available on the book companion website.

Putting it All Together – Developing Entrepreneurial Creativity

Creativity matters, whether we are starting a new entrepreneurial venture, trying to improve performance of an established organization, or help a mature one find new directions and "get out of the box." In this chapter, we've looked at some of the factors which affect our ability to draw out that creativity. People already have the capacity, but there is good evidence that this natural capability can be enhanced and developed through inputs targeted at individual, group, and environment. There is no single injection of magic which will make people more creative. Fostering creativity requires an integrated approach, creating the conditions and providing the framework within which people can sharpen and develop their skills.

Chapter Summary

- The dictionary defines creativity as *"the use of imagination or original ideas to create something,"* and in practice, we can see it as the ability to produce work that is both novel and *useful*.

- It is a combination of thinking skills including associating, pattern recognition, and divergent and convergent thinking. Its application can range from incremental to radical, from simple problem-solving to breakthrough insights.

- Although often portrayed as a flash of inspiration, creativity follows a process of recognition/preparation, incubation, insight, and validation/refinement.

- Everyone is naturally capable of creative thinking, but there are differences in the ways people prefer to express their creativity (creative style) and differences associated with personality and prior experience.

- Developing creativity is less about injecting something new than in creating enabling conditions to support a natural process. At the individual level, thinking skills can be enhanced using techniques aimed at developing new ways of dealing with the core process.

- Group level creativity recognizes the potential of diversity, and interaction and tools to support this include those which enable "creative collisions."Brainstorming is the best known, but there are many others; recent developments in information technology provide new ways of bringing groups together.

- Building an environment to support creativity includes paying attention to factors like physical space, time and "permission," reward and recognition, establishing a process, and training and skills development.

Key Terms

Associations   key principle in creativity in which the brain makes unexpected connections between different thoughts

Brainstorming   an approach to group idea generation which emphasis postponement of judgment.

Bricolage   process used by entrepreneurs to "create something out of nothing" by making use of whatever is at hand

Convergent and divergent thinking   Two complementary styles of thinking – convergent thinking is about focus, homing in on a single 'best' answer while divergent thinking is about making associations, often exploring round the edges of a problem

Creativity   'the use of imagination or original ideas to create something'

Effectuation theory of entrepreneurship which suggests that entrepreneurs do not have clear formal plans but interact with their environment, creating and modifying their approach through this

Flexibility the ability to come up with different types of idea

Fluency the ability to produce ideas

Lateral thinking approach to problem solving associated with Edward de Bono which emphasizes different strategies to defining and working through problems

Six thinking hats approach developed by Edward de Bono to help facilitate flexibility in switching between different thinking modes

References

1 Sarasvathy, S. (2008). *Effectuation: elements of entrepreneurial expertise*.Cheltenham: Edward Elgar.

2 Nelson, R. and Baker, T. (2005). Creating something from nothing: resource construction through entrepreneurial bricolage. *Administrative Science Quarterly*, 50(3), pp. 329–366.

3 Christensen, C., Dyer, J. and Gregerson, H. (2011). *The innovator's DNA*. Boston: Harvard Business School Press.

4 Sperry, R. (1969). Hemisphere deconnection and unity in conscious awareness. *American Psychologist*, 23, pp. 723–733.

5 Kirton, M. (1980). Adaptors and innovators. *Human Relations*, 3, pp. 213-224.

6 Leonard, D. and Swap, W. (2005). *Deep smarts: how to cultivate and transfer enduring business wisdom*. Boston: Harvard Business School Press.

7 Guilford, J. (1967). *The nature of human intelligence*. New York: McGraw-Hill.

8 Sternberg, R. (1999). Handbook of creativity. Cambridge, MA: Cambridge University Press.

9 Bessant, J. and Tidd, J. (2015). *Innovation and entrepreneurship*. Hoboken, NJ: Wiley.

10 Bessant, J. and Tidd, J. (2015). *Innovation and entrepreneurship*. Hoboken, NJ: Wiley.

11 de Bono, E.(1985). *Six thinking hats*. Harmondsworth, UK: Penguin.

12 Osborn, A. (1953). *Applied imagination: principles and procedures of creative problem solving*. New York: Charles Scribner and Sons.

13 Kingdon, M.E. (2002). *Sticky wisdom: how to start a creative revolution at work*. London: Capstone.

14 Lehrer, J.(2012). *Imagine: how creativity works*. Edinburgh: Canongate.

15 Allen, T. (1977). *Managing the flow of technology*. Cambridge, MA: MIT Press.

16 Birkinshaw, J. and Duke, L. (2013). Employee-led innovation. *Business Strategy Review*, 2013(2), pp. 46–50.

CHAPTER 4

Searching for Opportunities

LEARNING OBJECTIVES

By the end of this chapter you will be able to understand:

1. *Where innovations come from, the wide range of different sources which offer opportunities to entrepreneurs*

2. *Where could we innovate? The opportunity space available for innovation*

3. *How to search for opportunities to innovate*

4.0   Where Do Innovations Come From?

One definition of an entrepreneur is someone who sees an opportunity and does something about it. Whether it's an individual looking to find a new product or service to make his or her fortune, a social entrepreneur trying to change the world, or a large established organization looking for new market space, the challenge is one of finding opportunities for innovation.

So where do innovations come from? Do they just flash into life like the light bulb popping up above a cartoon character's head? Or strike with sudden inspiration, like Archimedes jumping up from his bath and running down the street, so enthused by his new idea that he forgot to get dressed? Such "Eureka!" moments are certainly a part of innovation folklore, and from time to time, they do lead somewhere.

For example, Percy Shaw's observation of the reflection in a cat's eye at night led to the development of one of the most widely used road safety innovations in the world.

Or George de Mestral, on a walk in the Swiss Alps, noticing the way plant burrs became attached to his dog's fur and developing from that inspiration the highly successful Velcro fastener.

But in reality, there's much more to innovation than simple inspiration or flashes of bright ideas, although these can be useful starting points. Creating value from ideas involves a process of actively searching for ideas, revising and refining them, weaving different strands of knowledge together towards a useful product, process or service. We've learned that opportunities exist in many different places and our challenge in searching is to make sure we spread our net as widely as possible in the early stages. **Figure 4.1** indicates the wide range of stimuli which can begin the innovation journey.

An important discussion in entrepreneurship concerns the extent to which entrepreneurs are "discoverers," better able to find opportunities which are already in the world and waiting to be found. The alternative is that they are creators of opportunity, able to reframe and open up new space for innovation. This corresponds a little to our "knowledge push" vs. "need pull" model. This theme is particularly associated with the work of Scott Shane.*

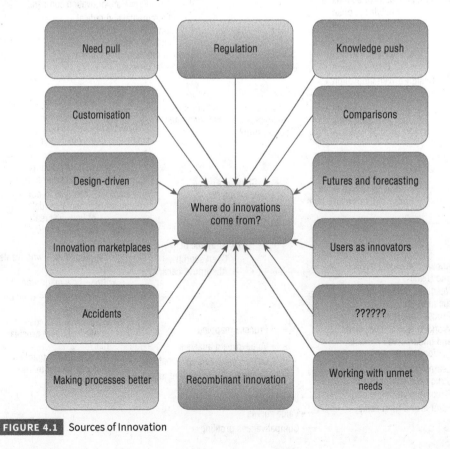

FIGURE 4.1   Sources of Innovation

*Shane, S., (2003). *A general theory of entrepreneurship: the individual-opportunity nexus.* Cheltenham: Edward Elgar.

Before we look at some tools to help us make use of these different sources it might be worth pausing for a moment to think about a second big question where *could* we innovate? How can we navigate across such a rich sea of innovation possibilities? How can we explore innovation space?

DEEPER DIVE: Sources of innovation

Read the Deeper Dive_Sources of innovation document in the ebook or from the book companion site.

VIDEO: Stephen Johnson, Popular Science Author and Media Theorist

Stephen Johnson (2010) discusses where innovations come from in his TED talk at https://www.ted.com/talks/steven_johnson_where_good_ideas_come_from?language=en.

4.1 | Where Could We Innovate?

One approach to finding an answer to the question of where we could innovate is to use a kind of "innovation compass" exploring different possible directions. **Figure 4.2** illustrates this innovation can take many forms, but we can map (**Table 4.1**) the options along four key dimensions.

For example, a new design of car, a new insurance package for accident-prone babies, and a new home-entertainment system would all be examples of *product innovation*. And change in the manufacturing methods and equipment used to produce the car or the home-entertainment system, or in the office procedures and sequencing in the insurance case, would be examples of *process innovation*.

Sometimes the dividing line is somewhat blurred. For example, a new jet-powered sea ferry is both a product and a process innovation. Services represent a particular case of this where the product and process aspects often merge. For example, is a new holiday package a product or process change?

Innovation can also take place by repositioning the perception of an established product or process in a particular user context. For example, an old-established product in the UK is Lucozade, originally developed as a glucose-based drink to help children and invalids in convalescence. These associations with sickness were abandoned by the brand owner, Beechams (part of GlaxoSmithKline), when it relaunched the product as a health drink aimed at the growing fitness market, where it is now presented as a performance-enhancing aid to healthy exercise. In 2014, the brand was sold to the giant Japanese firm Suntory for around $1.35 billion.

In similar fashion, Haagen-Dazs created a new market for ice cream, essentially targeted at adults, through *position innovation* rather than changing the product or core manufacturing

---

TABLE 4.1 **Mapping Innovation Space**

Dimension	Type of change
"Product" – What we offer the world	Changes in the things (products/services) an organization offers
"Process" – How we create and deliver that offering	Changes in the ways these offerings are created and delivered
"Position" – Who we provide our offering to and the story we tell around it	Changes in the context into which the products/services are introduced
"Paradigm" – Our core "business model" about who we are and how we create value	Changes in the underlying mental models which frame what the organization does

Source: Based on Francis, D. and Bessant, J. (2005). Targeting innovation and implications for capability development. *Technovation*, 25(3), pp. 171-183.

process. Reuben Mattus and his wife Rose founded the company in 1976 in New York and concentrated on high quality ingredients, aiming at the premium price market segment. They began with only three flavors but offered a rich taste and texture experience. By the 1990s, they had developed a niche typified by the "Lose Control" advertising campaign which was heavily influenced by fashion photography. Their message was that ice cream was no longer a treat for kids; it was a serious, luxury indulgence for adults.

His earlier background in marketing meant that he understood about positioning and brand image. He is quoted as saying, "If you're the same like everybody else, you're lost . . . the number one thing was to get a foreign sounding name." The name was an invention; it was chosen to sound like something Danish and carry associations to that world of good quality dairy products.

Sometimes opportunities for innovation emerge when we reframe the way we look at something. Henry Ford fundamentally changed the face of transportation not because he invented the motor car (he was a comparative latecomer to the new industry) or because he developed the manufacturing process to put one together (as a craft-based specialist industry, car-making had been established for around 20 years). His contribution was to change the underlying model from one which offered a hand-made, specialist product to a few wealthy customers to one which offered a car for Everyman at a price he could afford. The ensuing shift from craft to mass production was nothing short of a revolution in the way cars (and later countless other products and services) were created and delivered. Of course, making the new approach work in practice also required extensive product and process innovation, for example, in component design, in machinery building, in factory layout, and particularly in the social system around which work was organized.

CASE STUDY: Model T Ford

Read the Case Study_ Model T Ford document in the ebook or from the book companion site.

Examples of "paradigm" innovation – changes in mental models – include the shift to low-cost airlines, the provision of online insurance and other financial services and the repositioning of drinks like coffee and fruit juice as premium "designer" products. They involve a shift in the underlying vision about how innovation can create social or commercial value. The term "business model" is increasingly used and this is another way of thinking about "*paradigm innovation*" – we'll look at this in more detail in Chapter 12. Here (**Table 4.2**) are some examples:

What about not-for-profit and the public sector? The same ideas apply; there are examples of innovations along all the four dimensions and in the spaces in between.[†]

TABLE 4.2   **Examples of *Business Model Innovation***

Business model innovation	How it changes the rules of the game
"Servitization"	Traditionally, manufacturing was about producing and then selling a product. But increasingly, manufacturers are bundling various support services around their products, particularly for major capital goods. Rolls Royce, the aircraft engine maker, still produces high quality engines, but it has an increasingly large business around services to ensure those engines keep delivering power over the 30-plus year life of many aircraft. Caterpillar, the specialist machinery company, now earns as much from service contracts which help keep its machines running productively as it does from the original sale.
Ownership to rental	Spotify is one of the most successful music streaming companies, with around 8 million subscribers. They shifted the model from people's desire to own the music they listened to towards one in which they rent access to a huge library of music. In similar fashion, Zipcar and other car rental businesses have transformed the need for car ownership in many large cities.
Offline to online	Many businesses have grown up around the Internet and enabled substitution of physical encounters – for example, in retailing – with virtual ones.
Mass customization and co-creation	New technologies and a growing desire for customization have enabled the emergence not only of personalized products but platforms on which users can engage and co-create everything from toys (e.g., Lego), clothing (e.g., Adidas) to complex equipment like cars (Local Motors).

[†]Additional information and examples are available via the book companion website.

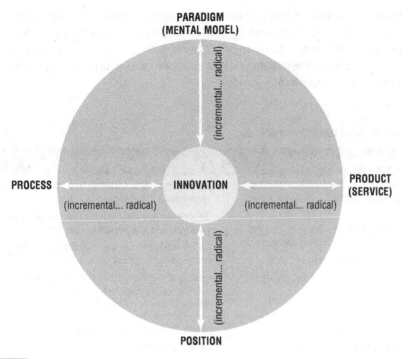

FIGURE 4.2 The 4Ps Model

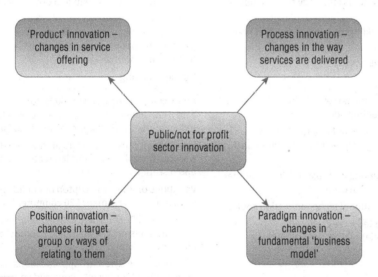

FIGURE 4.3 Exploring Innovation Space in Not-for-Profit and Public-Sector Organizations

Public-Sector Innovation

Read the Public public-sector innovation document in the ebook or from the book companion site.

What About the Small Stuff? The Importance of *Incremental Innovation*

It's easy to fall into the trap of thinking that innovation must be new to the world and incredibly dramatic. That's not the case. In fact, most innovations are improvements of ideas which already exist. "Doing what we do but better," is a rich seam of opportunities to be mined, and there are big advantages to this approach. It involves lower risk because we already know about the technology, the market, the competitors, etc. We still have to improve on what's there, but we have quite a lot of knowledge to help us get started.

Of course, in mature markets and competitive spaces, we will sometimes need to look for something radically different, something which rewrites the rules of the game. When this succeeds, it is great, but the path to get there is littered with the wreckage of many failures. And even when you get there, the challenge is that everyone else starts to follow your example and tries and find ways to improve on your idea!

TABLE 4.3   Some Examples of Innovations Mapped Onto the 4Ps Model

Innovation Type	Incremental: Do what we do but better	Radical: Do something different
Product: What we offer the world	Different Windows generations, for example, 7 and 8 replacing Vista and XP, essentially improving existing software New versions of established car models (e.g., the VW Golf essentially improving on established car design) Improved performance incandescent light bulbs CDs replacing vinyl records (essentially improving on storage technology)	New to the world software (e.g., the first speech-recognition program) Toyota Prius' hybrid engines (bringing a new concept) and the Tesla high-performance electric car LED-based lighting (using completely different and more energy efficient principles) Spotify and other music-streaming services (changing the pattern from owning to renting a vast library of music)
Process: How we create and deliver that offering	Improved fixed-line telephone services Extended range of stock-brokering services Improved auction house operations Improved factory operations efficiency through upgraded equipment Improved range of banking services delivered at branch banks Improved retailing logistics	Skype and other VOIP systems Online share trading eBay Toyota Production System and other "lean" approaches Online banking and now mobile banking in Kenya and the Philippines (using phones as an alternative to banking systems) Online shopping
Position: Where we target that offering and the story we tell about it	Haagen-Dazs changing the target market for ice cream from children to consenting adults Airlines segmenting service offering for different passenger groups – Virgin Upper Class, BA Premium Economy, etc. Dell and others segmenting and customizing computer configuration for individual users Online support for traditional higher education courses Banking services targeted at key segments (e.g., students, retired people)	Addressing underserved markets, for example, the Tata Nano aimed at emerging but relatively poor Indian market with car priced around $2000 Low-cost airlines opening up air travel to those previously unable to afford it (create new market and disrupt existing one) Variations on the "One Laptop per Child" project (e.g., Indian government $20 computer for schools) University of Phoenix and others building large education businesses via online approaches to reach different markets "Bottom of the pyramid" approaches using a similar principle but tapping into huge and very different high-volume/low-margin markets (e.g., Aravind Eye Clinics, Cemex construction products)
Paradigm: How we frame what we do	Bausch & Lomb moved from "eye wear" to "eye care" as its business model, effectively letting go of the old business of spectacles, sunglasses (Raybans) and contact lenses, all of which were becoming commodity businesses and moved into newer high-tech fields like laser surgery equipment, specialist optical devices and research in artificial eyesight. Dyson redefining the home appliance market in terms of high-performance engineered products Rolls Royce (from high-quality aero engines to becoming a service company offering "power by the hour") IBM (from being a machine maker to a service and solution company, selling off its computer making and building up its consultancy and service side)	Grameen Bank and other microfinance models (rethinking the assumptions about credit and the poor) iTunes platform (a complete system of personalized entertainment) Amazon, Google, Skype (redefining industries like retailing, advertising, and telecoms through online models) Linux, Mozilla, Apache (moving from passive users to active communities of users co-creating new products and services)

We can map this pattern of *incremental and radical innovation* ("do better" and "do different") onto our 4Ps model.

From Components to Systems?

Take a look at your mobile phone and think about the kind of innovation it represents. You'd probably say it's a product innovation, a change in the device we use to communicate. And you could plot its history from the earliest clunky fixed-line variants of a century ago to today's wristwatch and wearables.

You could also see it as a collection of product innovations which have converged over time. It now performs many different functions beyond simple voice communication: it's a clock, a calculator, a map, a library, a flashlight, and a terminal to access the huge information resources of the internet. It can do all of this because of the GPS, gyroscopes and all kinds of other sensors and actuators built in.

And you could also think in terms of what it represents: a platform on which you can build whatever you want your personal device to be. In your hand, you carry a kind of giant marketplace where sellers of every conceivable kind of app are trying to persuade you to purchase and use theirs. (Estimates for 2015 suggest there are nearly 2 million apps available for Android devices and a similar number for Apple!)

Pretty soon you might be feeling dizzy with all these layers and levels of innovation, each of which represents someone's entrepreneurial activity.

Innovation is often like a set of Russian dolls; we can change things at the level of components or we can change a whole system. For example, we can put a faster transistor on a microchip on a circuit board for the graphics display in a computer. Or we can change the way several boards are put together into the computer to give it particular capabilities: a games box, an e-book, a media PC. Or we can link the computers into a network to drive a small business or office. Or we can link the networks to others into the Internet. There's scope for innovation at each level, but changes in the higher-level systems often have implications for lower down. For example, if cars, as a complex assembly, were suddenly designed to be made from plastic instead of metal, it would still leave scope for car assemblers but would pose some sleepless nights for producers of metal components!

Figure 4.4 shows the range of choices, highlighting the point that such change can happen at the component or subsystem level or across the whole system.

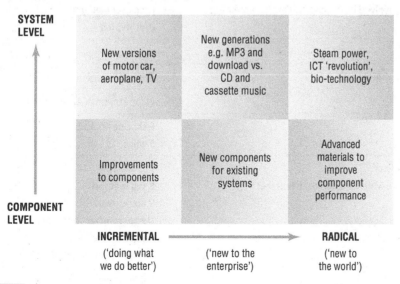

FIGURE 4.4 Dimensions of Innovation

4.2 How to Search: The opportunity Treasure Hunt

So far, we've looked at where innovations come from and at the wide range of innovation space across which we can look for these opportunities. Now we need to think about the question of how to carry out our search, and the good news here is that there is a rich toolkit on which we can draw. In **Table 4.3**, we look at some of the key sources of innovation and the questions we might want answers to in making use of them. And we link to some useful tools to help in answering these questions and some case examples. (In the workbook, there are some activities linked to these tools, so you have a chance to try them out for yourself.)

TABLE 4.4   **The Entrepreneur's Search Toolkit‡**

Source of innovation – and key questions about it	Useful Tools
Knowledge push	
Strategic fit – Why would deploying this knowledge be useful to us?	*Competency mapping*
Open search – Where is there useful knowledge outside our organization?	Open innovation tools like innovation marketplaces and knowledge mining
Absorptive capacity – How to acquire and use new knowledge from outside?	Absorptive capacity audit
Need pull	
Segmentation – Which people in the market might want our new product or service?	*Market segmentation*
Size – How many people want it?	Market surveys and focus groups
Concept testing – What do they want?	Concept testing Prototyping Minimum viable product
Hidden/latent needs – How do we help them articulate what they want?	*Ethnography* *Kano method* Value curves Outcome-driven innovation
Active user engagement – How can we get them involved in shaping and even co-creating our new product or service?	*Lead user methods* Prototyping
Process improvement	
What is the current process (and where could we improve it)?	Process mapping
Where is value created – or lost?	Value stream analysis
What are the root causes of process problems?	Fishbone analysis 5 whys
Working with unmet needs and underserved markets How can we find out about the needs people have which are not yet being met?	Ethnography Kano method Value curves *Outcome driven innovation* Frugal innovation Competitiveness profiling
Customization How can we configure our new offering to meet specific needs of different groups of people in the market?	Value curves Competitiveness profiling

TABLE 4.4   **The Entrepreneur's Search Toolkit**‡ *(continued)*

Source of innovation – and key questions about it	Useful Tools
Users as innovators How can we engage users as active players, contributors, even co-creators in the innovation process?	Crowdsourcing Lead user methods Prototyping
Mobilizing minds How can we gather ideas and inputs from many different people?	Innovation marketplaces Innovation contests Crowdsourcing
Learning from others through structured comparisons	
How can we design and carry out systematic comparisons to help us spot gaps and innovation opportunities?	Benchmarking Value curves Competitiveness profiling Blue Ocean strategy
Recombinant innovation	
How can we find similar problems in other areas and adapt solutions from these other worlds?	TRIZ Abstract-driven search/levels of abstraction
Futures and forecasting	
How can we explore the future in systematic fashion and use this to give some clues about innovation opportunities?	Scenarios Delphi methods Trend extrapolation

‡Further information on these tools and case illustrations are available on the book companion website.

Chapter Summary

- Innovations don't just appear perfectly formed, and the process is not simply a spark of imagination giving rise to changing the world. Instead, innovations come from a number of sources, and these interact over time.

- Sources of innovation can be resolved into two broad classes, knowledge push and need pull, although they almost always act in tandem. Innovation arises from their interplay.

- Entrepreneurs are both "discoverers" of opportunities (need pull) and "creators" of them (knowledge push).

- There are many variations on this theme, for example,"need pull" can include social needs, market needs, latent needs, "squeaking wheels," crisis needs, etc.

- While the basic forces pushing and pulling have been a feature of the innovation landscape for a long time, it involves a moving frontier in which new sources of push and pull come into play. Examples include the emerging demand pull from the "bottom of

the pyramid" and the opportunities opened up by an acceleration in knowledge production in R&D systems around the world.

- *User-led innovation* has always been important, but developments in communications technology have enabled much higher levels of engagement, via crowdsourcing, user communities, co-creation platforms, etc.

- Regulation is also an important element in shaping and directing innovative activity. By restricting what can and can't be done for legal reasons, new trajectories for change are established which entrepreneurs can take advantage of.

- Design-driven approaches and the related toolkit around prototyping are of growing importance.

- Accidents have always been a potential source of innovation, but converting them to opportunities requires an open mind. As Pasteur is reputed to have said, "Chance favors the prepared mind!"

Key Terms

Absorptive capacity   the extent to which an organization is able to make effective use of external knowledge

Business model innovation   changes in the whole architecture which describes a venture, how value is created and captured, for whom, underlying cost structure and market strategy, etc. (See Chapter 12 for more on this.)

Competency mapping   searching for opportunities by deploying elements of the organization's knowledge base

Component innovation   changes in one part of a wider system

Ethnography   approach to understanding user needs by observing what they do and how their world operates in terms of norms, values, behaviors, etc. Originally comes from the field of anthropology

Incremental innovation   small improvements to existing products, services or processes – "doing what we do but better."

Kano method   approach to understanding customer needs based on satisfying or delighting people in terms of what is offered

Lead user methods   tools linked to user-led innovation

Market segmentation   breaking the target market down into focused chunks rather than trying to address the needs of everyone

Outcome driven innovation   approach originally developed by Anthony Ulwick which finds opportunities through a rigorous analysis of the "jobs to be done" which people have rather than simple user needs research

Paradigm innovation   changes in the underlying mental or business model

Position innovation   changes in the context into which an innovation is launched – for example, a new market

Process innovation   changes in the way in which an offering is created or delivered

Product innovation   changes in what an organization offers the world

Radical innovation   significantly different changes to products, services or processes – "doing something completely different."

Recombinant innovation   type of innovation which transfers and applies well-known knowledge in one field into a different one in which it is novel

System innovation   (sometimes called architectural innovation) changes in the whole system, for example, moving from that computer design to a completely different way of processing information

User-led innovation   class of innovations which originate with early users whose interest or frustration leads them to create something new

CHAPTER 5

Building the Case

LEARNING OBJECTIVES

By the end of this chapter you will be able to:

1. *Develop a business plan to attract resources.*

2. *Assess market opportunities and competition.*

3. *Identify and manage critical risks and uncertainty.*

4. *Evaluate the costs, resources, and value of a project.*

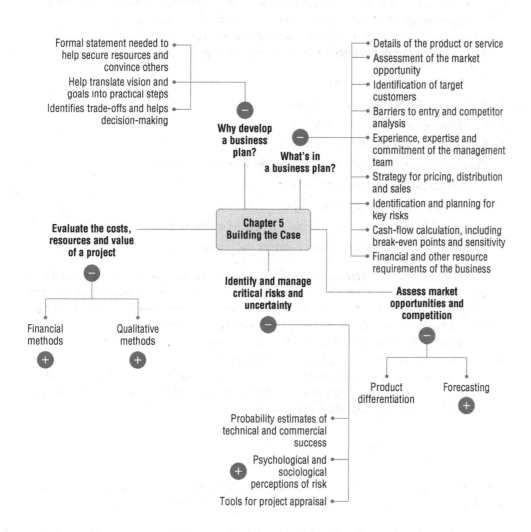

5.0 Why Develop a Business Plan?

Having identified an opportunity, the next stage in the entrepreneur's journey is trying to find the resources to make the new venture happen. And for that we need some kind of plan, a formal statement which we can use to secure support or funding for a project or venture. However, research is not unanimous on the role and effectiveness of business plans. Some studies indicate a positive relationship between the development of a formal business plan and the ability to attract external funding,[1] whereas others find no significant relationship.[2] Whatever the reality, the development of a convincing plan has become a rite of passage for a new venture.

In practice, business planning serves a much broader function than funding, and can help to translate abstract or ambiguous goals into more explicit operational needs, and support subsequent decision-making and identify trade-offs. A business plan can help to make more explicit the risks and opportunities, expose any unfounded optimism and self-delusion, and avoid subsequent arguments concerning responsibilities and rewards.

5.1 What's in a Business Plan?

No standard business plan exists, but in many cases venture capitalists will provide a pro forma for their business plan. Typically, a business plan should be relatively concise, say no more than 10–20 pages, begin with an executive summary, and include sections on the product, markets, technology, development, production, marketing, human resources, financial estimates with contingency plans, and the timetable and funding requirements.

A typical formal business plan will include the following sections:[3]

1. Details of the product or service.
2. Assessment of the market opportunity.
3. Identification of target customers.
4. Barriers to entry and competitor analysis.
5. Experience, expertise, and commitment of the management team.
6. Strategy for pricing, distribution, and sales.
7. Identification and planning for key risks.
8. Cash-flow calculation, including break-even points and sensitivity.
9. Financial and other resource requirements of the business.

Unfortunately, many entrepreneurs place too much emphasis on the novelty of the technology, product, or market, rather than more relevant factors such as experience and the assessment of market potential and risk. **Table 5.1** shows some of the criteria which venture capitalists actually use to help them make judgments about funding new ventures.

Fewer than half of the plans examined provide a detailed marketing strategy, and just half include any sales plan. Three-quarters of the plans fail to identify or analyze any potential competitors. As a result, most business plans contain only basic information. The lack of attention to marketing and competitor analysis is particularly problematic as research indicates that both factors are associated with subsequent success.[4]

A Question of Balance

When developing a business plan, it is necessary to balance the need for detail with the need for flexibility. This includes a number of trade-offs or "balancing acts":[5]

- *The appropriate degree of formalization.* Formalization is good because it facilitates transparency, order, and predictability – but in striving to enforce effectiveness, formalization

TABLE 5.1   **Criteria Used by Venture Capitalists to Assess Proposals**

Important Criteria for Funding	Mean Score
Entrepreneur able to evaluate and react to risk	3.6
Entrepreneur capable of sustained effort	3.6
Entrepreneur familiar with the market	3.5
Entrepreneur demonstrated leadership ability*	3.2
Financial return > 10 times within 10 years*	3.1
Entrepreneur has relevant track record*	3.0
Product prototype exists and functions*	3.0
Target market has high growth rate*	3.0
Product demonstrated market acceptance*	2.9
Product proprietary or can be protected*	2.7
Investment is easily made liquid* (e.g., made public or acquired)	2.7
Venture will stimulate an existing market	2.4
Little threat of competition within 3 years	2.3
Venture will create a new market*	1.9
Product is "high technology"	1.5

1 = irrelevant, 2 = desirable, 3 = important, 4 = essential. *Denotes significant difference in the ranking of European, US, and Asian criterion. Sample size = 348 venture capitalists
Source: Adapted from Knight, R. 1992, Criteria used by venture capitalists, In T. Khalil and B. Bayraktar (eds.), *Management of Technology III: The key to global competitiveness*, Industrial Engineering & Management Press, Georgia, pp. 574–583.

also risks inhibiting innovation and flexibility. From this it follows that entrepreneurs need to carefully consider the level of formalization they impose on the fuzzy front end.

- *Gentle or harsh screening of ideas.* On the one hand, firms need to get rid of bad ideas quickly, to save the costs associated with their further development. On the other hand, harsh screening may also kill good ideas too early. Ideas for new products often refine and gain momentum through informal discussion and testing.

- *Uncertainty reduction and equivocality.* Market and technological uncertainty can often be reduced through environmental scanning and increased information processing in the development team, but more information often increases the level of equivocality. An equivocal situation is one where multiple interpretations can be made. Therefore, firms need to balance their need to reduce uncertainty with the need to reduce equivocality.

- *Flexibility in product definition vs. the need to push it to closure.* A key objective in the fuzzy front end is a clear, robust, and unambiguous product definition, as such a definition facilitates the subsequent development phase. However, product features often need to be changed during development as market needs change or problems with underlying technologies are experienced.

- *Innovation vs. resource efficiency.* In essence, this concerns balancing competing value orientations, where innovation and creativity in the front end are enabled by organizational slack and an emphasis on people management, while resource efficiency is enabled by discipline and an emphasis on process management.

DEEPER DIVE: The fuzzy front end

Read the *Deeper Dive_The fuzzy front end* document in the ebook or from the book companion site.

5.2 Assess Market Opportunities and Competition

If we are going to construct a robust business plan, then it is clear from the above that we need to put considerable effort into understanding the potential market for our new idea. Forecasting the future has a pretty bad track record, but nevertheless has a central role in business planning for innovation. In most cases, the outputs (that is, the predictions made) are less valuable than the process of forecasting itself. If conducted in the right spirit, forecasting should provide a framework for gathering and sharing data, debating interpretations, and making assumptions, challenges, and risks more explicit.

There are many different methods to support forecasting, each with different benefits and limitations, and **Table 5.2** gives some examples.

There is no single best method. The most appropriate choice of forecasting method will depend on:

- What we are trying to forecast.
- Rate of technological and market change.
- Availability and accuracy of information.
- The company's planning horizon.
- The resources available for forecasting.

In practice, there will be a trade-off between the resources available and robustness of a forecast. The more common methods of forecasting such as trend extrapolation and time series are of limited use for new products, because of the lack of past data. The choice of method will also depend upon the type of business and the technological and market environment (**Figure 5.1**).

TABLE 5.2 Types, Uses, and Limitations of Different Methods of Forecasting

Method	Uses	Limitations
Market segmentation	Medium-term, product attributes & market segments understood	Sophistication of users, limitation of tools to distinguish noise & information
Trend extrapolation	Short-term, stable environment	Relies on past data & assumes past patterns
Competitor benchmarking	Medium-term, product & process improvement	Identifying relevant benchmarking candidates
Product and technology road-mapping	Medium-term, stable platform & clear trajectory	Incremental, fails to identify future uncertainties
Scenario development	Long-term, high uncertainty	Time-consuming, unpalatable outcomes

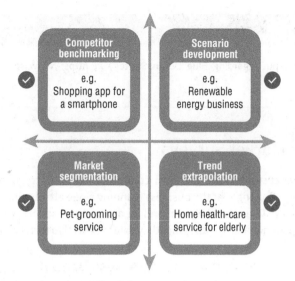

FIGURE 5.1 Choosing the Right Forecasting Method.

Entrepreneurship in Action: Cross-industry benchmarking

Rail services and Formula 1 racing do not appear to have much in common, other than wheels. However, train companies in the UK have begun to benchmark F1 practices and technology.

In an effort to improve train availability and utilization, train maintenance crews have studies how F1 teams conduct rapid pit-stops. As a result, turnaround times have been reduced from two days to as little as four hours.

Technology benchmarking is also improving performance. Use of telemetry is advanced in F1 racing to identify emerging problems and to anticipate and correct faults. Train companies are using similar techniques to try to reduce breakdowns and delays. Finally, F1 has pioneered the use of KERS – Kinetic Energy Recovery Systems – to capture wasted energy during braking and to re-use this for acceleration, and train manufacturers are researching how this can be adapted for their use.

A deeper technique, regression analysis, can be used to identify the main factors driving demand for a given product, and therefore provide some estimate of future demand, given data on the underlying drivers. For example, a regression might express the likely demand for the next generation of digital mobile phones in terms of rate of economic growth, price relative to competing systems, rate of new business formation, and so on. For each variable, a coefficient is derived, based on the relative influence of the variable. Thus, the reliability of the forecast depends a great deal on selecting the right variables in the first place. The advantage of regression is that, unlike simple extrapolation or time-series analysis, the forecast is based on cause-and-effect relations. Econometric models are simply bundles of regression equations, including their interrelationship. However, regression analysis is of little use where future values of an explanatory value are unknown, or where the relationship between the explanatory and forecast variables may change.

Leading indicators and analogues can improve the reliability of forecasts, and are useful guideposts to future trends in some sectors. In both cases, there is a historical relationship between two trends. For example, new business start-ups might be a leading indicator of the demand for fax machines in six months' time. Similarly, business users of mobile telephones may be an analogue for subsequent patterns of domestic use.

Such "normative" techniques are useful for estimating the future demand for existing products, or perhaps alternative technologies or novel niches, but are of limited utility in the case of more radical systems innovation. Exploratory forecasting, in contrast, attempts to explore the range of future possibilities. The most common methods are:

- customer or market surveys
- scenario development.

VIDEO: Liz Jones, Strategy Regeneration

Liz Jones, Strategy Regeneration(2015) has interesting input regarding Blue Ocean Strategy at https://www.ispim-innovation.com/single-post/2015/06/16/Liz-Jones-Blue-Ocean-Strategy.*

Customer or Market Surveys

Surveys of potential customers are the most common method of trying to assess a market opportunity. The key challenges at the business planning stage are obtaining usable estimates of demand and pricing. To assess likely demand for a product or service, we need to refine our view of the target customer and identify what they value. Central to this is market segmentation.

Segmenting the Potential Market to Assess Demand
Segmentation is more effective for routine development projects, and prototyping, industry experts, focus groups, and latent needs analysis are all more effective for novel development projects.[6] Market or buyer segmentation is simply the process of identifying groups of customers with sufficiently similar purchasing behavior so that they can be targeted and treated in a similar way. This is important because different groups are likely to have different needs. By definition, the needs of customers in the same segment will be highly homogeneous. In formal statistical terms, the objective of segmentation is to maximize across-group variance and minimize within-group variance.

In practice, segmentation is conducted by analyzing customers' buying behavior and then using factor analysis to identify the most significant variables influencing behavior – descriptive segmentation – and then using cluster analysis to create distinct segments which help identify unmet customer needs – prescriptive segmentation. The principle of segmentation applies to both consumer and business markets, but the process and basis of segmentation are different in each case.

Segmenting Consumer Markets
Much of the research on the buying behavior of consumers is based on theories adapted from the social and behavioral sciences. Utilitarian theories assume that consumers are rational and make purchasing decisions by comparing product utility with their requirements. This model suggests a sequence of phases in the purchasing decision: problem recognition, information search, evaluation of alternatives, and finally, the purchase. However, such rational processes do not appear to have much influence on actual buying behavior.

For example, consumers' associations routinely test a wide range of competing products, and make buying recommendations based on largely objective criteria. If the majority of buyers were rational, and the consumers' association successfully identified all relevant criteria, these recommendations would become best-sellers, but this is not so.

Behavioral approaches have greater explanatory power. These emphasize the effect of attitude, and argue that the buying decision follows a sequence of changing attitudes toward a product – awareness, interest, desire, and finally, action. The goal of advertising is to stimulate this sequence of events. However, research suggests that attitude alone explains only 10% of decisions and can rarely predict buyer behavior.

In practice, the balance between rational and behavioral influences will depend on the level of customer involvement. Clearly, the decision-making process for buying an aircraft or machine tool is different from the process of buying a toothpaste or shampoo. Many purchasing decisions involve little cost or risk, and are therefore, low involvement. In such cases, consumers try to minimize the financial, mental, and physical effort involved in purchasing. Advertising is most effective in such cases. In contrast, in high-involvement situations, in which there is a high cost or potential risk to customers, buyers are willing to search

---

*Link included with permission of ISPIM.

for information and make a more informed decision. Advertising is less effective in such circumstances, and is typically confined to presenting comparative information between rival products.

There are many bases of segmenting consumer markets, including groupings by socio-economic class, life-cycle groupings, and by lifestyle or psychographic (psychological–demographic) factors. An example of psychographic segmentation is the Taylor–Nelson classification that consists of self-explorers, social resisters, experimentalists, achievers, belongers, survivors, and the aimless.

Segmenting Business Markets   Business customers tend to be better informed than consumers and, in theory at least, make more rational purchasing decisions. Business customers can be segmented on the basis of common buying factors or purchasing processes. The basis of segmentation should have clear operational implications, such as differences in preferences, pricing, distribution, or sales strategy. For example, customers could be segmented on the basis of how experienced, sophisticated, or price-sensitive they are. However, the process is complicated by the number of people involved in the buying process:

- The actual customer or buyer, who typically has the formal authority to choose a supplier and agree to terms of purchase.
- The ultimate users of the product or service, who are normally, but not always, involved in the initiation and specification of the purchase.
- Gatekeepers, who control the flow of information to the buyers and users.
- Influencers, who may provide some technical support to the specification and comparison of products.

Therefore, it is critical to identify all relevant parties in an organization, and determine the main influences on each. For example, technical personnel used to determine the specification may favor performance, whereas the actual buyer may stress value for money.

The most common basis of business segmentation is by the benefits customers derive from the product, process, or service. Customers may buy the same product for very different reasons, and attach different weightings to different product features.

It is difficult in practice to identify distinct segments by benefit because these are not strongly related to more traditional and easily identifiable characteristics such as firm size or industry classification. Therefore, benefit segmentation is only practical where such preferences can be related to more easily observable and measurable customer characteristics. For example, in the case of the machine tool, analysis of production volumes, batch sizes, operating margins, and value added might help differentiate between those firms which value higher efficiency and those which seek improvements in quality.

Differentiating Our Offering From Competitors   Having identified our target customer through segmentation, we can better assess how they define value, and why they might purchase our offering rather than existing or competing offerings. In short, how do we differentiate our product or service from others?

Here we are concerned with the specific issue of how to differentiate a product from competing offerings where technologies and markets are relatively stable. It is in these circumstances that the standard tools and techniques of marketing are most useful. We assume the reader is familiar with the basics of marketing, so here we shall focus on product differentiation by quality and other attributes.

Differentiation measures the degree to which competitors differ from one another in a specific market. Markets in which there is little differentiation and no significant difference in the relative quality of competitors are characterized by low profitability, whereas differentiation on the basis of relative quality or other product characteristics is a strong predictor of high profitability in any market conditions. Where a firm achieves a combination of high differentiation and high perceived relative quality, the return on investment is typically twice that of non-differentiated products.

Analysis of the Strategic Planning Institute's database of more than 3000 business units helps us to identify the profit impact of market strategy (PIMS):[7]

- High relative quality is associated with a high return on sales. One reason for this is that businesses with higher relative quality are able to demand higher prices than their competitors. Moreover, higher quality may also help reduce costs by limiting waste and improving processes. As a result, companies may benefit from both higher prices and lower costs than competitors, thereby increasing profit margins.

- Good value is associated with increased market share. Plotting relative quality against relative price provides a measure of relative value: high quality at a high price represents average value, but high quality at a low price represents good value. Products representing poor value tend to lose market share, but those offering good value gain market share.

- Product differentiation is associated with profitability. Differentiation is defined in terms of how competitors differ from each other within a particular product segment. It can be measured by asking customers to rank the individual attributes of competing products, and to weight the attributes. Customer weighting of attributes is likely to differ from that of the technical or marketing functions.

The compound effect of such differences in real growth can have a significant impact on relative market share over a relatively short period of time. However, in consumer markets, maintaining high levels of new product introduction is necessary, but not sufficient. In addition, reputation, or brand image, must be established and maintained, as without it, consumers are less likely to sample new product offerings, whatever the value or innovativeness.

Scenario Development

Scenarios are a good way to incorporate flexibility into business planning, by making assumptions more explicit and exploring "what-if?" trends and branching points. A strong scenario plan can also provide a persuasive narrative or story to guide the development of a new venture.

Scenarios are internally consistent descriptions of alternative possible futures, based upon different assumptions and interpretations of the driving forces of change.[8] Inputs include quantitative data and analysis, and qualitative assumptions and assessments, such as societal, technological, economic, environmental, and political drivers. Scenario development is not, strictly speaking, prediction, as it assumes that the future is uncertain and that the path of current developments can range from the conventional to the revolutionary. It is particularly good at incorporating potential critical events which might result in divergent paths or branches being pursued.

Scenario development can be normative or explorative. The normative perspective defines a preferred vision of the future and outlines different pathways from the goal to the present. For example, this is commonly used in energy futures and sustainable futures scenarios. The explorative approach defines the drivers of change, and creates scenarios from these without explicit goals or agendas.

For scenarios to be effective, they need to inclusive, plausible, and compelling (as opposed to being exclusive, implausible, or obvious), as well as being challenging to the assumptions of the stakeholders. They should make the assumptions and inputs used explicit, and form the basis of a process of discussion, debate, policy, strategy, and ultimately, action. The output is typically two or three contrasting scenarios, but the process of development and discussion of scenarios is much more valuable.

A strong scenario will be:

- Consistent. Each scenario must be internally logical and consistent to be credible.

- Plausible. To be persuasive and support action, the scenarios and underlying assumptions must be realistic.

- Transparent. The assumptions, sources, and goals should be made explicit. Without such transparency, emotive or doomsday-style scenarios with catchy titles can be convincing, but highly misleading.

- Differentiated. Scenarios should be structurally or qualitatively different, in terms of assumptions and outcomes, not simply degree or magnitude. Probability assessment of scenarios should be avoided, such as "most or least probable." Different subjective assessments of probability will be made by different stakeholders, so probability assessment can close rather than open debate on the range of possible futures.

- Communicable. Typically develop between three and five scenarios, each with vivid titles to promote memory and dissemination.

- Practical, to support action. Scenarios should be an input to strategic or policy decision-making, so should have clear implications and recommendations for action.

Innovation in Action: Internet scenarios at Cisco

Cisco develops much of the infrastructure for the Internet, so has a strategic need to explore potential future Scenarios. However, almost all organizations rely on the Internet, so these Scenarios are relevant to most, including those providing technology, connectivity, devices, software, content or services.

They began with three focal questions:

1. What will the Internet be like in 2025?

2. How much bigger will the Internet have grown from today's 2 billion users and $3 trillion market?

3. Will the Internet have achieved its full potential to connect the world's entire population in ways that advance global prosperity, business productivity, education, and social interaction?

Next, they then identified three critical drivers:

1. Size and scope of broadband network build out;

2. Incremental or breakthrough technological progress;

3. Unbridled or constrained demand from Internet users.

This analysis resulted in four contrasting Scenarios:

1. Fluid Frontiers: The Internet becomes pervasive, connectivity and devices are ever more available and affordable, while global entrepreneurship and competition create a wide range of diverse businesses and services.

2. Insecure Growth: Internet demand stalls because users fear security breaches and cyber-attacks result in increasing regulation.

3. Short of the Promise: Prolonged economic stagnation in many countries reduces the diffusion of the Internet, with no compensating technological breakthroughs.

4. Bursting at the Seams: Demand for IP-based services is boundless, but capacity constraints and occasional bottlenecks create a gap between the expectations and reality of Internet use.

If you're interested in the implications and potential strategies which flow from these four Scenarios, see the full report on the Cisco website.

Source: Olsen, E. (2011). *Strategic Planning Kit for Dummies*. 2nd ed. Hoboken, NJ: Wiley. http://www.dummies.com/how-to/content/strategic-planning-case-study-ciscos-internet-scen.html.

For start-up entrepreneurs, scenarios are powerful tools to help explore the possible future context in which the new venture will be located. But the approach is also useful for established organizations and for entrepreneurs and change agents trying to explore and open up new directions for products, services or processes. Organizations using scenario techniques confirm that these are useful to explore future risks in the business environment, to identify trends, understand interdependent forces, and to evaluate the implications of different strategic decisions. Building scenarios with broad organizational inputs helps to stretch people's thinking collectively and individually.[9]

The concept of an entrepreneurial "pivot" has become popular in research and practice. The term is adapted from financial investment analysis, but essentially describes how young (and sometimes not so young) organizations often have to challenge their assumptions, revise their initial plans, and change direction and business model.[10] We discuss business model innovation in Chapter 12, but the idea of a pivot is relevant here because any business plan is simply work-in-progress, and has to be revised in response to feedback from the environment, such as customer responses, competitor behavior, regulatory challenges, and new opportunities. So, the key to a successful pivot is to test the model continuously, adapting and adjusting as necessary.[11]

DEEPER DIVE: Business Model Innovation

Read the Deeper Dive_Business model innovation document in the ebook or from the book companion site.

5.3 | Identify and Manage Critical Risks and Uncertainty

Dealing with risk and uncertainty is central to the development of a realistic business plan. Risk is usually considered to be possible to estimate, either qualitatively – high, medium, low–or better still, by probability estimates. Uncertainty is by definition unknowable, but nonetheless, the fields and degree of uncertainty should be identified to help to select the most appropriate methods of assessment and plan for contingencies. Traditional approaches to assessing risk focus on the probability of foreseeable risks, rather than true uncertainty, or complete ignorance – what Donald Rumsfeld memorably called the "unknown unknowns" (February 12, 2002, US Department of Defense news briefing).

Research on new product development and R&D project management have identified a broad range of strategies for dealing with risk. There are many approaches to risk assessment, but the most common issues to be managed include:

- Probabilistic estimates of technical and commercial success.
- Psychological (cognitive) and sociological perceptions of risk.

A number of approaches exist to help entrepreneurs to assess risk in a balanced way.

Risk as Probability

Even in established organizations with structures and procedures for project management the problem of managing risk is significant – and it's likely to be even more of a challenge for start-up entrepreneurs. Research on established organizations indicates that 30–45% of all projects fail to be completed, and over half of projects overrun their budgets or schedules by up to 200%. For example, **Figure 5.2** presents the results of a survey of R&D managers. While most appear to be relatively confident when predicting technical issues such as the development time and costs, a much smaller proportion are confident when forecasting commercial aspects of the projects.

We examined how different approaches to project assessment were commonly used in practice. We surveyed 50 projects in 25 companies, and assessed how often different criteria were used, and how useful they were thought to be. **Table 5.3** summarizes some of the results. Clearly probabilistic estimates of technical and commercial success are nearly universal, and considered to be of critical importance in all types of project assessment. These are usually combined with some form of financial assessment, and fit with the company strategy and capabilities.

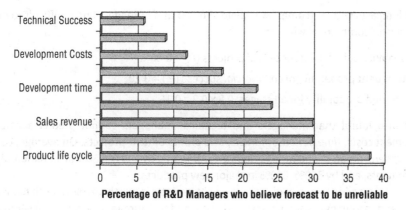

FIGURE 5.2   Managers' Perceptions of Sources of Uncertainty.

Source: Based on data from Freeman, C., & Soete, L. (1997). *The Economics of Innovation*, Cambridge, MA: MIT Press.

TABLE 5.3   **Use and Usefulness of Criteria Project Screening and Selection**

	High novelty		Low novelty	
	Usage (%)	Usefulness	Usage (%)	Usefulness
Probability of technical success	100	4.37	100	4.32
Probability of commercial success	100	4.68	95	4.50
Market share*	100	3.63	84	4.00
Core competencies*	95	3.61	79	3.00
Degree of commitment	89	3.82	79	3.67
Market size	89	3.76	84	3.94
Competition	89	3.76	84	3.81
NPV/IRR	79	3.47	68	3.92
Payback period/break-even*	79	3.20	58	4.27

Usefulness score: 5 = critical; 0 = irrelevant.
*denotes difference in usefulness rating is statistically significant at 5% level.
Source: Adapted from Tidd, J. & Bodley, K. (2002). The influence of project novelty on the new product development process. *R&D Management*, 32(2), pp. 127–38.

Question:

What do you conclude from Table 5.3 regarding the use of assessment criteria for different types of project?

The probabilities of technical and commercial success are widely used criteria, and generally relevant to all project types. Potential market size and share and payback period are commonly used criteria, but are more relevant to low novelty projects. Conversely, for more novel projects fit with competencies and commitment are more widely used and useful criteria.

Given the complexities involved, the outcomes of investments in innovation are uncertain, so that the forecasts (of costs, prices, sales volume, etc.) that underlie project and program evaluations can be unreliable. According to Joseph Bower, management finds it easier, when appraising investment proposals, to make more accurate forecasts of reductions in production cost than of expansion in sales, while their ability to forecast the financial consequences of new product introductions is very limited, indeed.[12] This last conclusion is confirmed by the study by Edwin Mansfield and his colleagues of project selection in large US firms.[13] By comparing project forecasts with outcomes, Mansfield showed that managers find it difficult to pick technological and commercial winners:

- Probability of *technical* success of projects (P_t) = 0.80
- Subsequent probability of *commercial* success (P_c) = 0.20
- Combined probability for all stages: 0.8 x 0.2 = 0.16

He also found that managers and technical managers cannot predict accurately the *development costs, time periods, markets,* and *profits* of R&D projects. On average, costs were greatly *underestimated*, and time periods *overestimated* by 140%–280% in incremental product improvements, and by 350%–600% in major new products.

Therefore, trying to get involved in the right projects is worth an effort, both to avoid wasting time and resources in meaningless activities, and to improve the chances of success.

Project appraisal and evaluation aims to:

1. Profile and gain an overall understanding of potential projects.
2. Prioritize a given set of projects, and where necessary reject projects.
3. Monitor projects, for example, by following up the criteria chosen when the project was selected.
4. Where necessary, terminate a project.
5. Evaluate the results of completed projects.
6. Review successful and unsuccessful projects to gain insights and improve future project management, that is, learning.

Entrepreneurship in Action: Very PC, learning from failure

Very PC is a family-owned start-up, created to provide information technology support for small and medium sized enterprises, and incorporated strong "environment and sustainable" ethical values.

It developed a "green" desk top computer that would operate with a fraction of the energy required for conventional desk top computers. Within the retail markets, using resellers under license, the company rode the "green IT" buzz and the demand for the "green" PCs looked secure.

The company was approached by the BBC *Dragon's Den* program to be a participant, and it agreed on the premise that it would raise public awareness and potentially increase sales. However, the experience was not positive, and the design concept of using existing components to design and build and lack of any intellectual property were criticized. The results led to a loss of customer and management confidence in the business. As a result, the company chose to focus on product re-development without changing the businesses operating model, but business performance continued to suffer.

Listening to their end-customers revealed that their resellers were using the green credentials to sell other companies products with higher margins, which contributed to forecast sales being twice actual sales. The business recovery began following a focus on direct sales and developing relationships with key customer accounts.

Source: Alexander, A., Berthod, O., Kunert, S., Salge, T. O. and Washington, A. L. (2015). *Failure-Driven Innovation*. Munich: Peter Pribilla Foundation.

Project evaluation usually assumes that there is a choice of projects to pursue, but where there is no choice, project evaluation is still important to help to assess the opportunity costs and what might be expected from pursuing a project. Different situations and contexts demand different approaches to project evaluation. We argued earlier that complexity and uncertainty are two of the most important dimensions for assessing projects. Different types of project will demand specific techniques, or at least different criteria for assessment.

A large number of techniques have been developed over the years, and are still being developed and used today. Most of these can be described by means of some common elements which form the core of any project evaluation technique:

- *Inputs* into the assessment include likely costs and benefits in financial terms, probability of technical and market success, market attractiveness, and the strategic importance to the organization.

- *Weighting*: Certain data may be given more relevance than other data (e.g., market inputs compared with technical factors), in order to reflect the company's strategy or the company's particular views. The data is then processed to arrive at the outcomes.

- *Balancing* a range of projects, as the relative value of a project with respect to other projects is an important factor in situations of competition for limited resources. Portfolio management techniques are specifically devoted to deal with this factor.

Economic and cost–benefit approaches are usually based on a combination of expected utility or Bayesian assumptions. Expected utility theory can take into account probabilistic estimates and subjective preferences, and therefore, deals well with risk aversion, but in practice, utility curves are almost impossible to construct, and individual preferences are different and highly subjective. Bayesian probability is excellent at incorporating the effects of new information, as we discussed earlier under the diffusion of innovations, but is very sensitive to the choice of relevant inputs and the weights attached to these.

As a result, no technique should be allowed to determine outcomes, as these decisions are a management responsibility. Many techniques used today are totally or partially software based, which have some additional benefits in automating the process. In any case, the most important issue, for any method, is the managers' interpretation.

There is no single "best" technique. The extent to which different techniques for project evaluation can be used will depend upon the nature of the project, the information availability, the company's culture, and several other factors. This is clear from the variety of techniques that are theoretically available and the extent to which they have been used in practice. In any case, no matter which technique is selected by a company, it should be implemented, and probably adapted, according to the particular needs of that organization. Most of the techniques in practical use incorporate a mixture of financial assessment and human judgment.

Entrepreneurship in Action: Espresso Mushroom Company*

A gourmet mushroom growing company fueled by waste coffee grounds. The Espresso Mushroom Company was founded by brothers Alex and Robbie Georgiou in 2012. Alex had first heard about the growing of mushrooms with byproducts of the coffee bean plant while working with Café Direct, but it took Robbie's discovery of the idea whilst reading Development Studies at Sussex University to prompt the two to create a start-up around the concept. As Robbie describes, "Because farmers only sell the bean from the coffee bush, they take the rest of the bush and process it to create mushroom compost, which is basically what we're doing. That's been going on since the eighties, but most people don't know about it." Alex and Robbie recognized an opportunity, but had little means to take their idea forward. Then began the lengthy trial and error process of learning how to grow high standard mushrooms with actual coffee grounds. At this time, Alex and Robbie were among a very few experimenting with the idea, a fact that gave credence to their tentative first steps.

The duo has described how much pressure, both financial and emotional, starting a business can create. According to one report, Alex and Robbie had each put in £10,000 of their own personal savings. Start-ups such as Alex and Robbie's both benefit and lose because of their small size; resources are at an absolute premium and in short supply, however, strong communication and a shared goal create an environment in which innovation and creativity can flourish.

After months of development, the first gourmet mushrooms were sold to a select few Brighton-based restaurants. It soon became clear however that significant growth could be achieved by adapting the business model, or pivoting. The Espresso Mushroom Company now make most of its income from their Kitchen Garden mushroom growing kits. That the product can be sold in trend-based clothing stores alongside ethical food companies is telling, and according to the duo, a particular choice to appeal to a wider audience than simply environmentalists.

That Robbie and Alex Georgiou were flexible enough to allow their business model to alter based on the initial success of their Kitchen Garden kits has permitted the Espresso Mushroom Company to achieve significant growth in their founding years, and to visualize a path for the future.

*A full case study on the Espresso Mushroom Company is available on the book companion website.

Perceptions of Risk

Probability estimates are only the starting point of risk assessment. Such relatively objective criteria are usually significantly moderated by psychological (cognitive) perceptions and bias, or overwhelmed altogether by sociological factors, such as peer pressure and cultural context. Studies suggest that different people (and animals) have different perceptions and tolerances for risk taking. For example, a study comparing the behaviors of chimpanzees and bonobos found that the chimps were more prepared to gamble and take risks.[14] At first sight, this appears to support the personality explanation for risk taking, but actually the two types of ape share more than 99% of their DNA. A more likely explanation is the very different environments in which they have evolved: in the chimp environment, food is scarce and uncertain, but in the bonobo habitats, food is plentiful. We are not suggesting that entrepreneurs are chimp-like, or accountants are ape-like, but rather that experience and context have a profound influence on the assessment of, and appetite for, risk.

At the individual, cognitive level, risk assessment is characterized by overconfidence, loss aversion, and bias. Overconfidence in our ability to make accurate assessments is a common failing, and results in unrealistic assumptions and uncritical assessment. Loss aversion is well documented in psychology, and essentially means that we tend to prefer to avoid loss rather than to risk gain. Finally, cognitive bias is widespread and has profound implications for the identification and assessment of risk. Cognitive bias results in us seeking and over-emphasizing evidence which supports our beliefs and reinforces our bias, but at the same time leads us to avoid and undervalue any information which contradicts our view. Therefore, we need to be aware of and challenge our own biases, and encourage others to debate and critique our data, methods, and decisions.

A common weakness is the oversimplification of problems characterized by complexity or uncertainty, and the simplification of problem-framing and evaluation of alternatives. This includes adopting a single prior hypothesis, selective use of information that supports this and devaluing alternatives, and illusion of control and predictability. Similarly, marketing managers are likely to share similar cognitive maps, and make the same assumptions concerning the relative importance of different factors contributing to new product success, such as the degree of customer orientation versus competitor orientation, and the implications of relationship between these factors, such as the degree of cross-functional coordination.

More generally, problems of limited cognition include:[15]

- *Reasoning by analogy*, which oversimplifies complex problems.
- *Adopting a single, prior-hypothesis bias*, even where information and trials suggest this is wrong.
- *Limited problem set*, the repeated use of a narrow problem-solving strategy.
- *Single outcome calculation*, which focuses on a simple single goal and a course of action to achieve it, while denying value trade-offs.
- *Illusion of control and predictability*, based on an overconfidence in the chosen strategy, a partial understanding of the problem, and limited appreciation of the uncertainty of the environment.
- *Devaluation of alternatives*, emphasizing negative aspects of alternatives.

At the group or social level, other factors also influence our perception and response to risk. How managers assess and manage risk is also a social and political process. It is influenced by prior experience of risk, perceptions of capability, status and authority, and the confidence and ability to communicate with relevant people at the appropriate times. In the context of managing innovation, risk is less about personal propensity for risk-taking or rational assessments of probability, and more about the interaction of experience, authority, and context. In practice, managers deal with risk in different ways in different situations. General strategies include delaying or delegating decisions, or sharing risk and responsibilities. Generally, when managers are performing well and achieving their targets, they have less incentive to take risks. Conversely, when under pressure to perform, managers will often accept higher risks, unless these threaten survival.

VIDEO: William Westgate, William Westgate & Associates, Inc.

William Westgate of William Westgate & Associates, Inc. (2017) offers his perspective on handling "super wicked problems" at https://www.ispim-innovation.com/single-post/2017/05/20/William-Westgate-Super-Wicked-Problems.*

5.4 Evaluate the Costs, Resources, and Value of A Project

Even in established organizations with structures and departments working on the task, the evidence is that financial appraisal of new ventures is difficult. For example, given their mathematical skills, one might have expected R&D managers to be enthusiastic users of quantitative methods for allocating resources to innovative activities. The evidence suggests otherwise: practicing R&D managers have been skeptical for a long time. An exhaustive report by practicing European managers on R&D project evaluation classifies and assesses more than 100 methods of evaluation and presents 21 case studies on their use.[16] However, it concludes that no method can guarantee success, that no single approach to pre-evaluation meets all circumstances, and that – whichever method is used – the most important outcome of a properly structured evaluation is improved communication.

In any plan, many of the variables in an evaluation cannot be reduced to a reliable set of figures to be plugged into a formula, but depend on expert judgements; hence the importance of communication, especially between innovative activities, on the one hand, and the allocation of financial resources, on the other.

Financial Methods

Financial methods are still the most commonly used method of assessing innovative projects, but usually in combination with other, often more qualitative approaches. The financial methods range from simple calculation of payback period or return on investment, to more complex assessments of net present value (NPV) through discounted cash flow (DCF).

Project appraisal by means of DCF is based on the concept that money today is worth more than money in the future. This is not because of the effect of inflation, but reflects the difference in potential investment earnings, that is, the opportunity cost of the capital invested.

The NPV of a project is calculated using:

$$NPV = \sum_{0}^{T} P_t / (1+i)^t - C$$

where:

P_t = Forecast cash flow in time period t

T = Project life

i = Expected rate of return on securities equivalent in risk to project being evaluated

C = Cost of project at time $t = 0$

In practice, rather than use this formula, it is easy to create standard NPV templates in a spreadsheet package such as Excel. For most new ventures, NPV is less useful than a simpler forecast of cash-flow, break-even, or return on investment. Spreadsheet analysis allows easy assessment of the sensitivity of the cost and income estimates. The accuracy of forecasts and level of environmental uncertainty will determine the degree of sensitivity analysis to perform.

---

* Link included with permission of ISPIM.

TABLE 5.4   **Calculation on NPV**

Year	Revenue	Costs	Cash flow	Discount	NPV
1	0	4 000	(4 000)	0.9091	(3 636)
2	2 000	4 000	(2 000)	0.8264	(1 653)
3	4 000	4 000	0	0.7513	0
4	8 000	4 000	4 000	0.6830	2 732
5	12 000	6 000	6 000	0.6209	3 725
Totals	**26 000**	**22 000**	**4 000**		**+1 168**

Example of Calculation of Net Present Value (NPV)   Assume a 10% discount rate over five years. The numbers in the "discount" column in **Table 5.4** are taken from standard tables. Brackets are normally used to show negative values.

As the NPV is positive, the project passes the test. However, first check the sensitivity to changes in the forecasted cash flow.

First, a 10% shortfall in sales.

Year	Revenue	Costs	Cash flow	Discount	NPV
1	0	4 000	(4 000)	0.9091	(3 636)
2	1 800	4 000	(2 200)	0.8264	(1 818)
3	3 600	4 000	(400)	0.7513	(300)
4	7 200	4 000	3 200	0.6830	2 186
5	10 800	6 000	4 800	0.6209	2 980
Totals	**23 400**	**22 000**	**1 400**		**(588)**

Alternatively, assume a **10% increase in costs**.

Year	Revenue	Costs	Cash flow	Discount	NPV
1	0	4 400	(4 400)	0.9091	(4 000)
2	2 000	4 400	(2 400)	0.8264	(1 983)
3	4 000	4 400	(400)	0.7513	(300)
4	8 000	4 400	3 600	0.6830	2 459
5	12 000	6 600	5 400	0.6209	3 353
Totals	**26 000**	**24 200**	**1 800**		**(471)**

Question:

What do you conclude from this analysis? What other information might you need to make an assessment?

The example is very sensitive to errors in the estimates of costs or sales, as a 10% change in either makes the NPV negative. This suggests that great care should be taken when making such estimates. Given the sensitivity we might want to check that the discount rate of 10% is appropriate. As with many projects, the costs occur much earlier than revenues, so the higher the discount rate the less likely the project will produce a positive NPV.

There are two main problems using DCF analysis:

- the accuracy of the cash flow forecasts
- the selection of an appropriate discount rate

Estimates of cash flow in the distant future will be far less accurate than estimates of cash flow closer to the present time. Consequently, it is usual to perform sensitivity analysis on key variables to determine the impact on cash flow. For example, it is common to calculate the impact a 10% fall or increase in projected sales, or a 10% reduction or increase in costs would have on NPV. In addition, calculation of NPV is very sensitive to the choice of discount rate, which, if set too high, can undervalue longer-term, more innovative projects.[17]

Qualitative Methods

A simple checklist could be one made up of a range of factors which have been formed to affect the success of a project and which need to be considered at the outset. In the evaluation procedure, a project is evaluated against each of these factors using a linear scale, usually 1 to 5 or 1 to 10. The factors can be weighted to indicate their relative importance to the organization.

The value in this technique lies in its simplicity, but by the appropriate choice of factors, it is possible to ensure that the questions address, and are answered by, all functional areas. When used effectively, this guarantees a useful discussion, an identification and clarification of areas of disagreement, and a stronger commitment, by all involved, to the ultimate outcome. **Table 5.5** shows an example of a checklist, developed by the Industrial Research Institute, which can be adapted to almost any type of project.

As with all techniques, there is a danger that project appraisal becomes a routine that a project has to suffer rather than an aid to designing and selecting appropriate projects. If this happens, people may fail to apply the techniques with the rigor and honesty required, and can waste time and energy trying to "cheat" the system. Care needs to be taken to communicate the reasons behind the methods and criteria used, and where necessary, these should be adapted to different types of project and to changes in the environment (**Table 5.6**).[18]

TABLE 5.5 **List of Potential Factors for Project Evaluation.**

	Score (1–5)	Weight (%)	S x W
Corporate objectives			
Fits into the overall objectives and strategy			
Corporate image			
Marketing and distribution			
Size of potential market			
Capability to market product			
Market trend and growth			
Customer acceptance			
Relationship with existing markets			
Market share			
Market risk during development period			
Pricing trend, proprietary problem, etc.			
Complete product line			
Quality improvement			
Timing of introduction of new product			
Expected product sales life			
Manufacturing			
Cost savings			
Capability of manufacturing product			
Facility and equipment requirements			
Availability of raw material			
Manufacturing safety			

(Continued)

TABLE 5.5 **List of Potential Factors for Project Evaluation** (continued)

	Score (1–5)	Weight (%)	S x W
Research and development			
Likelihood of technical success			
Cost			
Development time			
Capability of available skills			
Availability of R&D resources			
Availability of R&D facilities			
Patent status			
Compatibility with other projects			
Regulatory and legal factors			
Potential product liability			
Regulatory clearance			
Financial			
Profitability			
Capital investment required			
Annual (or unit) cost			
Rate of return on investment			
Unit price			
Payout period			
Utilization of assets, cost reduction, and cash flow			

TABLE 5.6 **Approaches to Project Selection**

Selection approach	Advantages	Disadvantages
Simple "gut feel," intuition	Fast	Lacks evidence and analysis, may be wrong
Simple qualitative techniques – for example, checklists and decision matrices	Fast and easy to share – provides a useful focus for initial discussions	Lacks factual information and little or no quantitative dimension
Financial measures – for example, return on investment or payback time	Fast and uses some simple measurement	Doesn't take account of other benefits which might come from the innovation – learning about new technologies, markets, etc.
Complex financial measures – for example, "real options" approach	Takes account of learning dimension – the benefits from projects may lie in improved knowledge which we can use elsewhere as well as in direct profits	More complex and time-consuming. Difficult to predict the benefits which might arise from taking options on the future
Multi-dimensional measures – for example, decision matrix	Compares on several dimensions to build an overall "score" for attractiveness	Allows consideration of different kinds of benefits, but level of analysis may be limited
Portfolio methods and business cases	Compares between projects on several dimensions and provides detailed evidence around core themes	Takes a long time to prepare and present

Chapter Summary

- A business plan, however informal, helps to articulate, share, and debate the key assumptions, aims, and resources of a new venture. It can also be useful to attract support and resources.

- Forecasting methods assist in the identification and assessment of market opportunities and potential competition, ranging from simple market research to scenario planning.

- It is critical not to ignore risks and uncertainty, but instead to identify the types, sources, and ways to avoid, transfer, mitigate, or accept such risks.

- Financial planning is essential, especially analysis of cash flow, but is not sufficient. In addition, more qualitative methods of assessing the potential value of a new venture are necessary.

Key Terms

Competitor benchmarking   systematic comparison of performance, product, or processes of a competitor, with a view to learning and improvement.

Market segmentation   to partition a market on the basis of buyer characteristics, preferences, and behavior, for example, by demographics.

Risk   is usually considered to be possible to estimate, either qualitatively – high, medium, low – or ideally by probability estimates. However, in practice, different stakeholders' perceptions of risk and hazard influence decisions more than simple probabilistic assessments.

Roadmapping   identifies resource inputs, especially technologies, required to achieve medium-term and long-term product or process plans.

Scenarios   are internally consistent descriptions of alternative possible futures, based upon different assumptions and interpretations of the driving forces of change. Scenario development can be normative or explorative.

Trend extrapolation   prediction of future trends based upon past trends, only useful in the short to medium term.

Uncertainty   is, by definition, unknowable, but nonetheless the sources, fields, and degree of uncertainty can be identified to help to select the most appropriate methods of assessment and plan for contingencies.

References

[1] Delmar, F. and Shane, S. (2003). Does business planning facilitate the development of new ventures? *Strategic Management Journal*, 24(12), pp. 1165–1185.

[2] Kirsch, D. B., Goldfarb, B. and Gera, A. (2009). Form or substance? The role of business plans in venture capital decision making. *Strategic Management Journal*, 30(5), pp. 487–515.

[3] Kaplan, J. M. and Warren, A. C. (2013). *Patterns of entrepreneurship*. John New York: Wiley & Sons, Inc.

[4] Roberts, E. B. (1991). *Entrepreneurs in high technology: lessons from MIT and beyond*. Oxford: Oxford University Press.

[5] Florén, H. and Frishammar, J. (2012). From preliminary ideas to corroborated product definition: managing the front-end of new product development. *California Management Review*, 54(4), pp. 20-43.

[6] Tidd, J. and Bodley, K. (2002). Effect of novelty on new product development processes and tools. *R&D Management*, 32(2), pp. 127–138.

[7] Clayton, T. and Turner, G. (2006). Brands, innovation, and growth. In: J. Tidd, ed., *From knowledge management to strategic competence: measuring technological, market, and organizational innovation*. London: Imperial College Press, pp. 77–93; Luchs, B. (1990). Quality as a strategic weapon. *European Business Journal*, 2(4), pp. 34–47; Buzzell, P. and Gale, B. (1987). *The PIMS principle*. New York: Free Press.

[8] Chermack, T. J. (2011). *Scenario planning in organizations: how to create, use, and assess scenarios*, Oakland, CA: Berrett-Koehler Publishers; Lindgren, M. and Bandhold, H. (2009). *Scenario planning: the link between future and strategy*. 2nd ed. Basingstoke: Palgrave Macmillan; Wright, G., Cairns, G. and Bradfield, R. (eds.) *Technological Forecasting and Social Change*, 79(1), January 2012, Special issue on scenario method: current developments in theory and practice.

[9] Visser, M. P. & Chermack, T. J. (2009). Perceptions of the relationship between scenario planning and firm performance: a qualitative study. *Futures*, 41(9), pp. 581–592; Godet, M. and Roubelat, F. (1996). Creating the future: the use and misuse of scenarios. *Long Range Planning*, 29(2), pp. 164–171.

[10] Arteaga, R. and Hyland, J. (2013). *Pivot: how top entrepreneurs adapt and change course to find ultimate success*. Hoboken, NJ: Wiley.

[11] Ries, E. (2011). *The lean startup: how constant innovation creates radically successful businesses*. London: Penguin.

[12] Bower, J. (1986). *Managing the resource allocation process*. Boston: Harvard Business School.

[13] Mansfield, E., Rapoport, J., Schnee, J., Wagner, S. and Hamburger, M. (1972). *Research and innovation in the modern corporation*. London: Macmillan.

[14] Heilbronner, S. R. (2008). A fruit in the hand or two in the bush? Divergent risk preferences in chimpanzees and bonobos. *Biology Letters*, 4(3), pp. 246–249.

[15] Walsh, J. P. (1995). Managerial and organizational cognition: notes from a field trip. *Organization Science*, 6(1), pp. 1–41; Genus, A. and Coles, A. M. (2006). Firm strategies for risk management in innovation. *International Journal of Innovation Management*, 10(2), pp. 113–126; Berglund, H. (2007). Risk conception and risk management in corporate innovation. *International Journal of Innovation Management*, 11(4), pp. 497–514.

[16] European Industrial Research Management Association. (1995). *Evaluation of R&D projects*. Paris: European Industrial Research Management Association.

[17] Christensen, C. M., Kaufmann, S. P. and Shih, W. C. (2008). Innovation killers: how financial tools destroy your capacity to do new things. *Harvard Business Review*, January, pp. 98–105

[18] Laslo, Z. & Goldberg, A. I. (2008). Resource allocation under uncertainty in a multi-project matrix environment: is organizational conflict inevitable? *International Journal of Project Management*, 26(4), pp. 773–788.

Raising Resources and Funding

LEARNING OBJECTIVES

By the end of this chapter you will be able to:

1. Identify the resources needed for a successful new venture.

2. Draw upon different sources of finance, especially crowd-funding.

3. Enlist the expertise of suppliers and partners.

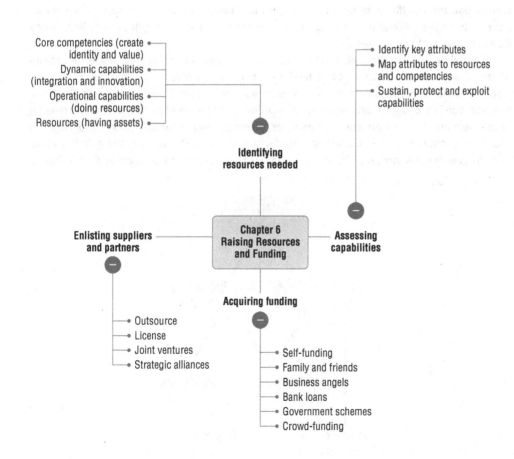

Core competencies (create identity and value)
Dynamic capabilities (integration and innovation)
Operational capabilities (doing resources)
Resources (having assets)

Identify key attributes
Map attributes to resources and competencies
Sustain, protect and exploit capabilities

Identifying resources needed

Enlisting suppliers and partners

Chapter 6 Raising Resources and Funding

Assessing capabilities

Outsource
License
Joint ventures
Strategic alliances

Acquiring funding

Self-funding
Family and friends
Business angels
Bank loans
Government schemes
Crowd-funding

6.0 Finding Resources

One of the central challenges for an entrepreneur is to identify and acquire the resources necessary to exploit an opportunity. The necessary resources include individual and collective knowledge and capabilities, as well as the more obvious but essential funding. By combining resources in novel ways, an entrepreneur is able to create value and differentiate from competing offerings.

6.1 Identifying Resources Needed

One way of looking at organizations is through what is called the "resource-based view"(RBV). This model suggests that competitive advantage is primarily driven by a firm's valuable, rare, inimitable, and non-substitutable *resources*.[1] The underlying assumption is that resources vary across organizations and that this heterogeneity can sustain competitiveness over time.

Resources are stocks that are *owned*, *controlled*, or *accessed on a preferential basis* by the firm. Resources are primarily *having* (stock) rather than *doing* (flow) forms.[2] "Having"resources can be tangible, like location, material, building, inventory, machinery, and low-cost employees, or less tangible like employee skills, patents, databases, licenses, brand, and copyright. These resources are normally available to most firms, tradable in the market and exogenous.

In contrast, "doing" resources, or capabilities, are more firm-specific, less tradable in the market and more difficult to imitate. Examples of "doing" resources are capabilities incorporated in organizational and managerial processes like product development, technology development, and marketing (**Figure 6.1**).

Capabilities refer to the organization's potential for *doing,* or carrying out a specific activity or set of activities. Such capabilities tend to consist of a combination or configuration of resources. At the most basic level, these can be the *basic operational or functional activities* of the firm, for example, design, manufacturing, or sales capability. These typically contribute directly to the creation of value from current processes, products, and services. For example, Zara has successfully integrated design, clothing manufacture, and IT to create a capability to introduce new clothing designs more rapidly and frequently than its competitors (so-called Fast-fashion).

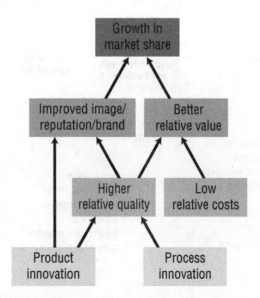

FIGURE 6.1   Resource base of the company, a hierarchical classification

Source: Adapted from Clayton, T. and Turner, G. (2012) in Tidd, J. From Knowledge management to strategic competence. Imperial College Press, London. Third edition.

Dynamic Capabilities

At a higher level, *dynamic capabilities* include abilities to improve, adapt, and innovate.[3] Dynamic capabilities are dedicated to the modification of operational capabilities and lead, for example, to changes in the firm's products or production processes.

David Teece's original definition as *"the firm's ability to integrate, build, and reconfigure internal and external competences to address rapidly changing environments"*[4] is rather broad and difficult to operationalize, so many authors have since offered their own definitions of dynamic capabilities.[5]

Rather than trying to define such a complex concept, a more useful way of identifying and operationalizing dynamic capabilities is to focus on the *functions* of dynamic capability. In other words, we ask, "What do dynamic capabilities do?" instead of "What is dynamic capability?"

6.2 Assessing Capabilities

One of the most difficult challenges in practice is to identify the capabilities necessary to create a new venture to exploit an opportunity. This technique for analyzing tangible and intangible resources is based on the identification and development of the strengths in the key product development and delivery system attributes and the intangible resources which produce them. The method consists of three parts:[6]

1. Identifying the key attributes of the most successful products and services offered by the organization.
2. Mapping these attributes to the resources or competencies of the organization, including tangible and intangible resources.
3. Assessing the potential for sustaining, protecting, and exploiting these resources, including knowledge management.

Identifying Key Attributes   A pragmatic view on the nature of competitive advantage was advanced by Coyne, whose argument started with the observation that any company which is making repeat sales in a competitive market must enjoy an advantage in the eyes of the customers who are making the repeat purchases.[7] He went on to argue that for a *sustainable* competitive advantage to exist three conditions must apply:

- Customers must perceive a consistent difference in important attributes between the producer's product/service and the attributes offered by competitors.
- This difference is the direct consequence of a capability gap between the producer and its competitors.
- Both the difference in important attributes and the capability gap can be expected to endure over time.

He suggested that there are four, and only four, types of resource capability:

- **Regulatory:** the possession of legal entities, e.g. patents & trademarks.
- **Positional:** the results of previous endeavor, e.g. reputation, trust, value chain configuration
- **Business systems:** the ability to do things well, e.g. consistent conformance to specification
- **Organizational characteristics:** e.g. the ability to manage change.

It is now possible to ask the question, "What is the nature of the package of product/delivery system attributes which customers' value?" and to go on to ask the question, "What is responsible for producing the valued attributes?" The product/delivery system attributes will include factors such as price, quality, specification, image, etc (see **Table 6.1**).

TABLE 6.1	Typical Product/Delivery System Attributes which Define Competitive Advantage
Image	What is the image of the product range? Is it important?
Price	Is a low selling price a key buying criterion?
User-friendliness	Is it important for the product to be user-friendly?
Availability	Is product range availability crucial?
Rapid response to inquiry	Is it important to produce designs, quotations, etc. very quickly?
Quick response to customer demand	Will sales be lost to the competition if they respond more quickly than you?
Width of product range	Is it important to offer a wide range of products and/or services to customers?
New product to market time	How important is the product development time?
Quality - the product's fitness for purpose	Does the product or service deliver exactly the benefits which the customers want?
Quality - the consistent achievement of defined specification	Is constant conformance to specification vital?
Safety	Is *safety in use* a major concern?
Regulatory requirements	Does meeting regulatory requirements earlier/better than the competition give a competitive advantage?
Degree of innovation	Is it important for the product or service to represent "state of the art?"
Ability to vary product specification	Is it important to produce product or service modifications easily and quickly?
Ability to vary product volume	Is it important to be able to increase or decrease production volume easily?
Customer service	Is the quality of the overall service which customers receive a key to winning business?
Before and after sales service	Is the supply of advice, spares, etc. a key aspect of winning business?

Source: Reproduced with permission from Tidd, J. (ed.) (2012). *From Knowledge Management to Strategic Competence*. Imperial College Press, London: Third edition.

The Valued Attributes   It may be necessary to identify different rankings for different categories of customers, e.g. new as opposed to long-standing customers, retailers as opposed to end users, etc. In carrying out this analysis of attributes, it is appropriate to seek consensus from the team with respect to questions such as:

- Can we agree on an importance weighting for each attribute?
- Can we agree on a benchmark score for each attribute compared with the competition?
- Can we agree on the *sustainability* of the advantage represented by each attribute?

The degree of congruence or dissonance in perceptions of these issues can in itself be illuminating. In addition to identifying the current strengths in the market place, it is also appropriate at this stage to identify known deficiencies in the product offering.

Mapping Attributes to Resources & Competencies   The important characteristics of strategic competencies are that they:

- Deliver a significant benefit to customers.
- Are idiosyncratic to the firm.

- Take time to acquire.
- Are sustainable because they are difficult and time-consuming to imitate.
- Comprise *configurations* of resources.
- Have a strong tacit content and are socially complex; they are the product of experiential learning.

The resources which produce product/delivery system attributes can now be placed in a framework of capabilities (see **Figure 6.2**):

(a) ***Regulatory capability:*** Resources which are legal entities.
- Tangible(on balance sheet)assets
- Intangible(off balance sheet) assets, e.g.:
  - Patents
  - Licenses
  - Trademarks
  - Contracts
  - Protectable data, etc.

(b) ***Positional capability:*** Resources which are not legal entities and which are the result of previous endeavor, i.e. with a high path dependency:
- Reputation of company
- Reputation of product
- Corporate networks
- Personal networks
- Unprotectable data
- Distribution network
- Supply chain network
- Formal and informal operating systems
- Processes

(c) ***Functional capability:***   Comprises resources which are either individual skills and know-how or team skills and know-how within the company, at suppliers, or at distributors, etc.
- Employee know-how & skills in:
  - Operations
  - Finance
  - Marketing
  - R & D, etc.
- Supplier know-how
- Distributor know-how
- Professional advisors' expertise, etc.

(d) ***Cultural capability:***   Comprises resources which are the characteristics of the organization:
- Perception of quality standards
- Tradition of customer service
- Ability to manage change
- Ability to innovate
- Team working ability
- Ability to develop staff, suppliers, and distributors
- Automatic response mechanisms

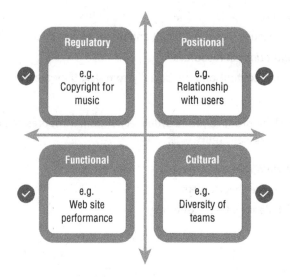

FIGURE 6.2 Mapping capabilities

Whilst it is possible for a valued product/delivery system attribute to be the result of a tangible asset, such as a building or a specialist manufacturing capability, research and experience suggest intangible resources, such as product reputation, employee know-how, etc., are the factors most often responsible for producing the attributes which are valued by customers. The identification of the intangibles which are responsible for each key product attribute results in a summary shown in **Table 6.2**.

The resources that occur frequently in the body of the matrix are those which, either by themselves or in combination with others, constitute the organization's strategic competencies.

TABLE 6.2 An Example of the Matrix of Attributes and Resources

Key Product/ Delivery Attributes	The Resources which Produce or Do Not Produce the Key Attributes:			
	Regulatory Capability	Positional Capability	Functional Capability	Cultural Capability
Strengths				
1. availability		Value chain Configuration	Forecasting skills	
2. quality				High perception of quality
3. specification	Patent 'abc'		Technology 'xyz'	
Etc.				
Weaknesses				

TABLE 6.2	An Example of the Matrix of Attributes and Resources *(continued)*			
Key Product/ Delivery Attributes	**The Resources which Produce or Do Not Produce the Key Attributes:**			
	Regulatory Capability	**Positional Capability**	**Functional Capability**	**Cultural Capability**
1.				
2.				
Summary of the key resources				

Source: Reproduced with permission from Tidd, J. (ed.) (2012). *From Knowledge Management to Strategic Competence.* Imperial College Press, London: Third edition.

DEEPER DIVE: Dynamic Capabilities and Entrepreneurial Effectuation

Read the Deeper Dive_ Dynamic capabilities and entrepreneurial effectuation document in the ebook or from the book companion site.

Sustaining, Protecting, and Exploiting Capabilities   Having identified the key resources, it is appropriate to examine development scenarios for our venture in terms of protection, sustenance, enhancement, and leverage (**Table 6.3**).

TABLE 6.3	Issues with Respect to the Development of Intangible Resources

With respect to protection

- Do all concerned recognize value of this intangible resource to the company?
- Can the resource be protected in law?

With respect to sustainability

- How long did it take to acquire this resource? Is it unique because of all that has happened in creating it?
- How durable is the resource? Will it decline with time?
- How easily may the resource be lost?
- How easily and quickly can others identify and imitate the resource?
- Can others easily "buy" the resource?
- Can others easily "grow" the resource?
- How appropriable is the resource? Can it "walk away?"
- Is the resource vulnerable to substitution?

With respect to enhancement

- Is the "stock" of this resource increasing?
- How can we ensure that the "stock" of this resource *continues* to increase?

(Continued)

TABLE 6.3	Issues with Respect to the Development of Intangible Resources *(continued)*
With respect to exploitation	

- Are we making the best use of this resource?
- How else could it be used?
- Is the scope for synergy identified and exploited?
- Are we aware of the key linkages which exist between the resources?

Source: Reproduced with permission from Tidd, J. (ed.) (2012). *From Knowledge Management to Strategic Competence.* Imperial College Press, London: Third edition.

This approach to the analysis of intangible resources is helpful for start-up entrepreneurs thinking through their business and the resources they need to put together. But it is also useful for established organizations, giving them new perspective and language that enable them to codify the tacit knowledge which they have of their companies. In particular, executives have welcomed the sometimes-new emphasis placed on issues such as:

- How can the key resource of reputation be protected, enhanced, and leveraged?
- How can management ensure that every employee is disposed to be both a promoter and custodian of the reputation which employs him/her?
- What are the key areas of employee know-how? Can they be codified? How long do they take to acquire?
- Is the business organized so that working and learning are the same?

Entrepreneurship in Action: WhatsApp

In February 2014, WhatsApp was sold to Facebook for $19 billion. Since its launch in 2009, WhatsApp has quietly grown to almost half the size of Facebook, with 450 million users.

Founders Jan Koum and Brian Acton are not typical of Silicon Valley technology-entrepreneurs. Both were well over 30 years old when they launched their messaging app in 2009. Koum and Acton met while working at Yahoo in 1997.

After almost ten years at Yahoo, in September 2007, Koum and Acton left to take a year of traveling around South America, funded by Koum's $400,000 savings from Yahoo. In early 2009, Koum realized that the seven-month-old Apple App Store could create a whole new industry of apps. He could develop the back-end of applications, but he recruited Igor Solomennikov, an iPhone developer from Russia, for the front-end development. WhatsApp, Inc. was registered on February 24, 2009, although the app had not yet been developed.

In October 2009, Acton convinced five ex-Yahoo friends to invest $250,000 in seed funding, and as a result, he was granted co-founder status and a stake. The two founders had a combined stake in excess of 60 percent, a large proportion for a technology start-up. By 2011, the app was in the Apple top ten and attracted the attention of many potential investors. Sequoia partner, Jim Goetz, promised not to push advertising models on them, and they agreed to take $8 million from Sequoia. WhatsApp raised additional funding of $50 million in 2013 from Sequoia Capital but with little publicity, valuing the company at $1.5 billion.

In 2012, Koum tweeted, "People starting companies for a quick sale are a disgrace to the Valley. . . . Next person to call me an entrepreneur is getting punched in the face by my bodyguard. Seriously."

Unlike most internet start-ups, they charged for their service rather than giving it away for free and relying on advertising. WhatsApp does not collect any of the personal or demographic information that Facebook, Google, and their rivals use to target ads. "No ads! No games! No gimmicks!" said Jan Koum, WhatsApp founder. "The simplicity and the utility of our product is really what drives us," Koum said at DLD, joking that WhatsApp was "clearly not doing that good a job" because it has not yet reached its goal of being on every smartphone in the world.

WhatsApp remains a lean operation, even by Silicon Valley standards. In early 2014, WhatsApp's still had only approximately 50 employees, 30 of which were engineers like its founders. It's funding of some $60 million is half as much as the much-smaller Snapchat. In 2014, it moved to a new building and plans to double staff to 100.

Sources: Bradshaw, T. (2014) What's up with the WhatsApp founders? *Financial Times*, February 2014; Olson, P. (2014) The rags-to-riches tale of how Jan Koum built WhatsApp into Facebook's new $19 billion baby, *Forbes*, February 2014.

6.3 | Acquiring Funding

The potential sources of initial funding for creating a new venture include (**Figure 6.3**):

- self-funding
- family and friends
- business angels
- bank loans
- government schemes
- crowd-funding

The initial funding to establish a new venture is rarely a major problem. Almost all are funded from personal savings or loans from family or friends. At this stage, few professional sources of capital will be interested, with the possible exception of government support schemes.

However, a new venture is likely to require financial restructuring every three years, if it is to develop and grow. Studies identify stages of development, each having different financial requirements:

1. Initial financing for launch.
2. Second-round financing for initial development and growth.
3. Third-round financing for consolidation and growth.
4. Maturity or exit.

In general, professional financial bodies are not interested in initial funding because of the high risk and low sums of money involved. It is simply not worth their time and effort to evaluate and monitor such ventures. However, as the sums involved are relatively small, typically of the order of tens of thousands of dollars, personal savings, remortgages, and loans from friends and relatives are often sufficient. In contrast, third-round finance for consolidation is relatively easy to obtain because by that time, the venture has a proven track record on which to base the business plan, and the venture capitalist can see an exit route.

Given their strong desire for independence, most entrepreneurs try to avoid external funding for their ventures. However, in practice this is not always possible, particularly in the later growth stages. The initial funding required to form a new venture includes the purchase of accommodation, equipment, and other start-up costs, plus the day-to-day running costs such

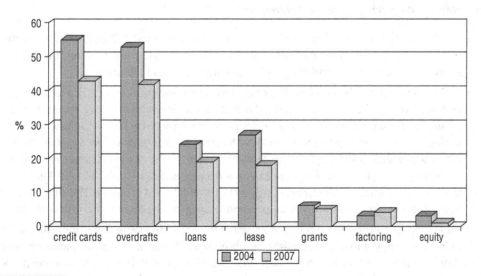

FIGURE 6.3 Source of finance for starting new ventures

Source: Centre for Business Research. (2008) *Financing UK small and medium-sized enterprises*. Cambridge: Centre for Business Research.

Entrepreneurship in Action: UnLtd – The UK Foundation for Social Entrepreneurs

UnLtd aims to help social entrepreneurs start up and run projects that deliver social benefit by providing funding and support.

The Foundation was established in 2000 through a partnership between seven leading UK non-profit organizations, including the School for Social Entrepreneurs, Ashoka, Senscot, The Scarman Trust, The Community Action Network, Comic Relief, and Changemakers, and funded by an endowment of £100 million from the UK Millennium Commission Award Scheme. The Foundation invests the money awarded to generate an income of £5 million a year to provide grants to individuals with projects to improve their community. These individual grants were launched in 2002 and range from £2500 to £15,000.

In addition to funding, UnLtd provides advice, training, and support, using its extensive network of resources and partner organizations throughout the UK. It has formed an Institute for Social Entrepreneurs to help to raise the effectiveness of the sector by building a deeper understanding of what works and what does not, translating that understanding into tools and performance measures, and promoting public and media awareness.

In the future, UnLtd plans to establish a Social Venture Fund to link social investors to more mature social entrepreneurs, whose projects have the potential to develop in scope and/or geography with significant financial backing. Current plans range from becoming a broker between different venture philanthropy funds to establishing its own VP fund.

Sources: *UnLtd corporate website*. http://www.unltd.org.uk;*A World Connected corporate website*. http://www.aworldconnected.org; *How to Change the World social network website*. http://www.howtochangetheworld.org;*The Institute for Social Entrepreneurs website*. http://www.socialent.org

---

as salaries, heating, light, and so on – usually referred to as the working capital. For these reasons, many ventures begin life as part-time businesses and are funded by personal savings, loans from friends and relatives, and bank loans, in that order. Around half also receive some funding from government sources. Venture capital is typically only made available at later stages to fund growth on the basis of a proven development and sales record.

Business Angels

Business angels are successful entrepreneurs who wish to re-invest in other new ventures, usually in return for some management role. The sums involved are usually relatively small (by venture capital standards), in the range $100,000–$250,000, but they can bring experience and expertise to a new venture in addition. They are usually able to introduce a venture to an established network of professional advisers and business contacts. In this way, they can provide a critical knowledge bridge between the venture and potential customers and investors.

Government Funding
There are several reasons why governments become involved in promoting and providing resources for new ventures:[8]

- Ideology or the broader desire to promote an entrepreneurial culture within a country or region to enhance employment. This can include small grant funding, tax breaks, management advice, or mentoring and equity rather than debt finance.

- There is an "equity gap" between the costs and risks involved in assessing and funding a new venture, and its potential return. The costs associated with the "due diligence" of assessing a venture and its subsequent management are relatively high and fixed, therefore professional venture capitalists are unlikely to consider proposals below a certain threshold, typically around $0.5 to $1 million. Similarly, where the risk of a new venture exceeds the expected return, professional venture capital is unlikely to be available. Table 12.3 indicates that this is a common problem, particularly in the UK and the rest of Europe. This suggests that government schemes may provide support and funding for smaller or higher-risk ventures.

- Professional venture capital tends to gravitate toward fashionable fields, for example, IT or biotechnology, and favor established centers of excellence, for example, Cambridge and Oxford in the UK or Boston in the USA. Table 10.3 indicates that this is a common problem, particularly in the USA and some emerging economies, where venture capital quickly follows technology trends and fads. This suggests there is a role for policy to broaden the availability of funding for ventures in a wider range of fields and regions.[9]

Entrepreneurship in Action: Instagram

Kevin Systrom, at age 27, and Mike Krieger, then just 24, launched Instagram, the photo- and video-sharing app in October 2010.

Systrom had the technical education and experience, a Stanford graduate in Management Science & Engineering, who had worked as an intern for Odeo(which became Twitter) and Google for two years. He developed an app that allowed location-aware text- and photo-sharing, dubbing it Burbn. Krieger, from São Paulo, Brazil, had a first degree and MSc in Symbolic Systems from Stanford University. Prior to founding Instagram, he worked at Meebo for 18 months as a user experience designer. Krieger was an early user of Burbn and met Systrom in the Stanford Mayfield Fellows Program for entrepreneurs. Together they decided to focus on the photo-sharing function of Burbn and to re-develop this as Instagram.

They received $500,000 initial seed funding in March 2010 from Baseline Ventures, and in February 2011, raised $7 million from Benchmark Capital and other investors. In April 2012, Instagram was sold to Facebook for around $1 billion in cash and stock. In 2015, Instagram was estimated to have more than 300 million users worldwide, with only 13 employees, but had yet to make any profit.

Crowd-Funding

Crowd-funding is a relatively recent potential source of resources but is now the first choice for half of all start-ups. Typically, it is mediated by a web portal on which projects can be posted to attract investors, often multiple non-professional investors who have some interest in the focus of the project. It is now a significant source of venture finance, with around 1,000 crowd-funding platforms worldwide, providing more than $5 billion of funding.[10]

One of the largest crowd-funding services is Kickstarter.com. Since its launch in 2009, Kickstarter has mediated the funding of 64,000 projects with pledges of $1 billion from 6.5 million investors. This suggests a mean investment of around $16,000 per project. The focus is on creative and media projects rather than high-technology. Seedups.com is another example but has a greater focus on technology start-ups. As a result, the sums raised are larger, in the range $25,000–$500,000, and investors have six months to review and bid for a stake in projects.

Some of these crowd-funding sites provide debt funding, i.e. loans to entrepreneurs, others provide equity finance, i.e. shares in the new venture. For social entrepreneurship, crowd-funding is more often through donations. In all cases, entrepreneurs have to provide an online pitch to attract investors. The application and project selection process is different on each platform, ranging from the completion of a simple form to meetings with advisers and background checks. All sites have time limits for raising finance. Therefore, the pitch has three distinct purposes: to attract crowd-funding, to market and build support for the new venture, and as a filter for more professional investors, such as business angels and venture capital.[11]Funding is more likely to be successful for shorter loan terms, e.g. 3 years rather than 5 years, or where there is other prior funding[12]. Significantly, the attention that a pitch receives in the funding stage, for example, the number of page views, is associated with the subsequent demand for the venture's products or services.[13]

The attention a pitch receives during the funding period is partly a function of individual social capital of entrepreneurs, for example, how well-connected they are on social media, and therefore, influences the likelihood of successful crowd-funding.[14]

The Uses and Limitations of Venture Capital

Venture capital has little relevance to the funding of the start-up or early stages of a new venture. Therefore, we will discuss this in more detail when we examine the factors which influence growth in Chapter 11.

General venture capital firms typically only accept 5% of the ventures they are offered, and the specialist technology venture funds are even more selective, accepting around 3%. While VCs receive many cold deals (without introduction), they rarely invest in them, so most proposals that are funded come by referral. The main reasons for rejecting proposals are the lack of intellectual property, the skills of the management team, and size of the potential market.

A survey of 136 venture capitalists, each with an average of 17 years' investment experience, identified five factors that influence funding:[15]

1. The quality of the business plan
2. Direct or indirect social ties between entrepreneur and potential investor
3. Technology and intellectual property
4. Size of funding required
5. Sector

Entrepreneurship in Action: Reuters' Corporate Venture Funds

Reuters established its first fund for external ventures, Greenhouse 1, in 1995. It has since added a further two venture funds, which aim to invest in related businesses such as financial services, media, and network infrastructure. By 2001, it had invested $432 million in 83 companies, and these investments contributed almost 10% to its profits. However, financial return was not the primary objective of the funds. For example, it invested $1 million in Yahoo! in 1995, and consequently Yahoo! acquired part of its content from Reuters. This increased the visibility of Reuters in the growing Internet markets, particularly in the USA where it was not well-known, and resulted in other portals following Yahoo!'s lead with content from Reuters. By 2001, Reuters' content was available on 900 web services and had an estimated 40 million users per month.

Source: Loudon, A. (2001). *Webs of Innovation: The networked economy demands new ways to innovate*. Harlow: Pearson Education. http://www.ft.com.

Venture capitalists are keen to provide funding for a venture with a proven track record and strong business plan, but will often require some equity or management involvement in return. However, the high fixed costs of assessing a venture means that professional venture capitalists tend to be more interested in funding later-stage ventures needing high levels of funding to grow, typically tens of millions of dollars (**Table 6.4**). Moreover, most venture capitalists are looking for a means to make capital gains after about five years, usually through a sale to a larger firm (trade sale) or, much less commonly, an initial public offering (IPO).

TABLE 6.4 **Examples of Venture Capital-Funded University Spin-Offs, 2011-2014**

University	Number of VC-funded university entrepreneurs	Number of VC-funded new ventures	Mean VC capital funding per new venture (US$m)
Stanford, USA	378	309	11.388
UC Berkeley, USA	336	284	8.493
MIT, USA	300	250	9.666
Indian Institute of Technology	264	205	15.36
Harvard, USA	253	229	14.13
Tel Aviv, Israel	169	141	8.89
Waterloo, Canada	122	96	10.50
Technion, Israel	119	98	8.133
McGill, Canada	74	72	7.458
Toronto, Canada	71	66	14.06
London, U.K.	71	67	15.94

Source: Derived from Pitchbook (2014).*Venture Capital Monthly August/September 2014 Report*. http://www. pitchbook.com.

DEEPER DIVE: Role of Venture Capital

Read the Deeper Dive: Role of venture capital document in the ebook or from the book companion site.

VIDEO: Muhammad Yunis

Muhammad Yunis, Nobel Prize winner, explains the concept of "microfinance" with the venture he established to implement it, the Grameen bank, "Banking on the Poor" (Journeyman Pictures 1997) at https://www.youtube.com/watch?v=MrUQKuvsmvw.

Entrepreneurship in Action: Alternative Investment Market (AIM)

The Alternative Investment Market (AIM) was established in London, UK, in 1995 as an alternative to the London Stock Exchange. It is designed to be simpler and cheaper than the main market, to have a less restrictive regulatory regime than the main exchange, and therefore, to be more suited to smaller firms at an earlier stage of development. AIM began with just 10 UK-based companies in 1995, but had 1500 firms listed by 2006, including 250 from overseas. The total market capitalization was £72 billion in 2006. About half of all firms on the AIM have a market capitalization of less than £15 million and a quarter of firms less than £5 million.

Listing on AIM is easier and cheaper than on most other exchanges, and costs around 5% of the funds raised on flotation. Admission to AIM takes around four months and involves a number of prescribed steps:

1. The business plan is developed.
2. Advisers are appointed – Nomad (nominated adviser, a unique and critical feature of AIM, regulated by the London Stock Exchange), broker, accountant, and lawyer.
3. Nomad prepares the timetable for admission.
4. Accountants prepare financial due diligence, including historical trading record.
5. Lawyers conduct the legal due diligence, including a review of all contracts, titles, and any litigation.
6. Accountants prepare the 18-month working capital requirements for the admission document.
7. Formal Admission Document is developed.
8. Marketing and completion, including institutional road-show and public relations.

There is no minimum capitalization or trading record requirement and no minimum proportion of shares which have to be held by the public. Institutional investors have been attracted to invest in AIM companies because of the many tax breaks available to investors, such as Venture Capital Trusts. However, a listing on AIM requires greater transparency than a private company, for example, in terms of accounting standards, corporate governance, and communication with investors.

In 2005, 29 Chinese or China-focused firms were listed on the London AIM, but regulation, language, and distance can make this more difficult and expensive than for local firms. The cost of listing is typically between £500,000 and £1 million, around twice that of a UK-based firm. AIM-style markets have been launched in Asia, including the SESDAQ in Singapore, Growth Enterprise Market in Hong Kong, and Mother Market in Japan.

6.4 | Enlisting Suppliers and Partners

Expertise, competence, and knowledge base all contribute to new venture creation. In much of the entrepreneurship literature, capabilities are conceived in the narrow sense of individual attributes, but it may be more realistic to consider these in the collective and aggregate sense, more commonly adopted in the strategy and innovation literatures on dynamic capabilities and a resource-based view of the firm.[16] Therefore, one of the challenges entrepreneurs face is how to identify relevant external knowledge, resources, and capabilities, and how to access or acquire these. **Figure 6.4** suggests four different ways to exploit such complementary capabilities.

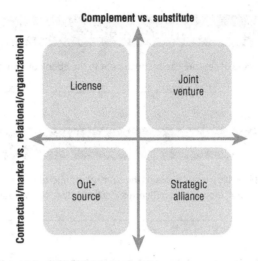

FIGURE 6.4 Strategies to enlist complementary capabilities

Outsource

The subcontracting or "outsourcing" of non-core activities has become popular in recent times. Typically, arguments for subcontracting are framed in terms of strategic focus, or "sticking to the knitting," but in practice most subcontracting or outsourcing arrangements are based on the potential to save costs: suppliers are likely to have lower overheads and variable costs, and may benefit from economies of scale if serving other firms.

The quality of the relationship with suppliers and the timing of their involvement in development are critical factors. Traditionally, such relationships have been short-term, contractual arm's-length agreements focusing on the issue of the cost, with little supplier input into design or engineering. In contrast, the "Japanese" or "partnership" model is based on long-term relationships, and suppliers make a significant contribution to the development of new products.

The latter approach increases the visibility of cost/performance trade-offs, reduces the time to market and improves the integration of components. In this case, some form of "partnership" or "lean" relationship is often advocated, based on the quality and development lead-time benefits experienced by Japanese manufacturers of consumer durables, specifically cars and electronics:[17]

- Fewer suppliers, longer-term relations
- Greater equity–real "cost transparency"
- Focus on value flows – the relationship, not the contract
- Vendor assessment, plus development
- Two-way or third-party assessment
- Mutual trust –sharing of experience, expertise, knowledge, and investment

License

Once you have acquired some form of formal legal IPR, you can allow others to use it in some way in return for some payment (a license), or sell the IPR outright (or assign it). Licensing IPR can have a number of benefits:

- Reduce or eliminate production and distribution costs and risks
- Reach a larger market

- Exploit in other applications
- Establish standards
- Gain access to complementary technology
- Block competing developments
- Convert competitor into defender

Considerations when drafting a licensing agreement include degree of exclusivity, territory, type of end use, period of license, and type and level of payments – royalty, lump sum, or cross-license. Next, calculate relative investment and weight according to share of risk. Finally, compare results to alternatives, e.g. return to licensee, imitation, litigation. There is no "best" licensing strategy, as it depends on the strategy of the organization and the nature of the technology and markets. This is discussed in detail in the chapter on exploiting knowledge and intellectual property. We will discuss the application of intellectual property in greater detail in Chapter 10.

Joint Ventures & Strategic Alliances

Joint ventures, whether formal or informal, typically take the form of an agreement between two or more organizations to co-develop a new technology, product, or service. There are two basic types of formal joint venture: a new company formed by two or more separate organizations, which typically allocate ownership based on shares of stock controlled; or a simpler contractual basis for collaboration. The critical distinction between the two types of joint venture is that an equity arrangement requires the formation of a separate legal entity. In such cases, management is delegated to the joint venture, which is not the case for other forms of collaboration.

Unlike more formal joint ventures, a strategic alliance typically has a specific end goal and timetable and does not normally take the form of a separate company. Doz and Hamel identify a range of motives for strategic alliances and suggest strategies to exploit each:[18]

- To build critical mass through co-option
- To reach new markets by leveraging co-specialized resources
- To gain new competencies through organizational learning

In a co-option alliance, critical mass is achieved through temporary alliances with competitors, customers, or companies with complementary technology, products, or services. Through co-option a company seeks to group together other relatively weak companies to challenge a dominant competitor. Co-option is common where scale or network size is important, such as mobile telephony and aerospace. For example, Airbus was originally created in response to the dominance of Boeing, Symbian and Linux in response to Microsoft's dominance, and the Open Handset alliance and Android in response to Apple's success. Greater international reach is a common related motive for co-option alliances. However, co-option alliances may be inherently unstable and transitory. Once the market position has been achieved, one partner may seek to take control through acquisition or to go unilateral.

In a co-option alliance, partners are normally drawn from the same industry, whereas in co-specialization, partners are usually from different sectors. In a co-specialized alliance, partners bring together unique competencies to create the opportunity to enter new markets, develop new products, or build new businesses. Such co-specialization is common in systems or complex products and services. However, there is a risk associated with co-specialization. Partners are required to commit to partners' technology and standards. Where technologies are emerging and uncertain and standards are yet to be established, there is a high risk that a partner's technology may become redundant.

There has been spectacular growth in strategic alliances, and at the same time more formal joint ventures have declined as a means of collaboration. There are a number of reasons for the increase in alliances overall, specifically the switch from formal joint ventures to more transitory alliances:[19]

- Speed–transitory alliances versus careful planning. Under turbulent environmental conditions, speed of response, learning, and lead time are more critical than careful planning, selection, and development of partnerships.
- Partner fit – network versus dyadic fit. Due to the need for speed, partners are often selected from existing members of a network or alternatively, reputation in the broader market.
- Partner type – complementarity versus familiarity. Transitory alliances increasingly occur across traditional sectors, markets, and technologies, rather than from within, e.g. Microsoft and LEGO to develop an Internet-based computer game, Deutsche Bank and Nokia to create mobile financial services.
- Commitment – aligned objectives versus trust. The transitory nature of relationships make the development of commitment and trust more difficult, and alliances rely more on aligned objectives and mutual goals.
- Focus – few, specific tasks versus multiple roles. To reduce the complexity of managing the relationships, the scope of the interaction is more narrowly defined, and focused more on the task than the relationship.

Whilst external sources of knowledge and capabilities are usually necessary for a new venture to develop, there are many challenges to navigate when working with other organizations, often with different strategies, business models, and ways of working (**Table 6.5**).

But alliances don't always work – as Table 6.5 shows, there are plenty of reasons why what looks good on paper fails to work out in practice!

Entrepreneurship in Action: Generative collaboration for app development–Apple versus Android

In a comparative case study of the mobile phone platforms iPhone and Android, the effects of different types of supplier relationships were assessed, focusing on the influence of innovation and value creation and capture.

The notion of generative capacity is introduced to the research on open innovation, suggesting that it is generativity rather than openness that drives value-creation through such collaboration. The two contrasting cases illustrate that generativity and innovation can be achieved in different ways: Apple is often characterized (by competitors) as being a proprietary closed system, or "walled-garden," but with the benefit of a more integrated user experience; Google's Android platform is more open and distributed, but is also criticized (by Apple and its followers) for being too fragmented and uncoordinated.

The study found that the issue is not only the degree of openness that matters, but both openness and control are important to facilitate generative supplier contributions. In the two cases of collaborative innovation, it is generativity, not openness, that creates the aggregate value of the innovation. To some extent, control hinders generativity, as when external suppliers of application software must seek permission to be accepted as content, but in other cases, control can facilitate generativity through toolkits, standards, and guidelines for suppliers. Similarly, openness can be both generative and hindering. It opens up for new ideas and possibilities, but in some cases, a lack of common strategy and coordination can hinder exploration and exploitation, and partners must create their own paths for innovation.

However, they find that the suppliers in the more open innovation networks such as Android and the Open Handset alliance tend to adopt a more active role as creative peer producers, rather than merely as contractual deliverers in the case of Apple's standard relationship.

Source: Bergquist, M., Kusschel, J., Ljungberg, J., and Remneland-Wikhamn, B. (2011). Open innovation, generativity and the supplier as peer: the case of iPhone and Android. *International Journal of Innovation Management*, 15(1), pp. 205–230.

TABLE 6.5 Common Reasons for the Failure of Alliances (review of 16 studies)

Reason for failure	% studies reporting factor (n = 16)
Strategic/goal divergence	50
Partner problems	38
Strong–weak relation	38
Cultural mismatch	25
Insufficient trust	25
Operational/geographical overlap	25
Personnel clashes	25
Lack of commitment	25
Unrealistic expectations/time	25
Asymmetric incentives	13

Source: Derived from Duysters, G., Kok, G., and Vaandrager, M. (1999). Crafting successful strategic technology partnerships. *R&D Management*, 29(4), pp. 343–51.

Chapter Summary

- It is critical to identify the resources needed for a successful new venture. This involves much more than acquiring funding, and includes an assessment of the broader but more specific capabilities required, such as skills, experience, reputation, processes, systems, suppliers, partners, and intellectual property.
- There are many sources of finance, but in the initial stages, the primary funding is likely to be from savings, loans, or crowd-funding. Venture capital becomes relevant much later.
- A new venture is likely to have to rely on a network of relationships and partners to develop and deliver its products or services. The mechanism include formal legal contracts such as subcontracting, outsourcing, licensing, and joint ventures, as well as less formal agreements and alliances.

Key Terms

Alternative Investment Market (AIM) established as a simpler and cheaper alternative to the London Stock Exchange

Business angels successful entrepreneurs who wish to re-invest in new ventures, usually in return for some management role. They are usually able to introduce a venture to an established network of professional advisers and business contacts

Capabilities are "doing" resources. By definition, they create value and are more firm-specific, less tradable in the market, and more difficult to imitate than other "having" resources or assets. Examples of

"doing" resources are capabilities incorporated in organizational and managerial processes like product development, technology development, and marketing

Crowd-funding provides new venture financing through either loans (debt) or equity (shares). Typically, it is mediated by a web portal on which projects can be posted to attract investors, often multiple non-professional investors who have some interest in the focus of the project

References

[1] Teece, D.J. (2012). Dynamic capabilities: routines versus entrepreneurial action. *Journal of Management Studies, Special issue on micro-origins of organizational routines and capabilities*, 49(8), pp. 1395–1401; Zahra, S.A., Sapienza, H.J., and Davidsson, P. (2006). Entrepreneurship and dynamic capabilities: a review, model and research agenda. *Journal of Management Studies*, 43(4),

pp. 917–955; Barney, J.B. (2001). Resource-based theories of competitive advantage: a ten-year retrospective on the resource-based view. *Journal of Management*, 27, pp. 643–650.

2 Amit, R. and Schoemaker, P.J.H. (1993). Strategic assets and organisational rent. *Strategic Management Journal*, 14, pp. 33–46; Helfat, C.E., Finkelstein, S., Mitchell, W., Peteraf, M.A., Singh, H., Teece, D.J. and Winter, S.G. (2007). *Dynamic capabilities: understanding strategic change in organizations*. Malden: Blackwell Publishing.

3 Zollo, M. and Winter, S.G. (2002). Deliberate learning and the evolution of dynamic capabilities. *Organization Science*, 13(3), pp. 339–351; Winter, S.G. (2003). Understanding dynamic capabilities. *Strategic Management Journal*, 24, pp. 991–995.

4 Teece, D.J., Pisano, G., Shuen, A. (1997). Dynamic capabilities and strategic management. *Strategic Management Journal*, 18(7), August, pp. 509–533.

5 Teece, D.J. and Pisano, G. (1994). The dynamic capabilities of firms: an introduction. *Industrial and Corporate Change*, 3, pp. 537–556; Teece, D.J. (2000). Strategies for managing knowledge assets: the role of firm structure and industrial context. *Long Range Planning*, 33(1), pp. 35–54; Teece, D.J. (2006). *Explicating dynamic capabilities: the nature and microfoundations of (long run) enterprise performance*. Berkeley: University of California, WP; Teece, D.J. (2007). Explicating dynamic capabilities: the nature and microfoundations of (sustainable) enterprise performance. *Strategic Management Journal*, 28(13), pp. 1319–1350; Pavlou, P.A. and Sawy, O.A.E. (2011). Understanding the elusive black box of dynamic capabilities. *Decision Sciences*, 42(1), pp. 239–273.

6 Tidd, J. (2012). What are compentencies? *From Knowledge Management to Strategic Competence*. 3rd ed. London: Imperial College Press; Hall, R. (1992). The strategic analysis of intangible resources. *Strategic Management Journal*, 13, pp. 135–144; Hall, R. (1993). A framework linking intangible resources and capabilities to sustainable competitive advantage. *Strategic Management Journal*, 14, pp. 607–618.

7 Coyne. (1986). Sustainable competitive advantage: what it is, and what it isn't. *Business Horizons*, 29(1), pp. 54–61.

8 Harding, R. (2000). *Venturing forward: the role of venture capital in enabling entrepreneurship*. London: Institute for Public Policy Research.

9 Lockett, A., Murray, G. and Wright, M. (2002). Do UK venture capitalists still have a bias against investment in new technology firms? *Research Policy*, 31, pp. 1009–1030.

10 Kshetri, N. (2015). Success of crowd-based online technology in fundraising: an institutional perspective. *Journal of International Management*, 21, pp. 100–116; Markowitz, E. (2013). 22 crowdfunding sites (and how to choose yours), *Inc.*, June, pp. 30–31.

11 Valanciene, L. and Jegeleviciute, S. (2014). Crowdfunding for creating value: stakeholder approach. *Procedia - Social and Behavioral Sciences*, 156, pp. 599–604; Crowdfund Capital Advisors (2014). *How does crowdfunding impact job creation, company revenue, and professional investor interest?* Available at: http://www.crowdfund-capitaladvisors.com [Accessed January 8, 2018].

12 Barasinska, N. and Schafer, D. (2014). Is crowdfunding different? Evidence on the relation between gender and funding success from a German peer-to-peer lending platform. *German Economic Review*, 15(4), pp. 436–452.

13 Burtch, G., Ghose, A., and Wattal, S. (2013). An empirical examination of the antecedents and consequences of contribution patterns in crowd-funded markets. *Information Systems Research*, 24(3), pp. 499–519.

14 Giudici, G., Guerini, M., and Rossi-Lamastra, C., (2013). Why crowdfunding projects can succeed: the role of proponents' individual and territorial social capital. *8th International Forum on Knowledge Asset Dynamics (IFKAD)*, pp. 285–299.

15 Shane, S. and Cable, D. (2002). Network ties, reputation and the financing of new ventures. *Management Science*, 48(3), pp. 364–381; Baum, J.A.C. and Silverman, B.S. (2004). Picking winners or building them? Alliance, intellectual and human capital as selection criteria in venture financing and performance of biotechnology startups. *Journal of Business Venturing*, 19, pp. 411–436.

16 Tidd, J. (2014). Conjoint innovation: bridging innovation and entrepreneurship. *International Journal of Innovation Management*, 18(1), pp. 1–20, DOI 10.1142/S1363919614500017; Tidd, J. (2012). It takes two to tango: entrepreneurial interaction and innovation. *European Business Review*, October.

17 Brem, A. and Tidd, J. (2012). *Perspectives on Supplier Innovation*. London: Imperial College Press; Lamming, R. (1993). *Beyond Partnership*. Upper Saddle River: Prentice Hall; Nishiguchi, T. (1994). *Strategic Industrial Sourcing: The Japanese Advantage*. Oxford: Oxford University Press.

18 Niesten, E. and Jolink, A. (2015). The impact of alliance management capabilities on alliance attributes and performance: a literature review. *International Journal of Management Reviews*, 17(1), pp. 69–100; Meier, M. (2011). Knowledge management in strategic alliances: a review of empirical evidence. *International Journal of Management Reviews*, 13(1), pp. 1–23; Doz, Y. and G. Hamel (1998). *Alliance Advantage: The Art of Creating Value through Partnering*, Boston: Harvard Business School Press.

19 Jenssen, J.I. and Nybakk, E. (2013). Inter-organizational networks and innovation in small, knowledge-intensive firms. *International Journal of Innovation Management*, 17(2), DOI 1350008; Duysters, G. and de Man, A. (2003). Transitionary alliances: an instrument for surviving turbulent industries? *R&D Management*, 33, pp. 49–58.

CHAPTER 7

Building the Team

LEARNING OBJECTIVES

By the end of this chapter you will be able to:

1. At the personal or individual level, understand how different leadership and entrepreneurial styles influence the ability to identify, assess, and develop new ideas and concepts.

2. At the partner level, combine the experience and expertise of entrepreneurial partners.

3. At the group or team level, identify how teams, groups, and processes each contribute to successful behaviors and outcomes.

4. At the venture level, assess how different factors can support or hinder innovation and entrepreneurship.

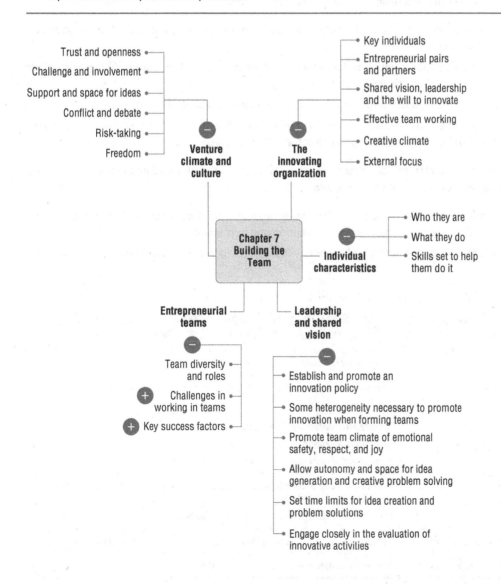

7.0 | The Innovating Organization

There is no universal ideal type of person or organization which promotes innovation and entrepreneurship. However, by examining case studies of entrepreneurs and innovative organizations and comparing these systematically with less successful ventures, we begin to identify consistent patterns of good leadership and organization. Larger-scale academic research confirms these factors contribute tend to superior performance (**Table 7.1**).

In this chapter, we focus on the contribution and interaction of four of these critical components: individual characteristics, entrepreneurial pairs, composition of teams, and influence of the creative climate. We discuss external focus and networks in Chapter 8.

7.1 | Individual Characteristics

Studies of innovation and entrepreneurship have tended to focus on the role of key individuals, in particular, inherent or given traits of inventors or entrepreneurs. Archetypical inventors include Thomas Edison and Alexander Graham Bell, or more recently, James Dyson and Steve Jobs. Each of these examples of inventors was also an innovator, translating the original technical inventions into new products, but each was also an entrepreneur, in the sense that they created and developed successful businesses based on the inventions and innovations.

Typical characteristics of an entrepreneur include:[1]

1. Passionately seeking to identify new opportunities and ways to profit from change and disruption.
2. Pursuing opportunities with discipline and focus on a limited number of projects, rather than opportunistically chasing every option.
3. Focusing on action and execution, rather than endless analysis.
4. Involving and energizing networks of relationships, exploiting the expertise and resources of others, while helping others to achieve their own goals.

These characteristics are consistent with what research tells us about the cognitive abilities necessary for creativity and innovation:

- Information acquisition and dissemination, including the capture of information from a wide range of sources, requiring attention and perception.
- Intelligence, the ability and capability to interpret, process, and manipulate information.

TABLE 7.1   **Anatomy of a Healthy New Venture**

Component	Key features
Key individuals	Entrepreneurs, promoters, champions, gatekeepers, and other roles which energize or facilitate innovation
Entrepreneurial Pairs and Partners	Complementary expertise, pooled resources and networks, better decisions
Shared vision, leadership, and the will to innovate	Clearly articulated and shared sense of purpose Stretching strategic intent 'Top management commitment'
Effective team working	Appropriate use of teams (at local, cross-functional, and inter-organizational levels) to solve problems Requires investment in team selection and building
Creative climate	Positive approach to creative ideas, supported by relevant motivation systems
External focus	Internal and external customer orientation

- Sense-making, giving meaning to information.
- Unlearning, the process of reducing or eliminating pre-existing routines or behaviors, including discarding information.
- Implementation, improvisation, autonomous behavior, experimentation, reflection, and action. Using information to solve problems, for example, during new product development or process improvement.

Personal orientation includes what are traditionally thought of as characteristics of the creative personas, as well as the creative abilities associated with creativity. These include personality traits such as openness to experience, tolerance of ambiguity, resistance to premature closure, curiosity, and risk-taking, among others. They also include such creative-thinking abilities as fluency, flexibility, originality, and elaboration. Expertise, competence, and knowledge base also contribute to creative efforts. Traditionally, people have been assessed and selected for different tasks on the basis of such characteristics, for example, using psycho-metric questionnaires or tests. For example, the Kirton Adapter-Innovator (KAI) scale assesses different dimensions of creativity, including originality, attention to detail, and reliance on rules.

The Kirton Adapter-Innovator scale is a psychometric approach for assessing the creativity of individuals. By a series of questions, it seeks to identify an individual's attitudes toward originality, attention to detail and following rules. It seeks to differentiate "adaptive" from "innovative" styles:

- Adaptors characteristically produce a sufficiency of ideas based closely on existing agreed definitions of a problem and its likely solutions, but stretching the solutions. These ideas help to improve and "do better."
- Innovators are more likely to reconstruct the problem, challenge the assumptions, and to emerge with a more novel solution. Innovators are less concerned with doing things better than with doing things differently.

It is important to recognize that creativity is an attribute that we all possess, but the preferred style of expressing it varies widely. Recognizing the need for different kinds of individual creative styles is an important aspect of developing successful innovations and new ventures. It is clear from a wealth of psychological research that every human being comes with the capability to find and solve complex problems, and where such creative behavior can be harnessed amongst a group of people with differing skills and perspectives, extraordinary things can be achieved. Some people are comfortable with ideas which challenge the whole

Entrepreneurship in Action: Personal creativity and entrepreneurship

A study of 800 senior managers revealed that there were significant differences between those in the top quartile (25%) and the rest of the sample. The more successful managers had achieved their goals within eight years, and most were in senior management positions by their early 30s. The key differences associated with the more successful managers were personality and cognitive, in particular the breadth and creativity of their thinking, and their social skills. However, the study does not conclude that creative thinking and social skills are inherent personality traits but rather dispositions, which can be developed and improved significantly.

Such abilities are critical in many contexts, including large organizations and small start-up companies. For example, Eon, the world's largest energy services company, has created a graduate training program to help to assess and develop their new recruits. Following psychometric assessment, graduate recruits follow specific programs aimed to improve their personal and social skills, including placements in different parts of the business. Alex Oakley, head of human resources at Eon, believes, "In this way, we get a balance between skills and personal attributes that helps people do the job. We don't just concentrate on skills." Similarly, Jamie Malcolm, an entrepreneur who co-founded the garden center, Shoots, in Sussex, argues that "anything new and innovative, like a start-up business, needs to take risks – you just can't succeed without it. I'll always be prepared to take risks in order to innovate. The innovation required to grow the business is what drives me. Risk can be dangerous if you're taking it because of your personal desire to do so. You don't have to lower your appetite for risk as the business grows – you just have to analyze it more as there's more at stake."

Source: Kaisen Consultants. (2006). *Kaisen Consultants corporate website*. https://www2.deloitte.com/uk/en/pages/human-capital/solutions/organisation-transformation-and-talent.html

way in which the universe works, whilst others prefer smaller increments of change – ideas about how to improve the jobs they do or their working environment in less radical ways. We discuss the role of creativity in more detail in Chapter 5.

Entrepreneurial Disposition

Research on successful entrepreneurs has identified some of the factors that affect the likelihood of establishing a venture. These include a combination of those which are largely inherent or given and those which can be more easily learned or influenced:

- Family and ethnic background
- Psychological profile
- Formal education and early work experience

Background

A number of other studies confirm that both family background and religion affect an individual's propensity to establish a new venture. A significant majority of technical entrepreneurs have a self-employed or professional parent. Studies indicate that 50–80% have at least one self-employed parent. For example, one seminal study found that four times as many technical entrepreneurs have a parent who is a professional, compared with other groups of scientists and engineers.[2] The most common explanation for this observed bias is that the parent acts as a role model and may provide support for self-employment.

Psychological Profile

Much of the research on the psychology of entrepreneurs is based on the experience of small firms in the USA, so the generalizability of the findings must be questioned. However, in the specific case of technical entrepreneurs, there appears to be some consensus regarding the necessary personal characteristics. The two critical requirements appear to be an internal locus of control and a high need for achievement. The former characteristic is common in scientists and engineers, but the need for high levels of achievement is less common. Entrepreneurs are typically motivated by a high need for achievement (so-called "n-Ach"), rather than a general desire to succeed. This behavior is associated with moderate risk-taking, but not gambling or irrational risk-taking. A person with a high n-Ach:

- Likes situations where it is possible to take personal responsibility for finding solutions to problems.
- Has a tendency to set challenging but realistic personal goals and to take calculated risks.
- Needs concrete feedback on personal performance.

Studies of the traits of successful entrepreneurs identify very similar profiles in a wide range of contexts, which typically feature innovativeness, risk-taking, and an ambition to achieve, compete, and grow.[3] For example, the General Enterprise Tendency test assesses five types of trait: need for achievement, drive and ambition, risk-taking, autonomy and creativity, and potential for innovation. This instrument has proven effective at identifying potential owner-managers, but fails to distinguish these from successful entrepreneurs. However, these are not the same characteristics as those who simply seek self-employment or manage small businesses, where the primary needs appear to be autonomy and independence.[4]

These differences are critical, because too often entrepreneurs, the self-employed, and SMEs are grouped together as a single group, whereas research confirms that these have very different characteristics, motives, and outcomes. For example, the Global Entrepreneurship Monitor (GEM) tracks entrepreneurship at the national level, and in addition to cultural, demographic, and educational factors, includes indicators of infrastructure and national context. However, the focus of the GEM is on start-up activity, rather than subsequent success or growth, so it also fails to differentiate small businesses from successful entrepreneurial activity. For example, despite their evident structural economic problems, the GEM ranked Greece and Ireland top of the EU for "total entrepreneurial activity."

Education and Experience

In general, the self-employed and managers of SMEs tend to be under-educated compared to the relevant population. One explanation for this is that either by choice or lack of ability or opportunity, those who do not pursue higher levels of education have fewer career options than those who do. This is often referred to as necessity-drive entrepreneurship, in contrast to opportunity-driven. Opportunity-driven entrepreneurs, in contrast to the self-employed and managers of SMEs, tend to be more educated than the relevant population, and technical entrepreneurs even more so: in general, those with a higher, college or university-level education are twice as likely to be successful entrepreneurs, and 85% of technical entrepreneurs have a degree.[5]

In addition to a master's-level education, a technical entrepreneur will have around 13 years of work experience on average before establishing a new venture. In the case of Route 128, the cluster of high-tech firms around the universities in Boston, the entrepreneurs' work experience is typically with a single incubator organization, whereas technical entrepreneurs in Silicon Valley tend to have gained their experience from a larger number of firms before establishing their own venture. This suggests that there is no ideal pattern of previous work experience. However, experience of development work appears to be more important than work in basic research. As a result of the formal education and experience required, a typical technical entrepreneur will be aged between 30 and 40 years when establishing his or her first venture. This contrasts with the popular notion that tech entrepreneurs are all fresh college graduates or drop-outs – it is relatively late in life compared to other types of venture but is due to a combination of ability and opportunity. On the one hand, it typically takes between 10 and 15 years for a potential entrepreneur to attain the necessary technical and business experience. On the other hand, many people begin to have greater financial and family responsibilities at this time, which reduces the appetite for risk. Thus, there appears to be a window of opportunity to start a new venture in the mid-thirties. Moreover, different fields of technology have different entry and growth potential. Therefore, the choice of a potential entrepreneur will be constrained by the dynamics of the technology and markets. The capital requirements, product lead times, and potential for growth are likely to vary significantly between sectors.

Numerous surveys indicate that around three-quarters of technical entrepreneurs claim to have been frustrated in their previous job. This frustration appears to result from the interaction of the psychological predisposition of the potential entrepreneur and poor selection, training, and development by the parent organization. Specific events may also trigger the desire or need to establish a new venture, such as a major reorganization or downsizing of the parent organization.

Entrepreneurial Pairs and Partners

Whilst much of the entrepreneurial research and policy focuses on individual entrepreneurs and their traits, numerous studies have identified "multiple founders" as a factor which contributes to the success of new ventures.[6] Reasons for the success of ventures created by multiple founders include complementary capabilities, contrasting cognitive and creative styles, greater credibility, and broader networks (**Table 7.2**).

Expertise, competence, and knowledge base all contribute to new venture creation, but in much of the entrepreneurship literature, capabilities are conceived in the narrow sense of individual attributes. Therefore, it may be more realistic and productive to consider these in the collective and aggregate sense, more commonly adopted in the strategy and innovation literatures on dynamic capabilities and resource-based view of the firm (see Chapter 6).

TABLE 7.2 Entrepreneurial Pairs and Partnerships

New Venture	Complementary capabilities
Apple: Jobs, Wozniak & Ive	Graphic design and showmanship; Computer science; Industrial design
Google: Page & Brin	Computer Science (PhD); Mathematics and Computer Science (PhD)
Facebook: Zuckerberg & Saverin	Computer science and psychology; Business studies and finance
Netflix: Randolph & Hastings	Engineering and Marketing; Mathematics and Computer Science (MSc)
Skype: Zennström & Friis	Computer science and telecommunications; Customer service and sales
Microsoft: Gates & Allen	Computer science and intellectual property; Computer science
Intel: Noyce, Moore, & Grove	Physics, math, and organization; Electrical engineering; Process engineering and strategy
Sony: Ibuka & Morita	Telecommunications R&D; Physics, electronics, and family business
Rolls Royce: Royce & Rolls	Engineering; Sales and finance
Marks and Spencer: Marks & Spencer	Retail sales; Finance and supply networks
Formula One: Ecclestone Mosley	Math, car sales, and motor racing; Physics, law, and motor racing
Electrification: Tesla & Westinghouse	Science, math, and showmanship; Business and finance
Steam power: Watt & Boulton	Engineering; Business and manufacturing

Sources: Tidd, J. (2014). Conjoint innovation: Building a bridge between innovation and entrepreneurship. *International Journal of Innovation Management*, 18(1), pp. 1–20; Tidd, J. (2012). It takes two to tango: how multiple entrepreneurs interact to innovate. *European Business Review*, 24(4), pp. 58–61.

Examination of Table 7.2 indicates that founders of many innovative, high-growth ventures have a tendency to have different capabilities, indicated by their prior education, work experience, and roles. Most typically, we find that a combination of technical and sales or marketing is a common coupling, although other variations exist, depending upon the maturity of technology and markets. For example, the initial opportunity recognition, at the interface of the research and opportunity framing phases, requires the ability to connect a specific technology or know-how to a commercial application and is based on a rare combination of skill, experience, aptitude, insight, and circumstances. A key issue here is the ability to synthesize scientific knowledge and market insights, which increases with the entrepreneur's social capital – linkages, partnerships, and other network interactions. This requires a delicate balance between differentiation and integration of capabilities, strong ties within disciplines to develop depth, and weaker ties across functions to promote innovation. Research confirms that the functional diversity of the founding team is associated with new venture success.[7]

Also, cognitive differences and behavioral interaction between founders appear to be relevant to entrepreneurial outcomes, including opportunity for debate and constructive conflict.[8] Debate focuses on issues and ideas, whereas conflict focuses on people and their relationships. Debate involves the productive use and respect for diversity of perspectives and points of view. Where debates are missing, people follow authoritarian patterns without questioning. Conflict in an organization refers to the presence of personal, interpersonal, or emotional tensions, and conflicts can occur over tasks, process, or relationships. Task conflicts focus on disagreements about the goals and content of work, the "what?" that needs to be done and "why?" Process conflicts are around "how?" to achieve a task, its means and methods. In general, some task and process conflict is constructive, helping to avoid groupthink, and to consider more diverse opinions and alternative strategies. In contrast, relationship conflict is generally energy-sapping and destructive, as emotional disagreements create anxiety and hostility. So, the goal is not necessarily to minimize debate and conflict and maximize consensus, but to maintain a level of constructive debate and conflict consistent with the need for diversity and a range of different preferences and styles of creative problem-solving. Group members with similar creative preferences and problem-solving styles are likely to be more harmonious but much less effective than those with mixed preferences and styles.

DEEPER DIVE: Creative Problem-Solving Styles

Read the Deeper Dive_Creative problem-solving styles document in the ebook or from the book companion site.

7.2 | Leadership and Shared Vision

The contribution that individuals make to the performance of their organizations can be significant. Upper echelons theory argues that decisions and choices by top management have an influence on the performance of an organization (positive or negative!) through their assessment of the environment, strategic decision making, and support for innovation. The results of different studies vary, but the reviews of research on leadership and performance suggest leadership directly influences around 15% of the differences found in performance of businesses and contributes an additional 35% through the choice of business strategy.[9] So directly and indirectly, leadership can account for half of the variance in performance observed across organizations. At higher levels of management, the problems to be solved are more likely to be ill-defined, demanding leaders to conceptualize more.

Researchers have identified a long list of characteristics that might have something to do with being effective in certain situations which include generic traits, such as seeking responsibility, social competence, and good communication. Although these lists may describe some characteristics of some leaders in certain situations, measures of these traits yield highly inconsistent relationships with being a good leader.[10] In short, there is no brief and universal list of enduring traits that all good leaders must possess under all conditions.

Studies in different contexts identify not only the technical expertise of leadership influencing group performance but also broader cognitive ability, such as creative problem-solving and information-processing skills. For example, studies of groups facing novel, ill-defined problems confirm that both expertise and cognitive-processing skills are key components of creative leadership and are both associated with effective performance of creative groups.[11] Moreover, this combination of expertise and cognitive capacity is critical for the evaluation of others' ideas. A study of scientists found that they most valued their leader's inputs at the early stages of a new project, when they were formulating their ideas and defining the problems, and at the later stage, where they needed feedback and insights to the implications of their work. Therefore, a key role of creative leadership in such environments is to provide feedback and evaluation, rather than to simply generate ideas.[12] This evaluative role is critical, but it is typically seen as not conducive to creativity and innovation, where the conventional advice is to suspend judgement to foster idea generation. Also, it suggests that the conventional linear view that evaluation follows idea generation may be wrong. Evaluation by creative leadership may precede idea generation and conceptual combination.

The quality and nature of the leader–member exchange (LMX) has also been found to influence the creativity of subordinates.[13] A study of 238 knowledge workers from 26 project teams in high-technology firms identified a number of positive aspects of LMX, including monitoring, clarifying, and consulting, but also found that the frequency of negative LMX was as high as the positive, around a third of respondents reporting these.[14] Therefore, LMX can either enhance or undermine subordinates' sense of competence and self-determination. However, analysis of exchanges perceived to be negative and positive revealed that it was typically how something was done rather than what was done, which suggests that task and relationship behaviors in leadership support and LMX are intimately intertwined, and that negative behaviors can have a disproportionate negative influence.

Intellectual stimulation by leaders has a stronger effect on organizational performance under conditions of perceived uncertainty. Intellectual stimulation includes behaviors that increase others' awareness of and interest in problems and develops their propensity and ability to tackle problems in new ways. It is also associated with commitment to an organization.[15] Stratified system theory (SST) focuses on the cognitive aspects of leadership and argues that conceptual capacity is associated with superior performance in strategic decision making where there is a need to integrate complex information and think abstractly in order to assess the environment. It also is likely to demand a combination of these problem-solving capabilities and social skills, as leaders will depend upon others to identify and implement solutions.[16] This suggests that under conditions of environmental uncertainty, the contribution of leadership is not simply, or even primarily, to inspire or build confidence, but rather to solve problems and make appropriate strategic decisions.

Rafferty and Griffin propose other sub-dimensions to the concept of transformational leadership that may have a greater influence on creativity and innovation, including articulating a vision and inspirational communication.[17] They define a vision as "the expression of an idealized picture of the future based around organizational values," and inspirational communication as "the expression of positive and encouraging messages about the organization, and statements that build motivation and confidence." They found that the expression of a vision has a negative effect on followers' confidence, unless accompanied with inspirational communication. Mission awareness increases the probability of success of R&D projects, but the effects are stronger at the earlier stages: in the planning and conceptual stage, mission awareness explained two-thirds of the subsequent project success.[18] Leadership clarity is associated with clear team objectives, high levels of participation, commitment to excellence, and support for innovation.[19]

The creative leader needs to do much more than simply provide a passive, supportive role to encourage creative followers. Perceptual measures of leaders' performance suggest that in a research environment, the perception of leader's technical skill is the single best predictor of research group performance, explaining around half of innovation performance.[20] Keller found that the type of project moderates the relationships between leadership style and project success, and that transformational leadership was a stronger predictor in research projects than in development projects.[21] This strongly suggests that certain qualities of transformational leadership may be most appropriate under conditions of high complexity, uncertainty, or novelty, whereas a transactional style has a positive effect in an administrative context and a negative effect in a research context.[22]

A review of 27 empirical studies of the relationships between leadership and innovation investigating when and how leadership influences innovation identified six factors leaders should focus on:[23]

1. Upper management should establish an innovation policy that is promoted throughout the organization. It is necessary that the organization, through its leaders, communicate to employees that innovative behavior will be rewarded.

2. When forming teams, some heterogeneity is necessary to promote innovation. However, if the team is too heterogeneous, tensions may arise. When heterogeneity is too low, more

directive leadership is required to promote team reflection, for example, by encouraging discussion and disagreement.

3. Leaders should promote a team climate of emotional safety, respect, and joy through emotional support and shared decision-making.

4. Individuals and teams have autonomy and space for idea generation and creative problem-solving.

5. Time limits for idea creation and problem solutions should be set, particularly in the implementation phases.

6. Finally, team leaders, who have the expertise, should engage closely in the evaluation of innovative activities.

Traditionally, people have been assessed and selected for different tasks on the basis of such characteristics, for example, using psychometric questionnaires or tests. A good example is the Kirton Adapter-Innovator (KAI) scale which we discussed earlier.

Entrepreneurship in Action: Opportunity and planning at Innocent

Innocent develops and sells fruit smoothies – healthy, premium-pulped fruit drinks with no additives. The company was created in 1999 by three friends from university, Adam Balon, Richard Reed, and Jon Wright. The company was founded with the help of £200,000 of venture capital, but Balon, Reed, and Wright still own 70% of the company. In 2006, Innocent had sales of around £70 million, representing a market share of 60%, and the company was valued at £175 million. It has since recruited more experienced managers from larger firms, and now employs 100 staff in West London. It also has bases in France and Denmark and planned to open offices in Germany and Austria in 2007. All production and packaging is outsourced, and the company focuses on development and marketing.

The company has cultivated a funky liberal image, in contrast to the large multinational firms that dominate the drinks market. They give 10% of company profits to charities, such as the Rainforest Alliance, and have developed a healthy dialogue with their customers through a weekly e-mail newsletter. In 2005, Reed won the title "Most Admired Businessman" from the UK National Union of Students (NUS). However, beneath the hippy image there is a well-educated and experienced management team. After university, Reed, now aged 33, gained experience in the advertising industry, and Balon and Wright both worked for large management consultants, respectively McKinsey and Bain. The likely exit or harvest for the business will be a trade sale similar to other so-called "ethical brands," such as Ben and Jerry's, which was bought by Unilever, and Green and Blacks acquired by Cadbury. In preparation, the owners sold 18% of the company to Coca-Cola for £30 million in April 2009.

7.3 | Entrepreneurial Teams

"It takes five years to develop a new car in this country. Heck, we won World War 2 in four years. . ."

Ross Perot's critical comment on the state of the US car industry in the late 1980s captured some of the frustration with existing ways of designing and building cars. In the years that followed, significant strides were made in reducing the development cycle with Ford and Chrysler succeeding in dramatically reducing time and improving quality. Much of the advantage was gained through extensive team working; as Lew Varaldi, project manager of Ford's Team Taurus project put it, "It's amazing the dedication and commitment you get from people. . .We will never go back to the old ways because we know so much about what they can bring to the party."[24]

Experiments indicate that teams have more to offer than individuals in terms of both fluency of idea generation and in flexibility of solutions developed. Focusing this potential on innovation tasks is the prime driver for the trend toward high levels of team working – in project teams, in cross-functional and inter-organizational problem-solving groups, and in cells and work groups where the focus is on incremental, adaptive innovation.

Many use the terms "group" and "team" interchangeably. In general, the word group refers to an assemblage of people who may just be near to each other. Groups can be a number of people that are regarded as unified or are classed together on account of any sort of similarity. For us, a team means a combination of individuals who come together or who have been brought together for a common purpose or goal in their organization. A team is a group that must collaborate in their professional work in some enterprise or on some assignment and share accountability or responsibility for obtaining results. There are a variety of ways to differentiate working groups from teams. One senior executive with whom we have worked described groups as individuals with nothing in common, except a zip/postal code. Teams, however, were characterized by a common vision.

Considerable work has been done on the characteristics of high-performance project teams for innovative tasks, and the main findings are that such teams rarely happen by accident.[25] They result from a combination of selection and investment in team building, allied to clear guidance on their roles and tasks, and a concentration on managing group process as well as task aspects.[26] For example, research within the Ashridge Management College developed a model for "superteams," which includes components of building and managing the internal team and its interfaces with the rest of the organization.[27]

Holti, Neumann, and Standing provide a useful summary of the key factors involved in developing team working.[28] Although there is considerable current emphasis on team working, we should remember that teams are not always the answer. In particular, there are dangers in putting nominal teams together where unresolved conflicts, personality clashes, lack of effective group processes, and other factors can diminish their effectiveness. Tranfield et al. look at the issue of team working in a number of different contexts and highlight the importance of selecting and building the appropriate team for the task and the context.[29]

Teams are increasingly being seen as a mechanism for bridging boundaries within the organization – and indeed, in dealing with inter-organizational issues. Cross-functional teams can bring together the different knowledge sets needed for tasks like product development or process improvement – but they also represent a forum where often deep-rooted differences in perspectives can be resolved.[30] Successful organizations were those which invested in multiple methods for integrating across groups – and the cross-functional team was one of the most valuable resources.

Self-managed teams working within a defined area of autonomy can be very effective. For example, Honeywell's defense avionics factory reports a dramatic improvement in on-time delivery – from below 40% in the 1980s to 99% in 1996 – to the implementation of self-managing teams.[31] In the Netherlands, one of the most successful bus companies, Vancom Zuid-Limburg, has used self-managing teams to both reduce costs and improve customer satisfaction ratings, and one manager now supervises over 40 drivers, compared to the industry average ratio of 1:8. Drivers are also encouraged to participate in problem finding and solving in areas like maintenance, customer service, and planning.[32]

Key elements in effective high-performance team working include:

- Clearly defined tasks and objectives
- Effective team leadership
- Good balance of team roles and match to individual behavioral style
- Effective conflict resolution mechanisms within the group
- Continuing liaison with external organization

Teams typically go through four stages of development, popularly known as "forming, storming, norming and performing."[33] That is, they are put together and then go through a phase of resolving internal differences and conflicts around leadership, objectives, etc. Emerging from this process is a commitment to shared values and norms governing the way the team will work, and it is only after this stage that teams can move on to effective performance of their task. Common approaches to team building can support innovation but are not sufficient.

Central to team performance is the make-up of the team itself, with good matching between the role requirements of the group and the behavioral preferences of the individuals involved. Belbin's work has been influential here in providing an approach to team role matching. He classifies people into a number of preferred role types – for example, "the plant" (someone who is a source of new ideas), "the resource investigator," "the shaper," and the "completer/finisher." Research has shown that the most effective teams are those with diversity in background, ability, and behavioral style. In one noted experiment, highly talented but similar people in "Apollo" teams consistently performed less well than mixed, average groups.[34]

With increased emphasis on cross-boundary and dispersed team activity, a series of new challenges is emerging. In the extreme case, a product development team might begin work in London, pass on to their US counterparts later in the day, who in turn pass on to their far Eastern colleagues – effectively allowing a 24-hour non-stop development activity. This makes for higher productivity potential – but only if the issues around managing dispersed and virtual teams can be resolved. Similarly, the concept of sharing knowledge across boundaries depends on enabling structures and mechanisms.[35]

Many people who have attempted to use groups for problem-solving find out that using groups is not always easy, pleasurable, or effective. **Table 7.3** summarizes some of the positive and negative aspects of using groups for innovation.

A survey of 1,207 firms aimed to identify how different organizational practices contributed to innovation performance.[36] It examined the influences of 12 common practices, including cross-functional teams, team incentives, quality circles, and ISO 9000 quality standards, on successful new product development. The study found significant differences in the effects of different practices, depending upon the novelty of the development project. For instance, both quality circles and ISO 9000 were associated with the successful development of incremental new products, but both practices had a significant negative influence on the success of radical new products. However, the use of teams and team incentives were found to have a positive on both incremental and radical new product development. This suggests that great care needs to be taken when applying so-called universal best practices, as their effects often depend on the nature of the project.

Our own work on high-performance teams, consistent with previous research, suggests a number of characteristics that promote effective teamwork:[37]

- *A clear, common, and elevating goal.* Having a clear and elevating goal means having understanding, mutual agreement, and identification with respect to the primary task a group faces. Active teamwork towards common goals happens when members of a group share a common vision of the desired future state. Creative teams have clear and common

TABLE 7.3 Potential Assets and Liabilities of Using A Group

Potential assets of using a group	Potential liabilities of using a group
1. Greater availability of knowledge and information	1. Social pressure toward uniform thought limits contributions and increases conformity
2. More opportunities for cross-fertilization, increasing the likelihood of building and improving upon ideas of others	2. Groupthink: groups converge on options, which seem to have greatest agreement, regardless of quality
3. Wider range of experiences and perspectives upon which to draw	3. Dominant individuals influence and exhibit an unequal amount of impact upon outcomes
4. Participation and involvement in problem-solving increases understanding, acceptance, commitment, and ownership of outcomes	4. Individuals are less accountable in groups, allowing groups to make riskier decisions
5. More opportunities for group development, increasing cohesion, communication, and companionship	5. Conflicting individual biases may cause unproductive levels of competition, leading to "winners" and "losers"

Source: Isaksen, S. and Tidd, J. (2006). *Meeting the Innovation Challenge*. Chichester: John Wiley & Sons, Ltd.

goals. The goals were clear and compelling but also open and challenging. Less creative teams have conflicting agendas, different missions, and no agreement on the end result. The tasks for the least creative teams were tightly constrained, considered routine, and were overly structured.

- *Results-driven structure*. Individuals within high-performing teams feel productive when their efforts take place with a minimum of grief. Open communication, clear coordination of tasks, clear roles and accountabilities, monitoring performance, providing feedback, fact-based judgement, efficiency, and strong impartial management combine to create a results-driven structure.

- *Competent team members*. Competent teams are composed of capable and conscientious members. Members must possess essential skills and abilities, a strong desire to contribute, be capable of collaborating effectively, and have a sense of responsible idealism. They must have knowledge in the domain surrounding the task (or some other domain which may be relevant) as well as with the process of working together. Creative teams recognize the diverse strengths and talents and use them accordingly.

- *Unified commitment*. Having a shared commitment relates to the way the individual members of the group respond. Effective teams have an organizational unity: members display mutual support, dedication, faithfulness to the shared purpose and vision, and a productive degree of self-sacrifice to reach organizational goals. Team members enjoy contributing and celebrating their accomplishments.

- *Collaborative climate*. Productive teamwork does not just happen. It requires a climate that supports cooperation and collaboration. This kind of situation is characterized by mutual trust, in which everyone feels comfortable discussing ideas, offering suggestions, and willing to consider multiple approaches.

- *Standards of excellence*. Effective teams establish clear standards of excellence. They embrace individual commitment, motivation, self-esteem, individual performance, and constant improvement. Members of teams develop a clear and explicit understanding of the norms upon which they will rely.

- *External support and recognition*. Team members need resources, rewards, recognition, popularity, and social success. Being liked and admired as individuals and respected for belonging and contributing to a team is often helpful in maintaining the high level of personal energy required for sustained performance. With the increasing use of cross-functional and inter-departmental teams within larger complex organizations, teams must be able to obtain approval and encouragement.

- *Principled leadership*. Leadership is important for teamwork. Whether it is a formally appointed leader or leadership of the emergent kind, the people who exert influence and encourage the accomplishment of important things usually follow some basic principles. Leaders provide clear guidance, support and encouragement, and keep everyone working together and moving forward. Leaders also work to obtain support and resources from within and outside the group.

- *Appropriate use of the team*. Teamwork is encouraged when the tasks and situations really call for that kind of activity. Sometimes the team itself must set clear boundaries on when and why it should be deployed. One of the easiest ways to destroy a productive team is to overuse it or use it when it is not appropriate to do so.

- *Participation in decision-making*. One of the best ways to encourage teamwork is to engage the members of the team in the process of identifying the challenges and opportunities for improvement, generating ideas, and transforming ideas into action. Participation in the process of problem-solving and decision-making actually builds teamwork and improves the likelihood of acceptance and implementation.

- *Team spirit*. Effective teams know how to have a good time, release tension, and relax their need for control. The focus at times is on developing friendship, engaging in tasks for mutual pleasure, and recreation. This internal team climate extends beyond the need for a collaborative climate. Creative teams have the ability to work together without major conflicts in personalities. There is a high degree of respect for the contributions of others. Less creative teams are characterized by animosity, jealousy, and political posturing.

- *Embracing appropriate change*. Teams often face the challenges of organizing and defining tasks. In order for teams to remain productive, they must learn how to make necessary changes to procedures.

There are also many challenges to the effective management of teams. We have all seen teams that have "gone wrong." As a team develops, there are certain aspects or guidelines that might be helpful to keep them on track. Hackman has identified a number of themes relevant to those who design, lead, and facilitate teams. In examining a variety of organizational work groups, he found some seemingly small factors that if overlooked in the management of teams, they will have large implications that tend to destroy the capability of a team to function. These small and often hidden "tripwires" to major problems include:[38]

- *Group versus team*. One of the mistakes that is often made when managing teams is to call the group a team but to actually treat it as nothing more than a loose collection of individuals. This is similar to making it a team "because I said so." It is important to be very clear about the underlying goal and reward structure. People are often asked to perform tasks as a team but then have all evaluation of performance based on an individual level. This situation sends conflicting messages and may negatively affect team performance.

- *Ends versus means*. Managing the source of authority for teams is a delicate balance. Just how much authority can you assign to the team to work out its own issues and challenges? Those who convene teams often "over manage" them by specifying the results as well as how the team should obtain them. The end, direction, or outer limit constraints ought to be specified but the means to get there ought to be within the authority and responsibility of the group.

- *Structured freedom*. It is a major mistake to assemble a group of people and merely tell them in general and unclear terms what needs to be accomplished and then let them work out their own details. At times, the belief is that if teams are to be creative, they ought not be given any structure. It turns out that most groups would find a little structure quite enabling, if it were the right kind. Teams generally need a well-defined task. They need to be composed of an appropriately small number to be manageable but large enough to be diverse. They need clear limits as to the team's authority and responsibility, and they need sufficient freedom to take initiative and make good use of their diversity. It's about striking the right kind of balance between structure, authority, and boundaries – and freedom, autonomy, and initiative.

- *Support structures and systems*. Often, challenging team objectives are set, but the organization fails to provide adequate support in order to make the objectives a reality. In general, high-performing teams need a reward system that recognizes and reinforces excellent team performance. They also need access to good quality and adequate information, as well as training in team-relevant tools and skills. Good team performance is also dependent on having an adequate level of material and financial resources to get the job done. Calling a group a team does not mean that they will automatically obtain all the support needed to accomplish the task.

- *Assumed competence*. Technical skills, domain-relevant expertise, experience, and abilities often explain why someone has been included within a team, but these are rarely the only competencies individuals need for effective team performance. Members will undoubtedly require explicit coaching on skills needed to work well in a team.

Entrepreneurship in Action: Organizational climate for innovation at Google

Google appears to have learned a few lessons from other innovative organizations, such as 3M. Technical employees are expected to spend 20% of their time on projects other than their core job, and similarly, managers are required to spend 20% of their time on projects outside the core business and 10% to completely new products and businesses. This effort devoted to new, non-core business is not evenly allocated weekly or monthly, but when possible or necessary. These are contractual obligations, reinforced by performance reviews and peer pressure, and integral to the 25 different measures of and targets for employees. Ideas progress through a formal qualification process, which includes prototyping, pilots, and tests with actual users. The assessment of new ideas and projects is highly data-driven and aggressively empirical, reflecting the IT basis of the firm, and is based on rigorous experimentation within 300 employee user panels, segments of Google's 132 million users, and trusted third parties. The approach is essentially evolutionary in the sense that many ideas are encouraged, most fail but some are successful, depending on the market response. The generation and market testing of many alternatives and tolerance of (rapid) failure are central to the process. In this way, the company claims to generate around 100 new products each year, including hits such as Gmail, AdSense, and Google News.

However, we need to be careful to untangle cause and effect and determine how much of this is transferable to other companies and contexts. Google's success to date is predicated on dominating the global demand for search engine services through an unprecedented investment in technology infrastructure – estimated at over a million computers. Its business model is based upon "ubiquity first, revenues later," and is still reliant on search-based advertising. The revenues generated in this way have allowed it to hire the best and to provide the space and motivation to innovate. Despite this, it is estimated to have only 120 or so product offerings, and the most recent blockbusters have all been acquisitions: YouTube for video content; DoubleClick for web advertising; and Keyhole for mapping (now Google Earth). In this respect, it looks more like Microsoft than 3M.

Source: Iyer, B. and Davenport, T.H. (2008). Reverse engineering Google's innovation machine. *Harvard Business Review*, April, pp. 58–68.

Question:

Cross-functional teams have many advantages, but they are not suitable for all types of projects. What do you think are the potential advantages and drawbacks of using cross-functional teams?

A study examined 40 development projects in the consumer electronics and pharmaceuticals industries to identify the roles and influences of cross-functional teams in different types of R&D project.

Common Benefits:

- Higher-risk projects are likely to have a higher return and are strengthened by using cross-functional teams
- Cross-functional cooperation tends to enhance information-processing capabilities

Potential drawbacks:

- Cross-functional teams are resource-intensive and are not necessary for all types of projects
- Undesirable psycho-social outcomes, such as increased conflict and group-member turnover

Conclusion:

- The benefits of cross-functional cooperation tend to outweigh the psycho-social costs in the case of high-risk and high-value projects with much technological and market newness

Source: Gemser, G. and Leenders, M. (2011). Managing cross-functional cooperation for new product development success. *Long Range Planning*, 44(1), pp. 26–41.

DEEPER DIVE: Team Diversity

Read the Deeper Dive_Team diversity document in the ebook or from the book companion site.

7.4 Venture Climate and Culture

Climate is defined as the recurring patterns of behavior, attitudes, and feelings that characterize life in the organization. These are the objectively shared perceptions that characterize life within a defined work unit or in the larger organization. Climate is distinct from culture in that it is more observable at a surface level within the organization and more amenable to change and improvement efforts. Culture refers to the deeper and more enduring values, norms, and beliefs within the organization. Climate and culture are different – traditionally, studies of organizational culture are more qualitative, whereas research on organizational climate is more quantitative – but a multidimensional approach helps to integrate the benefits of each perspective. What is needed is a common sense set of levers for change that leaders can exert direct and deliberate influence over.

Table 7.4 summarizes some research of how climate influences innovation. Many dimensions of climate have been shown to influence innovation and entrepreneurship, but here we discuss six of the most critical factors.

For each factor, the challenge is to achieve the appropriate level, rather than to maximize any dimension. Too much of each climate factor can be as dysfunctional as too little, although the reasons for poor performance will be different (**Figure 7.1**).

Trust and Openness

The trust and openness dimension refers to the emotional safety in relationships. These relationships are considered safe when people are seen as both competent and sharing a common set of values. When there is a strong level of trust, everyone in the organization dares to put

TABLE 7.4   Climate Factors Influencing Innovation

Climate factor	Most Innovative (score)	Least Innovative (score)	Difference
Trust and Openness	253	88	165
Challenge and Involvement	260	100	160
Support and space for ideas	218	70	148
Conflict and Debate	231	83	148
Risk-taking	210	65	145
Freedom	202	110	92

Source: Derived for Isaksen, S. and Tidd, J. (2006). *Meeting the Innovation Challenge*. Chichester: John Wiley & Sons, Ltd.

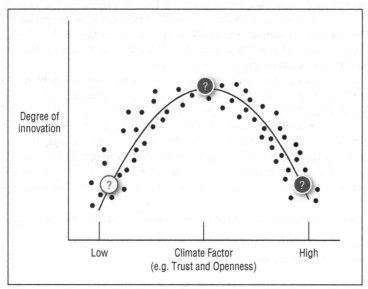

Each climate factor has an inverted U effect on innovation (curvi-linear relationship).

FIGURE 7.1   Getting the right level of climate factors to support entrepreneurship and innovation.

forward ideas and opinions. Initiatives can be taken without fear of reprisals and ridicule in case of failure. The communication is open and straightforward. Where trust is missing, count on high expenses for mistakes that may result. People also are afraid of being exploited and robbed of their good ideas.

When trust and openness are too low, you may see people hoarding resources (i.e., information, software, materials, etc.). However, trust can bind and blind. If trust and openness are too high, relationships may be so strong that time and resources at work are often spent on personal issues. It may also lead to a lack of questioning each other that, in turn, may lead to mistakes or less productive outcomes. Cliques may form where there are isolated "pockets" of high trust. In this case, it may help to develop forums for interdepartmental and intergroup exchange of information and ideas.

Challenge and Involvement

Challenge and involvement is the degree to which people are involved in daily operations, long-term goals, and visions. High levels of challenge and involvement mean that people are intrinsically motivated and committed to making contributions to the success of the organization. The climate has a dynamic and inspiring quality. However, if the challenge and involvement are too high, you may observe that people are showing signs of "burn out," they are unable to meet project goals and objectives, or they spend "too many" long hours at work. If challenge and involvement are too low, you may see that people are apathetic about their work, are not generally interested in professional development, or are frustrated about the future of the organization. One of the ways to improve the situation might be to get people involved in interpreting the vision, mission, purpose, and goals of the organization for themselves and their work teams.

Entrepreneurship in Action: Increasing challenge and involvement in an electrical engineering division

The organization was a division of a large, global electrical power and product supply company headquartered in France with 92 employees. It was losing about $8 million a year. A new general manager was bought in to turn the division around and make it profitable quickly.

An assessment of the organization's climate identified that it was strongest on the debate dimension but was very close to the stagnated norms when it came to challenge and involvement, playfulness and humor, and conflict. The quantitative and qualitative assessment results were consistent with their own impressions that the division could be characterized as conflict driven, uncommitted to producing results, and people were generally despondent. The leadership decided, after some debate, that they should target challenge and involvement, which was consistent with their strategic emphasis on a global initiative on employee commitment. It was clear to them that they also needed to soften the climate and drive a warmer, more embracing, communicative climate.

The management team re-established training and development and encouraged employees to engage in both personal and business-related skills development. They also provided mandatory safety training for all employees. They committed to increase communication by holding monthly all-employee meetings, sharing quarterly reviews on performance, and using cross-functional strategy review sessions. They implemented mandatory "skip level" meetings to allow more direct interaction between senior managers and all levels of employees. The general manager held 15-minute meetings with all employees at least once a year. All employee suggestions and recommendations were invited, and feedback and recognition was required to be immediate. A new monthly recognition and rewards program was launched across the division for both managers and employees that was based on peer nomination. The management team formed employee review teams to challenge and craft the statements in the hopes of encouraging more ownership and involvement in the overall strategic direction of the business.

In 18 months, the division showed a $7 million turnaround and won a worldwide innovation award. The general manager was promoted to a national position.

Source: Isaksen, S. and Tidd, J. (2006). *Meeting the Innovation Challenge*. Chichester: John Wiley & Sons, Ltd.

Support and Space for Innovation

Idea time is the amount of time people can (and do) use for exploring innovation. In the high idea-time situation, possibilities exist to discuss and test impulses and fresh suggestions that are not planned or included in the task assignment, and people tend to use these possibilities. When idea time is low, every minute is booked and specified. If there is insufficient time and space for generating new ideas, you may observe that people are only concerned with their current projects and tasks. Conversely, if there is too much time and space for new ideas, you may observe that people are showing signs of boredom, and that decisions are made through a slow, bureaucratic, processes.

Conflict and Debate

Conflict in an organization refers to the presence of personal, interpersonal, or emotional tensions. Although conflict is a negative dimension, all organizations have some level of personal tension. Conflicts can occur over tasks, processes, or relationships. Task conflicts focus on disagreements about the goals and content of work, the "what?" that needs to be done and "why?" Process conflicts are around "how?" to achieve a task, its means and methods. Relationship or affective conflicts are more emotional and are characterized by hostility and anger. In general, some task and process conflict is constructive, helping to avoid groupthink and to consider more diverse opinions and alternative strategies. However, task and process conflict only have a positive effect on performance in a climate of openness and collaborative communication, otherwise it can degenerate into relationship conflict or avoidance.

Relationship conflict is generally energy-sapping and destructive, as emotional disagreements create anxiety and hostility. If the level of conflict is too high, groups and individuals dislike or hate each other, and the climate can be characterized by "warfare." Plots and traps are common in the life of the organization. There is gossip and back-biting going on. You may observe gossiping at water coolers (including character assassination), information hoarding, open aggression, or people lying or exaggerating about their real needs. In these cases, you may need to take initiative to engender cooperation among key individuals or departments.

So, the goal is not necessarily to minimize conflict and maximize consensus, but to maintain a level of constructive debate consistent with the need for diversity and a range of different preferences and styles of creative problem-solving. Group members with similar creative preferences and problem-solving styles are likely to be more harmonious but much less effective than those with mixed preferences and styles. So, if the level of conflict is constructive, people behave in a more mature manner. They have psychological insight and exercise more control over their impulses and emotions.

Risk-Taking

Tolerance of uncertainty and ambiguity constitutes risk-taking. In a high risk-taking climate, bold new initiatives can be taken even when the outcomes are unknown. People feel that they can "take a gamble" on some of their ideas. People will often "go out on a limb" and be first to put an idea forward. In a risk-avoiding climate, there is a cautious, hesitant mentality. People try to be on the "safe side." They set up committees, and they cover themselves in many ways before making a decision. If risk taking is too low, employees offer few new ideas or few ideas that are well outside of what is considered safe or ordinary. In risk-avoiding organizations, people complain about boring, low-energy jobs and are frustrated by a long, tedious process used to get ideas to action.

Freedom

Freedom is described as the independence in behavior exerted by the people in the organization. In a climate with much freedom, people are given autonomy to define much of their own work. They are able to exercise discretion in their day-to-day activities. They take the initiative to acquire and share information, make plans and decisions about their work. If there is not enough freedom, people demonstrate very little initiative for suggesting new and better ways of doing things. They may spend a great deal of time and energy obtaining permission and gaining support or perform all their work "by the book." If there is too much freedom, people may pursue their own independent directions and have an unbalanced concern weighted toward themselves rather than the work group or organization.

Chapter Summary

- Leadership and organization of innovation is much more than a set of processes, tools, and techniques, and the successful practice of innovation demands the interaction and integration of three different levels of management: individual, collective, and climate.

- At the Personal or individual level, the key is to match the leadership styles with the task requirement and type of teams. General leadership requirements for innovative projects include expertise and experience relevant to the project, articulating a vision and inspirational communication, intellectual stimulation, and quality of leader–member exchange (LMX).

- At the Collective or social level, there is no universal best-practice, but successful teams require clear, common, and elevating goals, unified commitment, cross-functional expertise, collaborative climate, external support and recognition, and participation in decision-making.

- At the Context or Climate level, there is no "best innovation culture," but innovation is promoted or hindered by a number of factors, including Trust and Openness, Challenge and Involvement, Support and space for ideas, Conflict and Debate, Risk-taking and Freedom.

Key Terms

Climate recurring patterns of behavior, attitudes, and feelings that characterize life in the organization. These are the objectively shared perceptions that characterize life within a defined work unit or in the larger organization. Climate is distinct from culture in that it is more observable at a surface level within the organization and more amenable to change and improvement efforts.

Culture the deeper and more enduring values, norms, and beliefs within the organization.

Kirton Adapter-Innovator (KAI) scale a psychometric approach for assessing the creativity of individuals. By a series of questions, it seeks to identify an individual's attitudes towards originality, attention to detail, and following rules. It seeks to differentiate "adaptive" from "innovative" styles.

References

[1] Kaplan, J.M. and Warren, A.C. (2013). *Patterns of Entrepreneurship*. 4th ed. New Jersey: John Wiley & Sons, Inc.

[2] Roberts, E.B. (1991). *Entrepreneurs in High Technology: Lessons from MIT and beyond*. Oxford: Oxford University Press.

[3] Mueller, S.L. and Thomas, A.S. (2001). Culture and entrepreneurial potential: A nine-country study of locus of control and innovativeness. *Journal of Business Venturing*, 16(1), pp. 51–75; Robichaud, Y., McGraw, E., and Roger, A. (2001). Towards development of a measuring instrument for entrepreneurial motivation. *Journal of Developmental Entrepreneurship*, 5(2), pp. 189–202; Shane, S. and Venkataraman, S. (2000). The promise of entrepreneurship as a field of research. *Academy of Management Review*, 25, pp. 217–226; Georgelli, Y.P., Joyce, B., and Woods, A. (2000). Entrepreneurial action, innovation, and business performance. *Journal of Small Business and Enterprise Development*, 7(1), pp. 7–17; Gartner, W.B. (1988). Who is an entrepreneur is the wrong question. *Entrepreneurship Theory and Practice*, 13(1), pp. 47–64.

[4] Sarason, Y., Dean, T., and Dillard, F. (2006). Entrepreneurship as the nexus of individual and opportunity. *Journal of Business Venturing*, 21, pp. 286–305; Feldman, D.C. and Bolino, M.C. (2000). Career patterns of the self-employed. *Journal of Small Business Management*, 38(3), pp. 53–68.

[5] Harding, R. (2007). *GEM: Global Entrepreneurship Monitor*. London Business School; Storey, D. and Tether, B. (1998). New technology-based firms in the European Union. *Research Policy* 26, pp. 933–946.

[6] Astebro, T. and Serrano, C.J. (2015). Business partners: complementary assets, financing, and invention commercialization. *Journal of Economics and Management Strategy*, 24(2), pp. 228–252; Coad, A. and Timmermans, B. (2014). Two's company: composition, structure, and performance of entrepreneurial pairs. *European Management Review*, 11(2), pp. 117–138; Tidd, J. (2014). Conjoint innovation: building a bridge between innovation and entrepreneurship. *International Journal of Innovation Management*, 18(1), pp. 1–20; Tidd, J. (2012). It takes two to tango: how multiple entrepreneurs interact to innovate. *European Business Review*, 24(4), pp. 58–61.

[7] Patton, D. and Higgs, M. (2013). The role of shared leadership in the decision making processes of new technology based firms. *International Journal of Innovation Management*, 17(4), DOI 1350015; Coad, A. (2012). Two's company: directional diversity and performance of entrepreneurial pairs. SPRU seminar, 12 September, University of Sussex; Østergaard, C.R., Timmermans, B., and Kristinsson, K. (2011). Does a different view create something new? The effect of employee diversity on innovation. *Research Policy*, 40(3), pp. 500–509; Eisenhardt, K. and Schoonhoven, C.B. (1990). Organizational growth: linking founding team, strategy, environment, and growth. *Administrative Science Quarterly*, 35, pp. 504–529.

[8] Armstrong, S.J., Cools, E., and Sadler-Smith, E. (2012). Role of cognitive styles in business and management: reviewing 40 years of research. *International Journal of Management Reviews*, 14(3), pp. 238–262; Armstrong, S.J. and Hird, A. (2009). Cognitive style and entrepreneurial drive of new and mature business owner managers. *Journal of Business and Psychology*, 24, pp. 419–430; Dew, R. and Hearn, G. (2009). A new model of the learning process for innovation teams: networked nominal pairs. *International Journal of Innovation Management*, 13(4), pp. 521–536; Isaksen, S. and Tidd, J. (2006). *Meeting the Innovation Challenge: Leadership for Transformation and Growth*. Chichester: John Wiley & Sons, Ltd.

[9] Bowman, E.H. and Helfat, C.E. (2001). Does corporate strategy matter? *Strategic Management Journal*, 22, pp. 1–23.

[10] Mann, R.D. (1959). A review of the relationships between personality and performance in small groups. *Psychological Bulletin*, 56, pp. 241–270.

[11] Connelly, M.S., Gilbert, J.A., Zaccaro, S.J., Threlfall, K.V., Marks, M.A., and Mumford, M.D. (2000). Exploring the relationship of leader skills and knowledge to leader performance. *The Leadership Quarterly*, 11, pp. 65–86; Zaccaro, S.J., Gilbert, J.A., Thor, K.K., and Mumford, M.D. (2000). Assessment of leadership problem-solving capabilities. *The Leadership Quarterly*, 11, pp. 37–64.

[12] Farris, G.F. (1972). The effect of individual role on performance in creative groups. *R&D Management*, 3, pp. 23–28; Ehrhart, M.G. and Klein, K.J. (2001). Predicting followers' preferences for charismatic leadership: the influence of follower values and personality. *The Leadership Quarterly*, 12, pp. 153–180.

[13] Scott, S.G. and Bruce, R.A. (1994). Determinants of innovative behavior: a path model of individual innovation in the workplace. *Academy of Management Journal*, 37(3), pp. 580–607.

[14] Amabile, T.M., Schatzel, E.A., Moneta, G.B., and Kramer, S.J. (2004). Leader behaviors and the work environment for creativity: perceived leader support. *The Leadership Quarterly*, 15 (1), pp. 5–32.

[15] Rafferty, A.E. and Griffin, M.A. (2004). Dimensions of transformational leadership: conceptual and empirical extensions. *The Leadership Quarterly*, 15(3), pp. 329–354.

[16] Mumford, M.D., Zaccaro, S.J., Harding, F.D., and Jacobs, T.O., Fleishman, E.A. (2000). Leadership skills for a changing world: solving complex social problems. *The Leadership Quarterly*, 11, pp. 11–35.

[17] Rafferty, A.E. and Griffin, M.A. (2004). Dimensions of transformational leadership: conceptual and empirical extensions. *The Leadership Quarterly*, 15(3), pp. 329–354.

[18] Pinto, J. and Slevin, D. (1989). Critical success factors in R&D projects. *Research-Technology Management*, 32, pp. 12–18.

[19] West, M.A., Borrill, C.S., Dawson, J.F., Brodbeck, F., Shapiro, D.A., and Haward, B. (2003). Leadership clarity and team innovation in health care. *The Leadership Quarterly*, 14(4–5), pp. 393–410.

[20] Andrews, F.M. and Farris, G.F. (1967). Supervisory practices and innovation in scientific teams. *Personnel Psychology*, 20, pp. 497–515; Barnowe, J.T. (1975). Leadership performance outcomes in research organizations. *Organizational Behavior and Human Performance*, 14, pp. 264–280; Elkins, T. and Keller, R.T. (2003). Leadership in research and development organizations: a literature review and conceptual framework. *The Leadership Quarterly*, 14, pp. 587–606.

[21] Keller, R.T. (1992). Transformational leadership and performance of research and development project groups. *Journal of Management*, 18, pp. 489–501.

[22] Berson, Y. and Linton, J.D. (2005). An examination of the relationships between leadership style, quality, and employee satisfaction in R&D versus administrative environments. *R&D Management*, 35(1), pp. 51–60.

[23] Denti, L. and Hemlin, S. (2012). Leadership and innovation in organizations: a systematic review of factors that mediate or moderate the relationship. *International Journal of Innovation Management*, 16(3), DOI 1240007.

[24] Peters, T. (1988). *Thriving on Chaos*. New York: Free Press.

[25] Forrester, R. and Drexler, A. (1999). A model for team-based organization performance. *Academy of Management Executive*, 13(3), pp. 36–49; Conway, S. and Forrester, R. (1999). *Innovation and Teamworking: Combining Perspectives Through a Focus on Team Boundaries*. Birmingham: University of Aston Business School.

[26] Thamhain, H. and Wilemon, D. (1987). Building high performing engineering project teams. *IEEE Transactions on Engineering Management*, EM-34(3), pp. 130–137.

[27] Bixby, K. (1987). *Superteams*. London: Fontana.

[28] Holti, R., Neumann, J., and Standing, H. (1995). *Change Everything at Once: The Tavistock Institute's Guide to Developing Teamwork in Manufacturing*. London: Management Books 2000.

[29] Tranfield, D., Parry, I., Wilson, S., Smith, S., and Foster, M. (1998). Teamworked organizational engineering: getting the most out of teamworking. *Management Decision*, 36(6), pp. 378–384.

[30] Jassawalla, A. and Sashittal, H. (1999). Building collaborative cross-functional new product teams. *Academy of Management Executive*, 13(3), pp. 50–53.

[31] DTI. (1996). *UK Software Purchasing Survey*. London: Department of Trade and Industry.

[32] Van Beusekom, M. (1996). *Participation Pays! Cases of Successful Companies with Employee Participation*. The Hague: Netherlands Participation Institute.

[33] Tuckman, B. and Jensen, N. (1977). Stages of small group development revisited. *Group and Organizational Studies*, 2, pp. 419–427.

[34] Belbin, M. (2004). *Management Teams – Why they Succeed or Fail*. London: Butterworth-Heinemann.

[35] Smith, P. and Blanck, E. (2002). From experience: leading dispersed teams. *Journal of Product Innovation Management*, 19, pp. 294–304.

[36] Prester, J. and Bozac, M.G. (2012). Are innovative organizational concepts enough for fostering innovation? *International Journal of Innovation Management*, 16(1), pp. 1–23.

[37] Isaksen, S. and Tidd, J. (2006). *Meeting the Innovation Challenge: Leadership for Transformation and Growth*. Chichester: John Wiley & Sons, Ltd.

[38] Isaksen, S. and Tidd, J. (2006). *Meeting the Innovation Challenge: Leadership for Transformation and Growth*. Chichester: John Wiley & Sons, Ltd.

CHAPTER 8

Building and Working with Networks

LEARNING OBJECTIVES

By the end of this chapter you will be able to understand:

1. How networking helps the process of innovation through improving the range and scale of knowledge interaction.

2. How networking provides a powerful way of acquiring and amplifying the resources available to an entrepreneur.

3. How to build and work with effective networks.

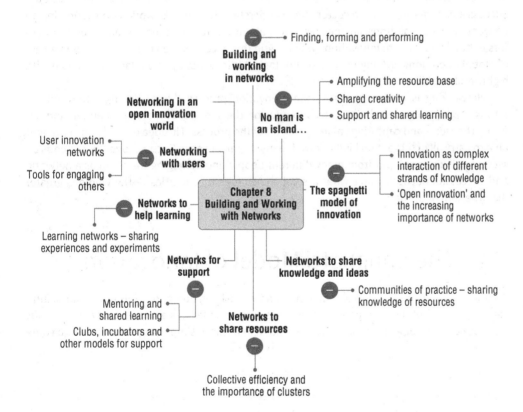

8.0 | No Man is an Island

It's easy to think of innovation as a solo act – the lone genius, slaving away in his or her garret, working on the idea which will change the world. Although that's a common image, it lies a long way from the reality. In reality, taking any good idea forward relies on all sorts of inputs from different people and perspectives. And it's about shared creativity – solving problems together and exploiting the fact that different people have different skills and experiences which they can bring to the party.

For example, the technological breakthrough which makes a better mousetrap is only going to mean something if people can be both made aware of it and persuaded that this is something they cannot live without. This side of things needs input from people with a marketing skill set. Making it happen is going to need skills in manufacturing, in procurement of the bits and pieces to make it, and in controlling the quality of the final product.

All of this will need funding, so other skills in getting access to finance – and the understanding of how to spend the money wisely – become important. Coordinating the diverse inputs needed to turn the mousetrap into a successful reality rather than a gleam in the eye will require project management skills, balancing resources against the clock, and facilitating a team of people to find and solve the thousand and one little problems which crop up as you make the journey.

Innovation is not a solo act but a multiplayer game. For start-up entrepreneurs, the challenge is one of amplifying the resource base – connecting with others who can bring complementary resources and energy to help make the new venture happen. But the same is true inside established organizations – bringing new products or services to life or changing internal processes depends on being able to make connections inside and outside the organization. Success means getting close to customers to understand their needs, working with suppliers to deliver innovative solutions, linking up with collaborators, research centers, and even competitors to build and operate innovation systems. And this becomes even more important in an era of global operations and high-speed technological infrastructures populated by people with highly mobile skills.

Networking is important across the innovation process – from finding opportunities, through pulling together the resources to develop the venture, to making it happen and diffusing the idea – and capturing value at the end of the process. The idea of a solo entrepreneur able to carry all of this out on his/her own is a myth; putting new ventures together depends on securing all kinds of input from many different people and managing this team as a network. And successful networks have what are called "emergent properties" – the whole is greater than the sum of the parts.

8.1 | The Spaghetti Model of Innovation

It's always nice to use simple, clear models – and we've been doing so in this book. Our picture (see **Figure 8.1**) of the entrepreneurial process suggests that it is a neat journey, allowing us to create value through innovation. That's helpful in terms of simplifying the picture into some

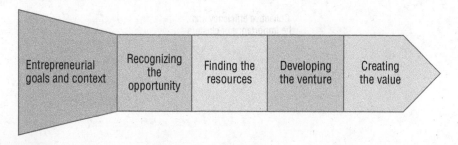

| Entrepreneurial goals and context | Recognizing the opportunity | Finding the resources | Developing the venture | Creating the value |

FIGURE 8.1 Simple model of the entrepreneurial process

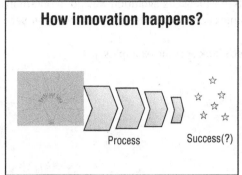
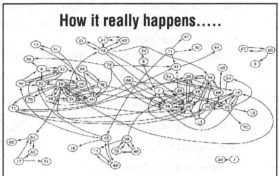

FIGURE 8.2 How innovation happens

clear stages and recognizing the key levers we may have to work with if we are going to manage the process successfully.

But like any simplification, the model isn't quite as complex as the reality. While our model works as an aerial view of what goes on and has to be managed, the close-up picture can look a lot more like the picture on the right (**Figure 8.2**). The ways knowledge actually flows around an innovation project are complex and interactive, woven together in a kind of social spaghetti where different people talk to each other in different ways, more or less frequently, and about different things.

This complex interaction is all about *knowledge* and how it is combined and deployed to make innovation happen. Whether it's our entrepreneur building a network to help get his mousetrap to market or a company like Apple bringing out the latest generation iPhone, the process will involve building running knowledge networks. As the innovation becomes more complex, the networks have to involve more and different players, many of whom may lie outside our organization.

8.2 | Working with Networks

A network can be defined as *a complex, interconnected group or system*, and networking involves using that arrangement to accomplish particular tasks.

At its simplest, networking happens in an informal way when people get together and share ideas as a by-product of their social and work interactions. But let's concentrate our attention on those networks which are deliberately set up to help make innovation happen, whether it is creating a new product or service or learning to apply some new process of thinking more effectively within organizations.

Innovation networks are more than just ways of assembling and deploying knowledge in a complex world. They also have "emergent properties" – in other words, the whole can be greater than the sum of its parts. Benefits that can come from an effective network include getting access to different and complementary knowledge sets, reducing risks by sharing them, accessing new markets and technologies, and otherwise pooling complementary skills and assets.

The idea of the lone inventor pioneering his or her way through to market success is something of a myth, not least because of the huge efforts and different resources needed to make innovation happen. While individual ideas, energy, and passion are key requirements, most successful entrepreneurs recognize the need to network extensively and to collect the resources they need via complex webs of relationships. They are essentially highly skilled at networking, both in building and in maintaining those networks to help create a sustainable business model.

These days one of the most powerful companies in the electronics world is ARM, whose chips are in almost all mobile phones and a host of other devices. Now a global player, ARM began as a spin-off from Cambridge University in the 1980s. Its evolution was not a one-man show, but the building and development of a complex network with links across countries, sectors, and technologies.

So how can networks help entrepreneurs? Let's look at some examples:

- Networks to share knowledge and ideas
- Networks to share resources
- Networks for support
- Networks to help learn
- Networking with users

8.3 Networks to Share Knowledge and Ideas

Networks form around people with similar interests. Think of all the different online communities that have sprung up to reflect common interests of all shapes and sizes. Entrepreneurs can make use of such "communities of practice" to find like-minded people with key knowledge resources which they may be willing to share.[1]

A great example of such a community is the one which has grown up to create and now support Linux software. Its origins lay with an entrepreneurial programmer, Linus Torvalds, who was working at the University of Helsinki in 1991; he became increasingly frustrated with the limitations of current operating systems and wanted to develop an open source version of the powerful UNIX language. He built a community of similarly frustrated programmers and users, and this has evolved over time to become one of the most powerful software platforms in the world – running almost all mobile phones, for example.

Entrepreneurship in Action: Many minds make light work...

Say the name Thomas Edison, and people instinctively imagine a great inventor, the lone genius who gave us so many 20th-century products and services – the gramophone, the light bulb, electric power, etc. But he was actually a very smart networker. His "invention factory" in Menlo Park, New Jersey, employed a team of engineers in a single room filled with workbenches, shelves of chemicals, books, and other resources. The key to their undoubted success was to bring together a group of young, entrepreneurial, and enthusiastic men from very diverse backgrounds and allow the emerging community to tackle a wide range of problems. Ideas flowed across the group and were combined and recombined into an astonishing array of inventions.

It's not just about external communities – in large organizations, communities of practice also play an increasingly important role. Public and private sector organizations wrestle with the paradox that they have hundreds or thousands of people spread across their organizations with all sorts of knowledge. The trouble is that, apart from some formal project activities which bring them together, many of these knowledge elements remain unconnected, like a giant jigsaw puzzle in which only a small number of the pieces have so far been fitted together.

It's back to the spaghetti model of innovation: how to ensure that people get to talk to others, share, and build on each other's ideas. This may not be too hard in a three- or four-person business, but it gets much harder across a sprawling multinational company. Although this is a long-standing problem, there has been quite a lot of movement in recent years toward understanding how to build more effective innovation networks within such businesses.

Entrepreneurship in Action: Using communities of practice

Procter & Gamble's successes with "connect and develop" (http://www.pgconnectdevelop.com/) owe much to its mobilizing rich linkages between people who know things within their giant global operations and increasingly outside it. P&G uses communities of practice – Internet-enabled "clubs" where people with different knowledge sets can converge around core themes – and deploys a small army of innovation "scouts" who are licensed to act as prospectors, brokers, and gatekeepers for knowledge to flow across the organization's boundaries. Intranet technology links around 10,000 people in an internal "ideas market," while sites like InnoCentive.com extend the principle outside the firm and enable a world of new collaborative possibilities.

3M – another firm with a strong innovation pedigree dating back over a century – similarly put much of its success down to making and managing connections. Larry Wendling, Vice President for Corporate Research, talks of 3M's "secret weapon": the rich formal and informal networking which links the thousands of R&D and market-facing people across the organization. Its long history of breakthrough innovations – from masking tape, through Scotchgard, Scotch tape, magnetic recording tape, to Post-its and their myriad derivatives – arises primarily out of people making connections.

8.4 Networks to Share Resources

The problem facing any start-up is inevitably a lack of resources; therefore, finding creative ways to share and leverage is a key skill. But the same challenge also faces small established firms which struggle to survive and grow; once again their big limitation is often resources. Networking offers an alternative to the costly business of acquiring and owning resources; for many key resources, there are benefits in sharing.

This idea is sometimes called "collective efficiency," and it means that small firms can become and remain competitive. There are many ways of organizing such networks – geographical proximity is clearly an important route, but they could also be grouped by sector or product/service type. The key point is that they come together – sometimes alone, sometimes with the help of network brokers and catalysts – to share and work together. The whole becomes much greater than the sum of the parts in such "clusters."

Entrepreneurship in Action: Small can be beautiful

"*The trouble with small firms isn't that they're small, it's that they're isolated!*" A powerful point: we know that small firms have lots of advantages in terms of focus, energy, and fast decision-making, but they often lack resources to achieve their full potential. This is where a concept the economists call collective efficiency comes in – the idea that you don't have to have all the resources under your own roof, only to know where and how to get hold of them.

Working with others can get you a lot further. For example, the world-beating Italian furniture industry shows how a network of small companies can compete in the high end of the market not through individual excellence but through sharing design expertise and facilities, and with collective materials purchasing and marketing.

An amazing 80% of the world's surgical instruments are made in one town, Sialkot, in Pakistan. This isn't a case of low-cost manufacturing; it is a high-precision, design-intensive business, and the small firms involved prosper by working together in a cooperative cluster.

In similar fashion, the Chinese motorcycle industry is becoming a world leader; most of its manufacturing takes place in the city of Chongqing. Once again, the dominant model is one of networking amongst a wide range of small, specialized producers, each taking responsibility for a particular system or component.

Innovation is also about taking risks and deploying what are often scarce resources on projects which may not succeed. So, another way in which networking can help is by helping to spread the risk and, in the process, extending the range of things which may be tried. This is particularly useful in the context of smaller businesses where resources are scarce, and it is one of the key features behind the success of many industrial clusters.

We think of places like Silicon Valley in the USA, Cambridge in the UK, or the island of Singapore as entrepreneurial powerhouses, but they are just the latest in a long-running list of regions which have grown through a continuous stream of innovation. It's not an accident of geography; what makes these places work is the networking which goes on amongst different players in the area.[2]

Entrepreneurship in Action: Networking for collective efficiency

Michael Best's fascinating account of the ways in which the Massachusetts economy managed to reinvent itself several times is one which places innovation networking at its heart. In the 1950s, the state suffered heavily from the loss of its traditional industries of textiles and shoes, but by the early 1980s, the "Massachusetts miracle" led to the establishment of a new high-tech industrial district. It was a resurgence enabled in no small measure by an underpinning network of specialist skills, high-tech research and training centers (the Boston area has the highest concentration of colleges, universities, research labs, and hospitals in the world), and by the rapid establishment of entrepreneurial firms keen to exploit the emerging "knowledge economy."[3]

But in turn this miracle turned to dust in the years between 1986 and 1992, when around one-third of the manufacturing jobs in the region disappeared as the minicomputer and defense-related industries collapsed. Despite gloomy predictions about its future, the region built again on its rich network of skills, technology sources, and a diverse local supply base. This allowed rapid new product development to emerge again as a powerhouse in high technology, such as special-purpose machinery, optoelectronics, medical laser technology, digital printing equipment, and biotech.

In each case, the process involved entrepreneurs creating new ventures – but they didn't do so in a vacuum. Instead they were able to mobilize networking to leverage and grow their enterprises, drawing on the collective efficiency effect.

8.5 Networks for Support

Being an entrepreneur can be a lonely occupation – trying to navigate through turbulent waters toward a destination which often seems to get lost in the storm clouds of day-to-day crises! Fortunately, networking is not just a way of providing leverage for entrepreneurs seeking to access resources; it can also offer support and encouragement. This could take a number of forms, ranging from members of the network acting as a sounding board through providing guidance and mentoring. An increasing number of networking clubs, often linked to entrepreneur incubators, are emerging to tap into this need for support networks.

VIDEO: Anil Gupta

Anil Gupta (2009) explains his approach for supporting entrepreneurs in solving some of the major social challenges facing India in his TED talk at https://www.ted.com/talks/anil_gupta_india_s_hidden_hotbeds_of_invention.

VIDEO: Chris Anderson: The Maker Revolution

Chris Anderson speaks about the "maker revolution" in his World Affairs 2013 keynote at https://www.youtube.com/watch?v=cjPk99jfFko.

8.6 Networks to Help Learning

Closely linked to support is the idea of using networks to help in a process of shared learning. While individual entrepreneurs might be trying to develop different ventures, the underlying experience and the challenges which they face is similar. So, it makes sense to share experiences and help each other in that learning journey.

Experience and research suggest that shared learning can help deal with some of the barriers to learning. For example:

- In shared learning, there is the potential for challenge and structured critical reflection from different perspectives
- Different perspectives can bring in new concepts (or old concepts which are new to the learner)
- Shared experimentation can reduce perceived and actual costs or risks in trying new things
- Shared experiences can provide support and open new lines of inquiry or exploration
- Shared learning helps explicate the systems principles, seeing the patterns (separating the wood from the trees)
- Shared learning provides an environment for surfacing assumptions and exploring mental models outside of the normal experience of individual organizations (helps prevent "not invented here" and other effects)
- Shared learning can reduce costs (e.g. in drawing on consultancy services and learning about external markets), which can be particularly useful for small/medium-sized enterprises (SMEs) and for developing country firms

Using shared learning can make a big difference, as shown in the following case studies.[4]

CASE STUDY: The Profitnet Programme

Read the Case Study_Profitnet programme document in the ebook or from the book companion site.

CASE STUDY: The Automotive Component Benchmarking Clubs

Read the Case Study_The Automotive Component Benchmarking Clubs document in the ebook or from the book companion site.

8.7 | Networking with Users

Innovation is not simply about technological knowledge; the other piece of the puzzle is knowledge of user needs. Users have always been an important source of innovation, and this role has accelerated in recent years as the technology and social networks allow for more participating in what is effectively a process of *co-creation*. However, although the potential of involving users is huge, the experience has often been that actively engaging with and working with communities beyond a front-end process of crowdsourcing ideas requires careful management.[5]

There are many different ways to build more open networks with users; **Figure 8.3** gives an overview of key strategies.

Working with lead users* can not only give us useful new insights in designing our new product or service, it can help give us early warning about changes we might need to make to enable our innovation to diffuse more widely or rapidly. It's for this reason that software companies make extensive use of beta testing – to work with lead users to get the final version right. In the lean start-up approach, the importance of early testing is stressed, but it also helps to have active and experienced lead users to work with.

---

*For an example of working with lead users, see Eric von Hippel's website: https://evhippel.mit.edu/teaching/

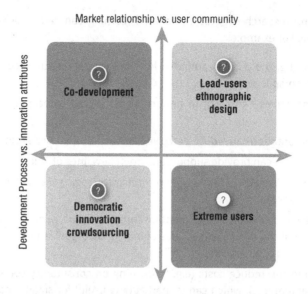

FIGURE 8.3 Different ways of networking with users

We mentioned extreme users as a source of innovation in Chapter 4, and it is clear they can give us valuable clues about what might be mainstream innovations in the future. For example, the whole concept of "mobile money" is of interest around the world, but in the extreme conditions of emerging countries in Africa, Asia, and Latin America, it is being brought to life because of the needs of "extreme users." M-PESA developed as a system to help provide more security for people not wishing to carry cash in Kenya but has since grown to become a powerful engine for mobile payments across the region and beyond.

CASE STUDY: M-PESA

Read the Case Study_MPESA document in the ebook or from the book companion site.

Another way of building such networks is via online communities; for example, a significant innovation community has been pulled together around the experience of living with or caring for those with rare diseases. User experiences of this kind can not only diffuse across the community to everyone's benefit but can also surface new directions for innovation.

The idea of user innovation often assumes a relationship in which suppliers are able, in some way or another, to harness the experience or ideas of users and apply them to their own product development efforts. But we are now seeing a dramatic shift toward more open, democratized forms of innovation that are driven by networks of individual users, not firms.[6] Users are now visibly active within all stages of the innovation process, from concept generation through development and diffusion. They may now be actively engaged with firms in the co-development of products and services, and the innovation agenda may no longer be entirely controlled by firms.

CASE STUDY: Lego

For a case study of Lego and how it is spawning a generation of user-innovators, co-creating new products at the design end.
Read the Case Study_Lego document in the ebook or from the book companion site.

CASE STUDY: Local Motors

For a case study of Local Motors, a community of enthusiastic entrepreneurs working in the automotive sector. Read the Case Study_Local Motors document in the ebook or from the book companion site.

We saw in Chapter 4 the emergence of the crowd as a source of innovation. Crowdsourcing can be implemented in many ways but is typically enabled by information and communication technology, which can extend the reach without losing some of the richness of user engagement.

One approach is to organize a competition, where a problem or challenge is set, and potential solutions or ideas are invited. Rewards range from peer or public recognition and community status, but more commonly feature some extrinsic motivation, such as free products or cash prizes. For example, Dell's crowdsourcing platform Idea Storm has received more than 15,000 ideas, of which over 400 have been implemented. Contributions and rewards tend to be more individual and competitive than in peer or user communities.

8.8 | Networking in an Open Innovation World

The innovation challenge – whether for a start-up entrepreneur or someone working inside an established organization trying to make change happen – is one of improving the knowledge flows in and out of the organization and trading in knowledge as much as goods and services. Great in theory, but what it implies is that we need to develop skills around making and managing connections.

One of the big shifts in the twenty-first century has been toward what is called "open innovation." (We saw some of this in Chapter 4, when we looked at how to search for opportunities.) Basically, the idea is simple: in a world where there is now so much knowledge being created, even the largest organization has to recognize that "not all the smart guys work for us." When we accept that, then the whole game changes and becomes all about networking. What do we know that someone else might be able to make use of, and how do we connect with them? Where is the knowledge that we might need, and how can we find it? We no longer have to do it all by ourselves, but we do have to learn how to build knowledge-sharing networks.

Opening up the game is not without its problems – first of all, in finding new ways to enable connections. There has been a huge rise in the role played by social and technological networking as mechanisms which enable closer linkages, and with it have sprung up new roles and groupings within organizations (gatekeepers, information managers, knowledge hubs, etc.) and new service businesses on the outside specializing in brokering and connecting. But improving knowledge flows also opens a can of worms as far as managing intellectual property is concerned. In a world of open source, who owns what, and how should you protect your hard-won knowledge assets?

For the lone entrepreneur, this raises a tantalizing mixture of threat and opportunity. On the one hand, he or she can make effective connections to resources, mobilize them, and act on a global basis. We've seen examples of this in the field of Internet businesses, which operate often with very small groups of people and amplify their efforts and presence through networking to a global community – sometimes running into billions of people. Developments around networking mean that the old problem for small businesses – their isolation – is removed. But on the other hand, the sheer scale and number of potential connections requires learning new skills in finding, forming, and getting networks to perform.

8.9 Building and Working in Networks

Building networks involves three steps: finding, forming, and performing.[7] The "finding" stage is essentially about setting up the network. Key issues here are around providing the momentum for bringing the network together and clearly defining its purpose. It may be crisis triggered, for example, perception of the urgent need to catch up via adoption of innovation. Equally, it may be driven by a shared perception of opportunity, the potential to enter new markets or exploit new technologies. Key roles here will often be played by third parties, that is network brokers, gatekeepers, policy agents, and facilitators.

"Forming" a network involves building a kind of organization with some structure to enable its operation.

Question:

What do you think are the key activities which need to be considered in running an effective network?

Key issues here are about trying to establish some core operating processes (about which there is support and agreement) to deal with:

- Network boundary management: how the membership of the network is defined and maintained
- Decision-making: how (where, when, who) decisions get taken at the network level
- Conflict resolution: how conflicts are resolved effectively
- Information processing: how information flows among members and is managed
- Knowledge management: how knowledge is created, captured, shared, and used across the network
- Motivation: how members are motivated to join/remain within the network
- Risk/benefit sharing: how the risks and rewards are allocated across members of the network
- Coordination: how the operations of the network are integrated and coordinated

---

Finally, the "performing" stage is about operating the network and allowing it to evolve. Networks need not last forever. Sometimes they are set up to achieve a highly specific purpose (e.g. development of a new product concept), and once this has been done, the network can be disbanded. In other instances, there is a case for sustaining the networking activities for as long as members see benefits. This may require periodic review and "re-targeting" to keep the motivation high.

Entrepreneurship in Action: Building entrepreneurial networks

Iain Edmondson looked at three Cambridge companies and the benefits they gained from networking at three different stages in their development:

- Conceptualization (the ideas)
- Start-up
- Growth

The benefits fell into two categories:

- "Harder" benefits: lead to customers, investors, partners, suppliers, employees, and technical and market knowledge/information
- "Softer" benefits: credibility/legitimacy, advice and problem-solving, confidence and reassurance, motivation/inspiration, and relaxation/interest

At the conceptualization stage, entrepreneurs tended to cast their net widely to try to establish themselves and their ideas in the entrepreneurial community and pave the way for the development of future business relationships. The role of networking groups here is in providing the softer benefits.

At the start-up stage, there is a shift toward using networks to gain more tangible benefits to develop new business relationships. Establishment of trust is crucial at this stage in sharing problems and solutions. The role of networking groups here is to provide both softer and harder benefits.

During the growth stage, there is no role for networking groups in providing the softer benefits. The focus for the entrepreneur is on PR, gaining new investors, suppliers, customers, and development partners.

Source: Edmondson, I. (2000). *The role of networking groups in the creation of new high technology ventures: the case of the Cambridge high tech cluster*. Cambridge: Judge Business School. MBA Individual Project.

Chapter Summary

- Innovation is not a solo act but a multiplayer game. Be it the entrepreneur who spots an opportunity or an established organization trying to renew its offerings or sharpen up its processes, making innovation happen depends on working with many different players. This raises questions about developing and making use of increasingly wide networks.

- The ways knowledge actually flows around an innovation project are complex and interactive, woven together in a kind of social spaghetti, where different people talk to each other in different ways, more or less frequently, and about different things. As the innovation becomes more complex, the networks have to involve more and different players.

- Networking can help entrepreneurs in a number of ways:
  - To share resources
  - To share knowledge and ideas
  - To provide support
  - To enhance learning

- Innovation networks are more than just ways of assembling and deploying knowledge in a complex world. They can also have what are termed "emergent properties," that is the potential for the whole to be greater than the sum of its parts. These include getting access to different and complementary knowledge sets, reducing risks by sharing them, accessing new markets and technologies, and otherwise pooling complementary skills and assets.

- Open innovation is a very broad concept but needs to be applied with care as its relevance is sensitive to the context. The appropriate choice of partner and specific mechanisms will depend on the type of innovation project and environmental uncertainty.

- Users can contribute to all phases of the innovation process, acting as sources, designers, developers, testers, and even the main beneficiaries of innovation.

- Operating within an innovation network is not easy. It needs a new set of management skills, and it depends on the starting point. The challenges include:
  - How to manage something we don't own or control
  - How to see system-level effects not narrow self-interests
  - How to build trust and shared risk-taking without tying the process up in contractual red tape

Key Terms

Clusters   networks which form because of the players being close to each other, for example, in the same geographical region. Silicon Valley is a good example of a cluster which thrives on proximity – knowledge flows amongst and across the members of the network but is hugely helped by the geographical closeness and the ability of key players to meet and talk.

Collective efficiency   where a group of (often small) players work together to share resources, risks, etc.

Communities of practice   networks which can involve players inside and across different organizations. What binds them together is a shared concern with a particular aspect or area of knowledge.

Emergent properties   a principle in systems that the whole is greater than the sum of the parts.

Learning network   a network formally set up for the primary purpose of increasing knowledge.

Network   a complex, interconnected group or system, and networking involves using that arrangement to accomplish particular tasks.

Open innovation   an approach which seeks to mobilize innovation sources inside and outside the enterprise.

User-led innovation   approach in which the ideas from interested or frustrated users create prototypes which represent new innovation possibilities. They are important not only as a source of innovation but also in shaping innovations which may diffuse widely.

References

[1] Wenger, E. (1999). *Communities of practice: learning, meaning, and identity*. Cambridge: Cambridge University Press.

[2] Saxenian, A. (1996). *Regional advantage: culture and competition in Silicon Valley and Route 128*. Boston: Harvard Business School Press.

[3] Best, M. (2001). *The new competitive advantage*. Oxford: Oxford University Press.

[4] Bessant, J., et al. (2012). *Constructing learning advantage through networks*. Journal of Economic Geography.

[5] Von Hippel, E. (2005). *The democratization of innovation*. Cambridge, MA: MIT Press.

[6] Flowers, D. and Henwood, F. (2010). Perspectives on user innovation. *International Journal of Innovation Management*, 12(3), pp. 5–10.

[7] Delbridge, R.I., Bessant, J., and Birkinshaw, J. (2007). Finding, forming, and performing: creating networks for discontinuous innovation. *California Management Review*, 49, pp. 67–84.

CHAPTER 9

Developing New Products and Services

LEARNING OBJECTIVES

After this chapter you should be able to:

1. Develop a formal process to support new venture development, such as stage-gate and the development funnel.

2. Identify the factors which influence success and failure in new venture development.

3. Choose and apply relevant tools to support each stage of new venture development.

4. Understand the differences between products and services and how these influence development.

5. Apply the lessons of diffusion research to promote the adoption of innovations.

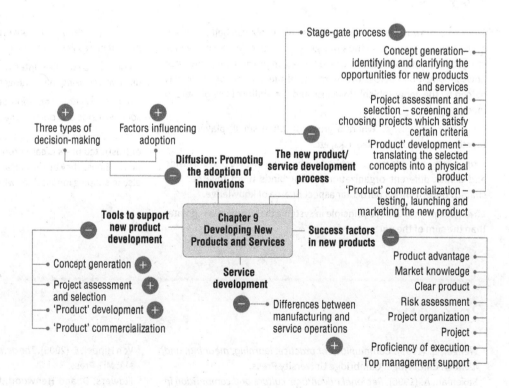

9.0 The New Product/Service Development Process

As we've seen, the process of new product or service development – moving from idea through to successful products, services or processes – is a gradual one of reducing uncertainty. The journey involves moving through a series of problem-solving stages around scanning, selecting, and implementation, linking market- and technology-related streams along the way.

At the outset, anything is possible, but growing commitment of resources during the life of the project makes it increasingly difficult to change direction. Managing new product or service development is a fine balancing act between the costs of continuing with projects, which may not eventually succeed (and which represent opportunity costs in terms of other possibilities), and the danger of closing down too soon, eliminating potentially fruitful options. With shorter life cycles and demand for greater product variety pressure is also placed upon the development process to work with a wider portfolio of new product opportunities and to manage the risks associated with progressing these through development to launch.

These decisions can be made on an *ad hoc* basis, but experience and research suggests some form of structured development system(with clear decision points and agreed rules on which to base go/no-go decisions) is a more effective approach. For start-ups, the idea of "lean start-up" has grown in popularity, essentially breaking down new venture formation into a series of short learning cycles, experimenting and pivoting towards something which will work.

DEEPER DIVE: The Lean Start Up

Read the Deeper Dive_The Lean Start Up document in the ebook or from the book companion site.

But the same challenge exists in established organizations seeking to update their product or service range or renew their processes. Attention on internal mechanisms for integrating and optimizing the process is critical, such as concurrent engineering, cross-functional working, advanced tools, early involvement, etc. To deal with this, attention has focused on systematic screening, monitoring, and progression frameworks, such as Cooper's "stage-gate" approach (**Figure 9.1**).[1]

As Cooper suggests, successful product development needs to operate some form of structured, staging process. As projects move through the development process, there are a number of discrete stages, each with different decision criteria or "gates" which they must pass. Many variations to this basic idea exist (e.g. "fuzzy gates"), but the important point is to ensure that there is a structure in place which reviews both technical and marketing data at each stage. A common variation is the "development funnel," which takes into account the reduction in uncertainty as the process progresses and the influence of real resource constraints (**Figure 9.2**).[2]

Whether we are working in commercial new product or service development, looking to improve or change processes within an organization, or create social value through innovation, the core message is that we need some form of structured development and review model to underpin our efforts. There are numerous other models in the literature, incorporating various stages ranging from three to 13. Such models are essentially linear and unidirectional, beginning with concept development and ending with commercialization. Such models suggest a simple, linear process of development and elimination. However, in practice the development of new products and services is inherently a complex and iterative process, and this makes it difficult to model for practical purposes.

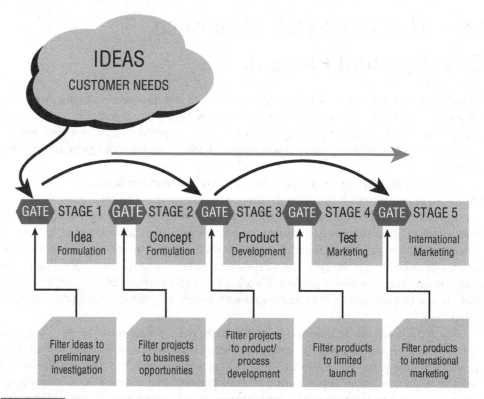

FIGURE 9.1 Stage-gate product development process

Sources: Derived from Cooper, R. (2001). *Winning at New Products: Accelerating the Process from Idea to Launch*. New York: Perseus Books; Cooper, R. (2000). Doing it right: winning with new products. *Ivey Business Journal*, 64(6), pp. 1–7.

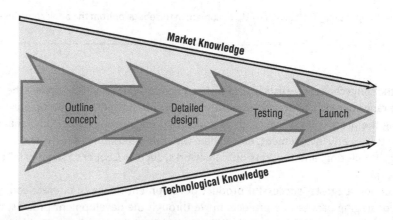

FIGURE 9.2 Product development funnel

Source: Derived from Cooper, R. (2001). *Winning at New Products: Accelerating the Process from Idea to Launch*. Perseus Books; Cooper, R. (2000). Doing it right: winning with new products. *Ivey Business Journal*, 64(6), pp. 1–7.

For ease of discussion and analysis, we will adopt a simplified four-stage model which we believe is sufficient to discriminate between the various factors that must be managed at different stages:[3]

1. *Concept generation* – identifying and clarifying the opportunities for new products and services

2. *Project assessment and selection* – screening and choosing projects which satisfy certain criteria

3. *"Product" development* – translating the selected concepts into a physical product
4. *"Product" commercialization* – testing, launching, and marketing the new product

We are using the term "product" here to describe the innovation, but the stages are common whether we are considering new services or changes to processes. There are some variations between these different types of innovation, and we'll explore these shortly.

9.1 | Concept Generation

Much of the marketing and product development literatures concentrate on monitoring market trends and customer needs to identify new product concepts. However, there is a well-established debate in the literature about the relative merits of "market-pull" versus "technology-push" strategies for new product development. A review of the relevant research suggests that the best strategy to adopt is dependent on the relative novelty of the new product. For incremental adaptations or product line extensions, "marketpull" is likely to be the preferred route, as customers are familiar with the product type and will be able to express preferences easily. However, there are many "needs" that the customer may be unaware of or unable to articulate, and in these cases, the balance shifts to a "technology-push" strategy. Nevertheless, in most cases, customers do not buy a technology, they buy products for the benefits that they can receive from them; the "technology-push" must provide a solution for their needs. Thus, some customer or market analysis is also important for more novel technology. This stage is sometimes referred to as the "fuzzy front end" because it often lacks structure and order, but a number of tools are available to help systematically identify new product concepts, and we'll look at these a little later in the chapter.

Entrepreneurship in Action: Learning from users at IDEO

IDEO is one of the most successful design consultancies in the world. Based in Palo Alto, California, and London, UK, it helps large consumer and industrial companies worldwide to design and develop innovative new products and services. Behind its rather typical Californian wackiness lies a tried and tested process for successful design and development:

1. Understand the market, client, and technology.
2. Observe users and potential users in real-life situations.
3. Visualize new concepts and the customers who might use them, using prototyping, models, and simulations.
4. Evaluate and refine the prototypes in a series of quick iterations.
5. Implement the new concept for commercialization.

The first critical step is achieved through close observation of potential users in context. As Tom Kelly of IDEO argues, "We're not big fans of focus groups. We don't much care for traditional market research either. We go to the source. Not the 'experts' inside a (client) company, but the actual people who use the product or something similar to what we're hoping to create. . .We believe you have to go beyond putting yourself in your customers' shoes. Indeed, we believe it's not even enough to ask people what they think about a product or idea. . .customers may lack the vocabulary or the palate to explain what's wrong, and especially what's missing."

The next step is to develop prototypes to help evaluate and refine the ideas captured from users. "An iterative approach to problems is one of the foundations of our culture of prototyping. . .you can prototype just about anything – a new product or service, or a special promotion. What counts is moving the ball forward, achieving some part of your goal."

Source: Kelly, T. (2002). *The Art of Innovation: Lessons in Creativity from IDEO.* New York: HarperCollinsBusiness.

9.2 Project Selection

This stage includes the screening and selection of product concepts prior to subsequent progress through to the development phase. Two costs of failing to select the "best" project set are:

- The actual cost of resources spent on poor projects
- The opportunity costs of marginal projects which may have succeeded with additional resources

There are two levels of filtering. The first is the aggregate product plan, in which the new product development portfolio is determined. The aggregate product plan attempts to integrate the various potential projects to ensure the collective set of development projects will meet the goals and objectives of the firm and help to build the capabilities needed. The first step is to ensure resources are applied to the appropriate types and mix of projects. The second step is to develop a capacity plan to balance resource and demand. The final step is to analyze the effect of the proposed projects on capabilities to ensure this is built up to meet future demands.

The second lower level filters are concerned with specific product concepts. The two most common processes at this level are the development funnel and variations on the stage-gate approach. The development funnel is a means to identify, screen, review, and converge development projects as they move from idea to commercialization. It provides a framework in which to review alternatives based on a series of explicit criteria for decision-making. Similarly, the stage-gate system provides a formal framework for filtering projects based on explicit criteria. The main difference is that where the development funnel assumes resource constraints, the stage-gate system does not.

9.3 Product Development

This stage includes all the activities necessary to take the chosen concept and deliver a product for commercialization. It is at the working level, where the product is actually developed and produced, that the individual R&D staff, designers, engineers, and marketing staff must work together to solve specific issues and to make decisions on the details. Whenever a problem appears, a gap between the current design and the requirement, the development team must take action to close it. The way in which this is achieved determines the speed and effectiveness of the problem-solving process. In many cases this problem-solving routine involves iterative design–test–build cycles, which make use of a number of tools.

9.4 Product Commercialization and Review

In many cases, the process of new product development blurs into the process of commercialization. For example, customer co-development, test marketing, and use of alpha, beta, and gamma test sites yield data on customer requirements and any problems encountered in use, but also help to obtain customer buy-in and prime the market. It is not the purpose of this section to examine the relative efficacy of different marketing strategies, but rather to identify those factors which influence directly the process of new product development. We are primarily interested in what criteria firms use to evaluate the success of new products, and how these criteria might differ between low and high novelty projects. In the former case, we would expect more formal and narrow financial or market measures, but in the latter case, we find a broader range of criteria are used to reflect the potential for organizational learning and future new product options.

Entrepreneurship in Action: Samsung and the rise of the smartphone

Smartphones are a good example of continuous product development and innovation, often with life cycles measured in months rather than years. Apple's entry into the mobile phone market with its various iPhone generations has received the most attention, but Samsung is an equally interesting example of a product development-led success strategy.

There is no accepted definition of a smartphone or distinction between these and feature-rich phones. However, many accept that Samsung entered the global smartphone market in October 2006 with its BlackJack phone, which at that time was similar in name, appearance, and features to the RIM Blackberry (and resulted in a legal challenge from RIM, similar to the legal disputes between of Apple and Samsung in 2012). The BlackJack smartphone was launched first in the USA via the operator AT&T and ran Windows Mobile. In 2007, it won the Best Smart Phone award at CTIA in the U.S. Just over a year later, the imaginatively-named BlackJack II was launched in December 2008, followed by the third-generation Samsung Jack in May 2009, which became the highest-selling Windows Mobile phone series to date.

Another major milestone was in November 2007, when Samsung became a founding member of the Open Handset Alliance (OHA), which was created to develop, promote, and license Google's Android system for smartphones and tablets. Another member company, HTC, launched the first Android smartphone in August 2008, but Samsung followed with its own in May 2009, the I7500, which included the full suite of Google services, 3.2" AMOLED display, GPS, and a 5-megapixel camera. However, Samsung has been promiscuous in its choice of operating systems, and in addition to adopting Windows and Android systems, developed and uses its own. In May 2010, Samsung launched the Wave, its first smartphone based on its own Bada platform, designed for touchscreen interfaces and social networking. Six more Wave phones were launched the following year, with sales in excess of 10 million units.

The real success story is Samsung's Android-based Galaxy S sub-brand, introduced in March 2010 and followed by the Galaxy S II in 2011 and S II in 2012, as a direct competitor to Apple's iPhone. In the first quarter of 2012, Samsung sold more than 42 million smartphones worldwide, which represented 29% of global sales, compared to Apple with 35 million (24% market share). By 2012, the OHA had 84 member firms, and the Android system accounted for around 60% of global sales, compared to Apple's iOS with 26%. However, estimates of market share differ between analysts, depending on whether they measure share of new sales or existing user-base, and market shares also fluctuate significantly with new product launches. For example, in the month of the launch of the new iPhone, Apple's share of new sales in the USA leaped from 26% to 43%, and Android collapsed from 60% to 47% (NPD, 2012). This clearly demonstrates the impact of a new product launch.

Moreover, this product-led strategy is not easy to sustain. Nokia and Blackberry were past leaders in their respective markets for many years but have recently suffered significant declines in sales and profitability. Despite high levels of research and development and strong brands, these two past market-leaders have failed to maintain their lead through new product development. In a single year (2011–2012), Nokia's market share fell from 24% to just 8%, and RIM, makers of the Blackberry, from 14% to below 7%. In part this decline reflects their proprietary operating systems which have failed to add new features and functions, such as Cloud storage, and provide access to far fewer apps than Apple's iTunes store or Google's Play for Android. In 2016, Samsung also suffered a significant fall in sales following the battery problems with its flagship Galaxy Note 7 model, and had to withdraw it from sale.

9.5 Success Factors in New Products

There have been numerous studies that have investigated the factors affecting the success of new products. Most have adopted a "matched-pair" methodology, in which similar new products are examined but one is much less successful than the other. This allows us to discriminate between good and poor practice and helps to control for other background factors.[4]

These studies have differed in emphasis and sometimes contradicted each other, but despite differences in samples and methodologies, it is possible to identify some consensus of what the best criteria for success are (see **Figure 9.3**):

- *Product advantage* – product superiority in the eyes of the customer, real differential advantage, high performance-to-cost ratio, delivering unique benefits to users appears to be the primary factor separating winners and losers. Customer perception is the key.

- *Market knowledge* – the homework is vital: better predevelopment preparation, including initial screening, preliminary market assessment, preliminary technical appraisal, detailed market studies, and business/financial analysis. Customer and user needs assessment and understanding is critical. Competitive analysis is also an important part of the market analysis.

- *Clear product definition* –This includes defining target markets, clear concept definition and benefits to be delivered, clear positioning strategy, a list of product requirements, features and attributes, or use of a priority criteria list agreed before development begins.

- *Risk assessment* – market-based, technological, manufacturing, and design sources of risk to the development project must be assessed, and plans made to address them. Risk assessments must be built into the business and feasibility studies so they are appropriately addressed with respect to the market and the firms' capabilities.

- *Project organization* – the use of cross-functional, multidisciplinary teams carrying responsibility for the project from beginning to end.

- *Project resources* – sufficient financial and material resources and human skills must be available; the firm must possess the management and technological skills to design and develop the new product.

- *Proficiency of execution* – quality of technological and production activities and all pre-commercialisation business analyses and test marketing; detailed market studies underpin new product success.

- *Top management support* – from concept through to launch. Management must be able to create an atmosphere of trust, coordination and control; key individuals or champions often play a critical role during the innovation process.

These factors have all been found to contribute to new product success, and should, therefore, form the basis of any formal process for new product development. Note that successful new product and service development requires the management of a blend of product or service characteristics, such as product focus, superiority, and advantage, and organizational issues, such as project resources, execution, and leadership. Managing only one of these key contributions is unlikely to result in consistent success.

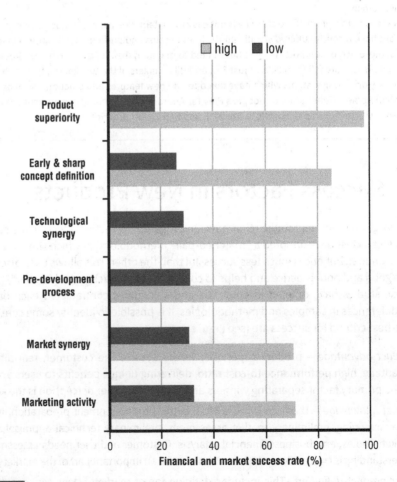

FIGURE 9.3 Factors Influencing new product success

Source: Based on data from van der Panne, G., van Beers, C., and Kleinknecht, A. (2003). Success and failure of innovation: a literature review. *International Journal of Innovation Management*, 7(3), pp. 309–338.

9.6 | Service Development

So far we've been looking at the case of physical products, but what about services? Employment trends in all the so-called advanced countries indicate a move away from manufacturing, construction, mining, and agriculture, toward a range of services, including retail, finance, transportation, communication, entertainment, professional, and public services. This trend is in part because manufacturing has become so efficient and highly automated, which generates proportionately less employment, and partly because many services are characterized by high levels of customer contact, are reproduced locally, and are, therefore, often labor-intensive. In the most advanced service economies, such as the USA and the UK, services create up to three-quarters of the wealth and 85% of employment, and yet we know relatively little about managing innovation in this sector. The critical role of services, in the broadest sense, has long been recognized, but service innovation is still not well understood.

Innovation in services in much more than the application of information technology (IT). In fact, the disappointing returns to IT investments in services has resulted in a widespread debate about its causes and potential solutions – the so-called "productivity paradox" in services. Frequently, service innovations, which make significant differences to the ways customers use and perceive the service delivered, will demand major investments in process innovation and technology by service providers, in skills and methods of working to change the business model, and major marketing changes. Estimates vary, but returns on investment on IT alone are around 15% (with a typical lag of two to three years, when productivity often falls). When combined with changes in organization and management, these returns increase to around 25%.[5]

In the service sector, the impact of innovation on growth is generally positive and consistent, with the possible exception of financial services. The pattern across retail and wholesale distribution, transport, communication services, and the broad range of business services is particularly strong. More recent research has identified the "hidden innovation" in the creative industries and media, for example, film and TV program development, which is not captured by traditional policy or measures, such as R&D or patents.

Most research and management prescriptions have been based on the experience of manufacturing and high-technology sectors. Most simply assume that such practices are equally applicable to managing innovation in services, but some researchers argue that services are fundamentally different. There is a clear need to distinguish what, if anything, of what we know about managing innovation in manufacturing is applicable to services, what must be adapted, and what is distinct and different.

We suggest that generic good practices do exist, which apply to both the development of manufactured and service offerings, but that these must be adapted to different contexts, specifically the scale and complexity, degree of customization of the offerings, and the uncertainty of the technological and market environments. It is critical to match the configuration of management and organization of development to the specific technology and market environment. For example, service development in retail financial services is very similar to product development for consumer goods.

The service sector includes a very wide range and a great diversity of different activities and businesses, ranging from individual consultants and shopkeepers, to huge multinational finance firms and critical non-profit public and third-sector organizations such as government, health, and education. Therefore, great care needs to be taken when making any generalization about the service sectors. We will introduce some ways of understanding and analyzing the sector later, but it is possible to identify some fundamental differences between manufacturing and service operations:

- *Tangibility*. Goods tend to be tangible, whereas services are mostly intangible, even though you can usually see or feel the results.

- *Perceptions* of performance and quality are more important in services, in particular, the difference between expectations and perceived performance. Customers are likely to regard a service as being good if it exceeds their expectations. Perceptions of service quality are affected by:

- tangible aspects – appearance of facilities, equipment, and staff
- responsiveness – prompt service and willingness to help
- competence – the ability to perform the service dependably
- assurance – knowledge and courtesy of staff and ability to convey trust and confidence
- empathy – provision of caring, individual attention

- *Simultaneity*. The lag between production and consumption of goods and services is different. Most goods are produced well in advance of consumption, to allow for distribution, storage, and sales. In contrast, many services are produced and almost immediately consumed. This creates problems of quality management and capacity planning. It is harder to identify or correct errors in services, and more difficult to match supply and demand.

- *Storage*. Services cannot usually be stored, for example, a seat on an airline, although some, such as utilities, have some potential for storage. The inability to hold stocks of services can create problems matching supply and demand – capacity management. These can be dealt with in a number of ways. Pricing can be used to help smooth fluctuations in demand, for example, by providing discounts at off-peak times. Where possible, additional capacity can be provided at peak times by employing part-time workers or outsourcing. In the worst cases, customers can simply be forced to wait for the services, by queuing.

- *Customer contact*. Most customers have low or no contact with the operations which produce goods. Many services demand high levels of contact between the operations and ultimate customer, although the level and timing of such contact varies. For example, medical treatment may require constant or frequent contact, but financial services only sporadic contact.

- *Location*. Because of the contact with customers and near simultaneous production and consumption of services, the location of service operations is often more important than for operations which produce goods. For example, restaurants, retail operations, and entertainment services all favor proximity to customers. Conversely, manufactured goods are often produced and consumed in very different locations. For these reasons, the markets for manufactured goods also tend to be more competitive and global, whereas many personal and business services are local and less competitive. For example, only around 10% of services in the advanced economies are traded internationally.

Question:

Which of the differences between the development of new products and new services is the most significant for management?

Answer: Whilst the applications may differ significantly, the relevance of many of the core principles is the same in product and service development. However, a fundamental difference is the balance between intangible and tangible attributes.

These service characteristics should be taken into account when designing and managing the organization and processes for new service development, as some of the findings from research on new product development will have to be adapted or may not apply at all. Also, because of the diversity of service operations, we need also to tailor the organization and management to different types of service context (**Table 9.1**).

In terms of performance, innovation, and quality appear to be improved by cross-functional teams and sharing information, raised by involvement with customers and suppliers, and by encouraging collaboration in teams.[6] Service delivery is improved by customer focus and project management and by knowledge sharing and collaboration in teams. Time to market is reduced by knowledge sharing and collaboration, customer focus, and project organization, but cross-functional teams can prolong the process. Costs are reduced by setting standards for projects and products and by involvement of customers and suppliers, but can be increased by using cross-functional teams.

TABLE 9.1   Characteristics of Service "High Innovators"

Business Descriptor	Low Innovators	High Innovators
Innovation outcomes		
% sales from services introduced < 3 years ago	<1%	17%
% new services versus competitors	>0%	5%
Customer base		
Focus on key customers	Average	High
Relative customer base	Similar to competitors	More focused than competitors
Value chain		
Focus on key suppliers	Average	High/strategic
Value-added/sales %	72%	60%
Operating cost added/sales	36%	25%
Vertical integration versus competitors	Same or more	Same or less
Innovation input		
'What' R&D	0.1% sales	0.7% sales
'How' R&D	0.1% sales	0.5% sales
Fixed assets/sales	growing at 10% p.a.	growing at >20% p.a.
Overheads/sales %	8%	11%
Innovation context		
Recent technology change	20%	40%
Time to market	>1 year	<1 year
Competition		
Competitor entry	10%	40%
Imports/exports versus market	2%	12%
Quality of offer		
Relative quality versus competitors	Declining	Improving
Value for money	Just below competitors	Better than competitors
Output		
Real sales	9%	15%

Source: Clayton, T. in Tidd, J. and Hull, F.M. (eds). (2003). *Service Innovation: Organizational Responses to Technological Opportunities and Market Imperatives*. Imperial College Press/World Scientific Publishing Co. Reproduced with permission.

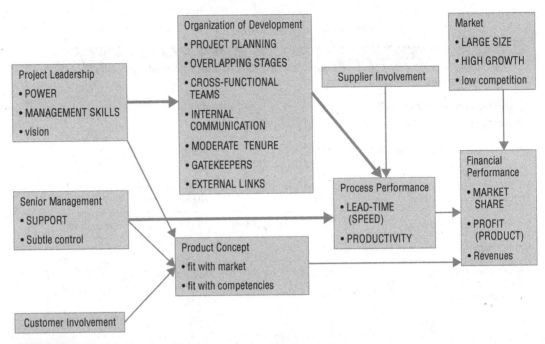

FIGURE 9.4 A framework for assessing new service development

Source: Brown, S.L> and Eisenhardt, K.M. (1995) Product development: Past research, present findings and future directions, Academy of Management Review, 20, 343–378.

Although individual practices can make a significant contribution to performance (**Figure 9.4**), it is clear that it is the coherent combination of practices and their interaction that creates superior performance in specific contexts. These research findings can be used to help assess the effectiveness of existing strategies, processes, organization, tools, technology, and systems (SPOTS), and to identify where and how to improve.

9.7 | Tools to Support New Product Development

(a) Concept Generation

Most studies have highlighted the importance of understanding users' needs. Designing a product to satisfy a perceived need has been shown to be an important discriminator of commercial success. Common approaches include:

- *Surveys and focus groups* – where a similar product exists, surveys of customers' preferences can be a reliable guide to development. Focus groups allow developers to explore the likely response to more novel products where a clear target segment exists.
- *Latent needs analysis* – are designed to uncover the unarticulated requirements of customers by means of their responses to symbols, concepts, and forms.
- *Lead users* – are representative of the needs of the market but some time ahead of the majority, and so represent future needs. Lead users are one of the most important sources of market knowledge for product improvements.
- *Customer-developers* – in some cases, new products are partly or completely developed by customers. In such cases, the issue is how to identify and acquire such products.
- *Competitive analysis* – of competing products, by reverse engineering or benchmarking features of competing products.
- *Industry experts or consultants* – who have a wide range of experience of different users' needs. The danger is that they may have become too immersed in the users world to have the breadth of vision required to assess and evaluate the potential of the innovation. The

use of "proxy experts" can help overcome the problem. They suggest selecting a specific group of respondents who have knowledge of the product category or usage context.

- *Extrapolating trends* – in technology, markets, and society to guess the short to medium term future needs.
- *Building scenarios* – alternative visions of the future, based on varying assumptions to create robust product strategies. Most relevant to long-term projects and product portfolio development.
- *Market experimentation* – testing market response with real products, but able to adapt or withdraw rapidly. Only practical where development costs are low, lead times short, and customers tolerant of product under performance or failure. Sometimes referred to as "expeditionary marketing," or more modestly "test marketing."

(b) Project Selection

Different combinations of criteria are used to screen and assess projects prior to development. The most common are based on discounted cash flows, such as Net Present Value/Internal Rate of Return, followed by cost-benefit analysis, and simple calculations of the payback period. In addition to these financial criteria, most organizations also use a range of additional measures:

- *Ranking* – a means of ordering a list of candidate projects in relative value or worthiness of support, broken down into several factors, so both objective and judgmental data can be assessed. These techniques are likely to be of most use in the early stages of the process since they are fairly "rough-cut" methods.
- *Profiles* – projects are given scores on each of several characteristics and are rejected if they fail to meet some pre-determined threshold. The projects which dominate on all or most of the factor scores are selected. These methods can be used at all stages of the development process.
- *Simulated outcomes* – alternative outcomes to which probabilities can be attached or alternate paths, depending on chance outcomes and when the projects have different pay-offs for different outcomes. The range of possible outcomes and the likelihood of a specific outcome is found. It is used especially in the analysis of sets of projects which are interdependent (the aggregate project plan).
- *Strategic clusters* – projects not selected solely for maximization of some financial measure but for the support they give to the strategic position. Groups are clustered according to their support for specific objectives, and then these groups are rated according to strategic importance and funded accordingly (again, this is important at the aggregate project plan level).
- *Interactive* – an iterative process between the R&D Director and project managers, where project proposals are improved at each stage to more closely align with the objectives. The aim of this is to develop projects that more nearly fit the strategic and tactical objectives of the firm. These methods are used mainly at the aggregate project plan level or at the early stages of specific projects.

Question:

Why do you think it is good practice to have clear criteria for selecting potential new products, rather than to rely exclusively on the judgement of senior managers?

Answer: Relying only on the judgement of managers is dangerous as it tends to politicize the decision-making process. Also, we all have our own biases as a result of personal, technical, and commercial knowledge and experience. For these reasons, clear criteria are important. There are two costs of failing to select the most appropriate projects:

1. The actual cost of resources spent on poor projects which wrongly pass the screening
2. The opportunity costs of marginal projects which are wrongly rejected by the screening process

The former tend to be the most visible and contribute to the high rate of failure in most organizations. The latter are difficult to assess but are no less important. For these reasons, the criteria used for screening proposals are critical.

(c) Product/Service Development

There are a number of tools, or methodologies, which have been developed to help solve the problems, and most require the integration of different functions and disciplines (**Table 9.2**). The most significant tools and methods used are:

- *Design for X* – thinking ahead about the downstream implications of the project in terms of various aspects and then bringing relevant knowledge from those areas to the early stage design. A good example is design for manufacture (DFM) which embraces "the full range of policies, techniques, practices, and attitudes that cause a product to be designed for the optimum manufacturing cost, the optimum achievement of manufactured quality, and the optimum achievement of life-cycle support (serviceability, reliability, and maintainability)." Studies from the car industry indicate that up to 80% of the final production costs are determined at the design stage. Other variations include Design for Assembly (DFA), Design for Producibility (DFP), and Whole Life Design, which explores recyclability and re-use. Similar principles can be used in the development of services.

- *Rapid Prototyping* – is the core element of the design-build-test cycle, and can increase the rate and amount of learning that occurs in each cycle. The first design is unlikely to be complete, and so designers go through several iterations, learning more about the problem and alternative solutions each time. The number of iterations will depend on the time and cost constraints of the project. Approaches like this lie at the heart of the "lean start-up" and "agile innovation" models for development and rely heavily on the interaction between producers and users in a process of shared exploration.

- *Digital tools* – a wide range of computer and internet-enabled tools are now available to support product and service design. These include simulation software, computer-aided design and development (CAD), and a wide range of computer-aided manufacturing tools, including 3-D printing of various kinds. Potential benefits include reduction in development lead times, economies in design, ability to design products too complex to do manually, and the combination of CAD with production automation Computer-aided Manufacture (CAM) to achieve the benefits of integration.

- *Quality Function Deployment (QFD)* – is a set of planning and communications routines, which are used to identify critical customer attributes and create a specific link between these and design parameters. It focuses and co-ordinates the skills within the organization to design, manufacture, and then market products to customers. The aim is to answer three

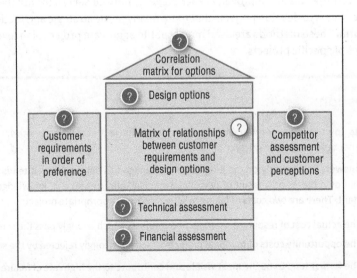

FIGURE 9.5 Quality function deployment

primary questions: What are the critical attributes for customers? What design parameters drive these attributes? What should the design parameter targets be for the new design (See **Figure 9.5**)?

DEEPER DIVE: Quality function deployment

Read the Deeper Dive: Quality function deployment document in the ebook or from the book companion site.

CASE STUDY: Joseph's

Read the Case Study_Joseph's document in the ebook or from the book companion site.

TABLE 9.2   Use and Usefulness of Techniques for Product and Service Development

	High Novelty		Low Novelty	
	Usage (%)	Usefulness	Usage (%)	Usefulness
Segmentation*	89	3.42	42	4.50
Market Experimentation	63	4.00	53	3.70
Industry Experts	63	3.83	37	3.71
Surveys/Focus groups*	52	4.50	37	4.00
User-practice Observation	47	3.67	42	3.50
Partnering Customers*	37	4.43	58	3.67
Lead Users*	32	4.33	37	3.57
Probability of technical success	100	4.37	100	4.32
Probability of commercial success	100	4.68	95	4.50
Market share*	100	3.63	84	4.00
Core competencies*	95	3.61	79	3.00
Degree of internal commitment	89	3.82	79	3.67
Market size	89	3.76	84	3.94
Competition	89	3.76	84	3.81
Gap Analysis	79	2.73	84	2.81
Strategic Clusters*	42	3.63	32	2.67
Prototyping*	79	4.33	63	4.08
Market Experimentation	68	4.31	63	4.08
QFD	47	3.33	37	3.43
Cross-functional Teams*	63	4.47	37	3.74
Project Manager (Heavyweight)*	52	3.84	32	3.05

Usefulness Scale: 1-5, 5=critical, based on manager assessments of 50 development projects in 25 firms.
*denotes difference in usefulness rating is statistically significant at 5% level
Source: Adapted from Tidd, J. and Bodley, K. (2002). The influence of project novelty on the new product development process. *R&D Management*, 32(2), pp. 127–138.

Entrepreneurship in Action: Pokémon Go

Pokémon Go is a location-based augmented reality mobile phone game developed by a start-up company called Niantic and commercialized by Nintendo, which owns much of the intellectual property for the characters. It was launched in July 2016 for iOS and Android devices, and the app has been downloaded more than 100 million times and generated over $10 million daily in in-app purchases. As a result, in 2016 Nintendo's share valuation has risen by $12 billion and Niantic's to $3.65 billion. The key to its success has been combining mapping and gaming technologies to create augmented reality and to promote social interaction in the real world, rather than simply online.

Niantic was founded by John Hanke in 2010 as an internal venture at Google, and was spun-off from Google in 2015. Hanke earned a degree in Liberal Arts at Austin Texas in 1989, as a Plan II student he completed an interdisciplinary arts and science honours major, and later an MBA from the Haas School of Business at the University of California, Berkeley, in 1996. He gained extensive experience with online games and mapping, and in 2001, founded the start-up Keyhole, which created the Earth Viewer program. Keyhole was acquired by Google in 2004 for $35 million, and Earth Viewer was renamed Google Earth.

9.8 Diffusion: Promoting the Adoption of Innovations

A better understanding of why and how innovations are (or are not) adopted can help us to develop and implement more realistic business plans for new ventures.

Diffusion is the means by which innovations are translated into social and economic benefits. We know that the impact of the *use* of innovations is around four times that of their generation,[7] and the widespread adoption of process innovations has the most significant benefit:[8] technological innovations are the source of productivity and quality improvements; organizational innovations are the basis of many social, health, and educational gains; and commercial innovations create new service and products. However, the benefits of innovations can take 10–15 years to be fully effected,[9] and in practice, most innovations fail to be adopted widely, so have limited social or economic impact.[10]

Conventional marketing approaches are adequate for promoting many products and services but are not sufficient for the majority of innovations. Marketing texts often refer to "early adopters" and "majority adopters," and even go so far as to apply numerical estimates of these, but these simple categories are based on the very early studies of the state-sponsored diffusion of hybrid-seed varieties in farming communities and are far from universally applicable. To better plan for innovations, we need a deeper understanding of what factors promote and constrain adoption, and how these influence the rate and level of diffusion within different markets and populations.

Rogers[11] definition of diffusion is used widely: "the process by which an innovation is communicated through certain channels over time among members of a social system. It is a special type of communication, in that the messages are concerned with new ideas" (2003, p. 5). The Economists' view of the innovation process begins with the assumption that it is simply the cumulative aggregation of individual, rational calculations. These individual decisions are influenced by an assessment of the costs and benefits, under conditions of limited information and environment uncertainty. However, this perspective ignores the effects of social feedback, learning, and externalities. The initial benefits of adoption may be small, but with improvement, re-invention, and growing externalities, the benefits can increase over time, and the costs decrease.

In contrast, Rogers conceptualizes diffusion as a social process, in which actors create and share information through communication. Therefore, a focus on the relative advantage of an innovation is insufficient, as different social systems will have different values and beliefs. This will influence the costs, benefits, and compatibility of an innovation, and different social structures will determine the most appropriate channels of communication and the type and influence of opinion leaders and change agents. Rogers distinguishes between three types of decision-making relevant to adoption of an innovation:

1. *Individual* – in which the individual is the main decision-maker, independent of peers. Decisions may still be influenced by social norms and interpersonal relationships, but the individual makes the ultimate choice, for example, the purchase of a consumer durable, such as a mobile phone.

2. *Collective* – where choices are made jointly with others in the social system, and there is significant peer pressure or formal requirement to conform, for example, the sorting and recycling of domestic waste.

3. *Authoritative* – where decisions to adopt are taken by a few individuals within a social system, due to their power, status, or expertise, for example, adoption of ERP systems by businesses or MRI systems by hospitals.

There is much evidence that opinion leaders are critical to diffusion, especially for changes in behavior or attitudes. Therefore, they tend to be a central feature of social and health change programs, such as sex education. However, they are also evident in more routine examples of product diffusion, ranging from athletic shoes to hybrid cars. Opinion leaders carry information across boundaries between groups, much like a knowledge bridge. They operate at the edge of groups, rather than from the top – not leaders within a group but brokers between groups. In the language of networks, they have many weak ties rather than a few strong ties. They tend to be accessible, have extended personal networks, and have high levels of social participation. They are recognized by peers as being both competent and trustworthy. They have access and exposure to mass media.

The time dimension is important, and many studies are particularly interested to understand and influence the rate of adoption. It can take years for a new drug to be prescribed after license, a decade for a new crop variety, or fifty years for educational or social changes. This leads to a focus on the communication channels and the decision-making criteria and process. Generally, mass-marketing media channels are more effective for generating awareness and disseminating information and knowledge, whereas interpersonal channels such as social media are more important in the decision-making and action stages.

Research on diffusion attempts to identify what influences the rate and direction of adoption of an innovation. The diffusion of an innovation is typically described by an S-shaped (logistic) curve (**Figure 9.6**).

Hundreds of marketing studies have attempted to fit the adoption of specific products to the S-curve, ranging from television sets to new drugs. In most cases, mathematical techniques can provide a relatively good fit with historical data, but research has so far failed to identify robust generic models of adoption. In practice, the precise pattern of adoption of an innovation will depend on the interaction of demand-side and supply-side factors:

- Demand-side factors – direct contact with or imitation of prior adopters, adopters with different perceptions of benefits and risk
- Supply-side factors – relative advantage of an innovation, availability of information, barriers to adoption, feedback between developers and users

The basic epidemic S-curve model is the earliest and is still the most commonly used. It assumes a homogeneous population of potential adopters, and that innovations spread by information transmitted by personal contact, observation, and the geographical proximity of existing and potential adopters. This model suggests that the emphasis should be on communication, and the provision of clear technical and economic information. However, the epidemic model has been criticized because it assumes that all potential adopters are similar and have the same needs, which is unrealistic.

The most influential marketing model of diffusion was developed by Frank Bass in 1969, and has been applied widely to the adoption of consumer durables.[12] The Bass model assumes that potential adopters are influenced by two processes: individual independent adopters, influenced mostly by personal, private assessment and trials; and later adopters,

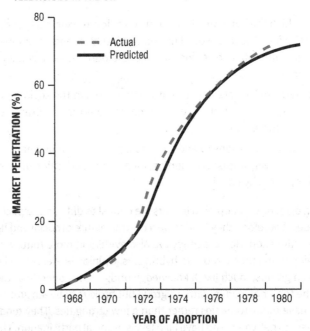

**DIFFUSION OF COLOUR
TELEVISIONS IN THE UK**

FIGURE 9.6 Typical diffusion curve

Source: Meade, N. and Islam, T. (2006). Modeling and forecasting the diffusion of innovation – a 25 year review. *International Journal of Forecasting*, 22(3), pp. 519–545. Reprinted with permission from Elsevier.

more influenced by interpersonal communication, social media, and mass marketing channels. Combining these two type of adopters produces a skewed S-curve because of the early adoption by innovators and suggests that different marketing processes are needed for the innovators and subsequent imitators. The Bass model is highly influential in economics and marketing research, and the distinction between the two types of potential adopters is critical in understanding the different mechanisms involved in the two user segments.

Bandwagons may occur where an innovation is adopted because of pressure caused by the sheer number of those who have already adopted an innovation, rather than by individual assessments of the benefits of an innovation. In general, as soon as the number of adopters has reached a certain threshold level, the greater the level of ambiguity of the innovations benefits and the greater the subsequent number of adopters. This process allows technically inefficient innovations to be widely adopted, or technically efficient innovations to be rejected. Examples include the QWERTY keyboard, originally designed to prevent professional typists from typing too fast and jamming typewriters; and the DOS operating system for personal computers, designed by and for computer enthusiasts.

Bandwagons occur due to a combination of competitive and institutional pressures.[13] Where competitors adopt an innovation, a firm may adopt because of the threat of lost competitiveness rather than as a result of any rational evaluation of benefits. For example, many firms adopted business process reengineering (BPR) in the 1980s in response to increased competition, but most failed to achieve significant benefits. The main institutional pressure is the threat of lost legitimacy, for example, being considered by peers or customers as being less progressive or competent.

The critical difference between bandwagons and other types of diffusion is that they require only limited information to flow from early to later adopters. Indeed, the more ambiguous the benefits of an innovation, the more significant bandwagons are on rates of adoption. In short, with bandwagons, a better product does not necessarily result in higher level of adoption.

> ## Question:
>
> Why is the idea of "bandwagons" important to consider when commercializing new products? What type of forecasting technique might best anticipate such bandwagons?
>
> **Answer:** A "bandwagon" is important because it suggests that once a threshold number of products have been purchased, the process of adoption changes – earlier adopters tend to evaluate the cost and benefits, but later adopters are influenced more by peer pressure. Examples include social media, fashion clothing, luxury cars, holiday destinations, and MBAs. Scenario planning and the Delphi method are probably the best forecasting methods to help anticipate bandwagons (see Chapter 5).

Factors Influencing Adoption

Characteristics of an innovation found to influence adoption include relative advantage, compatibility, complexity, observability, and trialability. Individual characteristics include age, education, social status, and attitude to risk. Environmental and institutional characteristics include economic factors, such as the market environment, and sociological factors, such as communications networks. However, whilst there is a general agreement regarding the relevant variables, there is very little consensus on the relative importance of the different variables, and in some cases, disagreements over the direction of relationships.

In predicting the rate of adoption of an innovation, five factors explain 49-87% of the variance:

- Relative advantage
- Compatibility
- Complexity
- Trialability
- Observability

However, the contextual or environmental factors are also important, as demonstrated by the fact that diffusion rates of different innovations are highly variable, and the rates for the same innovation in different contexts also vary significantly.

Relative Advantage

Relative advantage is the degree to which an innovation is perceived as better than competing products or the product it supersedes. Relative advantage is typically measured in narrow economic terms, for example, cost or financial payback, but non-economic factors, such as convenience, satisfaction, and social prestige, may be equally important. In theory, the greater the perceived advantage, the faster the rate of adoption.

It is useful to distinguish between the primary and secondary attributes of an innovation. Primary attributes, such as size and cost, are invariant and inherent to a specific innovation irrespective to the adopter. Secondary attributes, such as relative advantage and compatibility, may vary from adopter to adopter, being contingent upon the perceptions and context of adopters. In many cases, a so-called "attribute gap" will exist. An attribute gap is the discrepancy between a potential user's perception of an attribute or characteristic of an item of knowledge and how the potential user would prefer to perceive that attribute. The greater the sum of all attribute gaps, the less likely a user is to adopt the knowledge. This suggests that preliminary testing of an innovation is desirable in order to determine whether significant attribute gaps exist. The idea of pre-testing information for the purposes of enhancing its value and acceptance is not widely practiced.

Compatibility

Compatibility is the degree to which an innovation is perceived to be consistent with the existing values, experience, and needs of potential adopters. There are two distinct aspects of compatibility: existing skills and practices; and values and norms. The extent to which the innovation fits the existing skills, equipment, procedures, and performance criteria of the potential adopter is important and relatively easy to assess.

However, compatibility with existing practices may be less important than the fit with existing values and norms.[14] Significant misalignments between an innovation and an adopting organization will require changes in the innovation or organization, or both. In the most successful cases of implementation, mutual adaptation of the innovation and organization occurs. However, few studies distinguish between compatibility with value and norms, and compatibility with existing practices. The extent to which the innovation fits the existing skills, equipment, procedures, and performance criteria of the potential adopter is critical. Few innovations initially fit the user environment into which they are introduced. Significant misalignments between the innovation and the adopting organization will require changes in the innovation or organization, or in the most successful cases of implementation, mutual adaptation of both. Initial compatibility with existing practices may be less important, as it may provide limited opportunity for mutual adaptation to occur.

In addition, so-called "network externalities" can affect the adoption process. For example, the cost of adoption and use, as distinct from the cost of purchase, may be influenced by the availability of information about the technology from other users; of trained skilled users; of technical assistance and maintenance; and of complementary innovations, both technical and organizational.

Complexity

Complexity is the degree to which an innovation is perceived as being difficult to understand or use. In general, innovations which are simpler for potential users to understand will be adopted more rapidly than those which require the adopter to develop new skills and knowledge.

However, complexity can also influence the direction of diffusion, not only the rate of adoption. Evolutionary models of diffusion focus on the effect of "network externalities," that is the interaction of consumption, pecuniary and technical factors which shape the diffusion process. For example, within a region the cost of adoption and use, as distinct from the cost of purchase, may be influenced by the availability of information about the technology from other users; of trained skilled users; of technical assistance and maintenance; and of complementary innovations, both technical and organizational.

Trialability

Trialability is the degree to which an innovation can be experimented with on a limited basis. An innovation that is trialable represents less uncertainty to potential adopters and allows learning by doing. Innovations which can be trialed will generally be adopted more quickly than those which cannot. The exception is where the undesirable consequences of an innovation appear to outweigh the desirable characteristics. In general, adopters wish to benefit from the functional effects of an innovation but avoid any dysfunctional effects. However, where it is difficult or impossible to separate the desirable from the undesirable consequences, trialability may reduce the rate of adoption.

Developers of an innovation may have two different motives for involving potential users in the development process. First, to acquire knowledge from the users needed in the development process, to ensure usability and to add value. Second, to attain user "buy-in," that is user acceptance of the innovation and commitment to its use. The second motive is independent of the first because increasing user acceptance does not necessarily improve the quality of the innovation. Rather, involvement may increase users tolerance of any inadequacies. In the case of point-to-point transfer, typically both motives are present.

However, in the case of diffusion, it is not possible to involve all potential users, and therefore, the primary motive is to improve usability rather than attain user buy-in. But even the representation of user needs must be indirect, using surrogates, such as specially selected users groups. These groups can be problematic for a number of reasons. First, because they may possess atypically high levels of technical knowledge and, therefore, are not representative. Second, where the group must represent diverse user needs, such as both experienced and novice users, the group may not work well together. Finally, when user representatives work closely with developers over a long period of time, they may cease to represent users and instead absorb the developer's viewpoint. Thus, there is no simple relationship between user involvement and user satisfaction. Typically, very low levels of user involvement are associated with user dissatisfaction, but extensive user involvement does not necessarily result in user satisfaction.

Observability

Observability is the degree to which the results of an innovation are visible to others. The easier it is for others to see the benefits of an innovation, the more likely it will be adopted. The simple epidemic model of diffusion assumes that innovations spread as potential adopters come into contact with existing users of an innovation.

Peers who have already adopted an innovation will have what communication researchers call "safety credibility," because potential adopters seeking their advice will believe they know what it is really like to implement and utilize the innovation. Therefore, early adopters are well positioned to disseminate "vicarious learning" to their colleagues. Vicarious learning is simply learning from the experience of others, rather than direct personal experimental learning. However, the process of vicarious learning is neither inevitable nor efficient because, by definition, it is a decentralized activity.

Demonstrations of innovations are highly effective in promoting adoption. Experimental, private demonstrations or pilots can be used to assess attributes of an innovation and the relative advantage for different target groups and to test compatibility. Exemplary, public demonstrations can improve observability, reduce perceived complexity, and promote private trials. However, note the different purpose and nature of experimental and exemplary demonstrations. Resources, urgency, and uncertainty should determine the appropriate type of demonstration. Public demonstrations for experimental purposes are ill-advised and are likely to stall diffusion.

On the demand side, the uncertainty of potential adopters, and communication with and between them also needs to be managed. Whilst early adopters may emphasize technical performance and novelty above other factors, the mainstream mass market is more likely to be concerned with factors such as price, quality, convenience, and support. This transition from the niche market and needs of early adopters, through to the requirements of more mass markets has been referred to as crossing the chasm by Moore.[15] Moore studied the successes and many more failures of Silicon Valley and other high-technology products, and argued that the critical success factors for early adopters and mass markets were fundamentally different and that most innovations failed to make this transition. Therefore, the successful launch and diffusion of a systemic or network innovation demands attention to traditional marketing issues such as the timing and positioning of the product or service, but also significant effort to demand-side factors, such as communication and interactions between potential adopters.

Innovation in Action: Why innovations fail to be adopted

This research examined the factors which influence the adoption and diffusion of innovations drawing upon cases studies of successful and less successful consumer electronics products, such as the Sony PlayStation and MiniDisc, Apple iPod and Newton, TomTom GO, TiVo, and RIM Blackberry.

The study finds that a critical factor influencing successful diffusion is the careful management of acceptance by the early adopters, which in turn influences the adoption by the main market. Strategic issues such as positioning, timing, and management of the adoption network are identified as being important. The adoption network is defined as a configuration of users, peers, competitors, complementary products and services, and infrastructure. However, the positioning, timing, and adoption networks are different for the early and main market adopters, and failure to recognize these differences is a common cause of the failure of innovations to diffuse widely. Also, innovation contingencies such as the degree of radicalness and discontinuity affect how these factors interact and how these need to be managed to promote acceptance. The relevant assessment of the radicalness and discontinuity of an innovation is not based on the technological aspects, but rather the effects on user behavior and consumption.

To promote use by early adopters, the research recommends that four enabling factors need to be managed: legitimize the innovation through reference customers and visible performance advantage; trigger word of mouth within specialist communities of practice; stimulate imitation to increase the user base and peer pressure; and collaborate with opinion leaders. Significantly, the study argues that the subsequent successful diffusion of an innovation into the mainstream market has very little to do with the merits of the product itself, and much more to do with the positive acceptance of early adopters and repositioning and targeting for the main market by influencing the relevant adoption network.

Source: Frattini, F. in Tidd, J. (ed.) (2010). Achieving adoption network and early adopters acceptance for technological innovations. *Gaining Momentum: Managing the Diffusion of Innovations*. Imperial College Press.

Chapter Summary

There is a vast amount of management research on new product and service development, and we are now pretty certain what works and what does not. There are no guarantees that following the suggestions in this chapter will produce a blockbuster product, service, or business, but if these elements are not managed well, your chances of success will be much lower. This is not supposed to discourage experimentation and calculated risk-taking, but rather to provide a foundation for evidence-based practice. Research suggests that a range of factors affect the success of a potential new product or service:

- Some factors are product-specific, e.g. product advantage, clear target market, and attention to pre-development activities.

- Other factors are more about the organizational context and process, e.g. senior management support, formal process, and use of external knowledge.

- A formal process for new product and service development should consist of distinct stages, such as concept development,

business case, product development, pilot, and commercialization, separated by distinct decision points or gates, which have clear criteria, such as product fit, product advantages, and so on.

- Different stages of the process demand different criteria and different tools and methods. Useful tools and methods at the concept stage include segmentation, experimentation, focus groups, and customer-partnering; and at the development stage, useful tools include prototyping, design for production, and QFD.

- Services and products are different in a number of ways, especially intangibility and perceived benefits, and will demand the adaptation of the standard models and prescriptions for new product development.

- The relative advantage, compatibility, complexity, trialability, and observability of an innovation all affect the rate of diffusion.

Key Terms

Bandwagons occur during the diffusion of an innovation when an innovation is adopted because of the cumulative volume of previous adoptions, through peer pressure and expectations, rather than by any individual rational assessment of costs and benefits.

Bass model this model of diffusion assumes that potential adopters are influenced by two processes: by individual independent decisions and by interpersonal communications and channels.

Diffusion is the process by which a focal innovation is adopted by a focal social system or market segment and includes the rate and direction of change.

Development funnel an alternative to the stage-gate model, which takes into account the reduction in uncertainty as the process progresses and the influence of real resource constraints.

Quality Function Deployment (QFD) is a set of planning and communications routines, which are used to identify critical customer attributes and create a specific link between these and design parameters. It aims to answer three primary questions: What are the critical attributes for customers? What design parameters drive these attributes? What should the design parameter targets be for the new design?

Stage-gate process a structured, staging process. As projects move through the development process, there are a number of discrete stages, each with different decision criteria or "gates" which they must pass.

References

1. Cooper, R.G. (2000). Doing it right: winning with new products. *Ivey Business Journal*, 64(6), pp. 1–7.
2. Ibid., and Cooper, R. (2001). *Winning at New Products: Accelerating the Process from Idea to Launch*. Perseus Books.
3. Tidd, J. and Bodley, K. (2002). The affect of project novelty on the new product development process. *R&D Management*, 32(2), pp. 127–138.
4. van der Panne, G., van Beers, C., and Kleinknecht, A. (2003). Success and failure of innovation: a literature review. *International Journal of Innovation Management*, 7(3), pp. 309–338.
5. Crespi, G., Criscuolo, C., and Haskel, J. (2006). Information technology, organisational change and productivity growth: evidence from UK firms. *The Future of Science, Technology and Innovation Policy: Linking Research and Practice*. Brighton, UK: SPRU 40th Anniversary Conference.
6. Tidd, J. and Hull, F.M. (2006). Managing service innovation: the need for selectivity rather than "best-practice". *New Technology, Work and Employment*, 21(2), pp. 139–161; Tidd, J. and Hull, F.M. (2003). *Service Innovation: Organizational Responses to Technological Opportunities and Market Imperatives*. London: Imperial College Press.
7. Geroski, P.A. (2000). Models of technology diffusion. *Research Policy*, 29, pp. 603–625; Geroski, P. (1991). Innovation and the sectoral sources of UK productivity growth. *Economic Journal*, 101, pp. 1438–1451; Geroski, P. (1994). *Market Structure, Corporate Performance and Innovative Activity*. Oxford: Oxford University Press.
8. Griliches, Z. and Pakes, A. (1984). *Patents R&D and Productivity*. Chicago: University of Chicago Press; Stoneman, P. (1983). *The Economic Analysis of Technological Change*, Oxford: Oxford University Press.
9. Jaffe, A.B. (1986). Technological opportunity and spillovers of R&D: evidence from firms' patents, profits and market values. *American Economic Review*, 76, pp. 948–999.
10. Ortt, J.R. (2009). Understanding the pre-diffusion phases, in Tidd, J. (ed.) *Gaining Momentum: Managing the Diffusion of Innovations*. London: Imperial College Press. pp. 47–80.
11. Rogers, E.M. (2003). *Diffusion of Innovations*. New York: Free Press.
12. Bass, F.M. (1980). The relationship between diffusion rates, experience curves, and demand elasticities for consumer durable technological innovations. *Journal of Business*, 53, pp. 51–67; Bass, F.M. and Bultez, A.V. (1982). A note on optimal strategic pricing of technological innovations. *Marketing Science*, 1, pp. 371–378; Bass, F.M., Krishnan, T., and Jain, D. (1994). Why the Bass model fits without decision variables. *Marketing Science*, 13(3), pp. 203–223; Bass, F.M. (1969). A new product growth model for consumer durables. *Management Science*, 15, pp. 215–227.
13. Abrahamson, E. and Plosenkopf, L. (1993). Institutional and competitive bandwagons: using mathematical modelling as a tool to explore innovation diffusion. *Academy of Management Journal*, 18(3), pp. 487–517; Lee, Y. and O'Connor, G.C. (2003). New product launch strategy for network effects products. *Journal of the Academy of Marketing Science*, 31(3), pp. 241–255.
14. Chakravorti, B. (2003). *The Slow Pace of Fast Change: Bringing Innovation to Market in a Connected World*. Boston: Harvard Business School Press.; Chakravorti, B. (2004). The new rules for bringing innovations to market. *Harvard Business Review*, 82(3), pp. 58–67; Leonard-Barton, D. and Sinha, D.K. (1993). Developer-user interaction and user satisfaction in internal technology transfer. *Academy of Management Journal*, 36(5), pp. 1125–1139.
15. Moore, G. (1991). *Crossing the Chasm: marketing and selling technology products to mainstream customers*. New York: HarperBusiness; Moore, G. (1998). *Inside the Tornado: Marketing Strategies from Silicon Valley's Cutting Edge*. Chichester: Capstone, Wiley.

CHAPTER 10

Creating a New Venture

LEARNING OBJECTIVES

When you have completed this chapter you will be able to:

1. Distinguish between different entrepreneurial motives and goals for creating a new venture.

2. Identify the contextual factors which influence the creation of a new venture.

3. Choose an appropriate structure for a new venture.

4. Recognize and manage the key challenges at each stage of new venture development.

5. Identify and exploit a range of intellectual property.

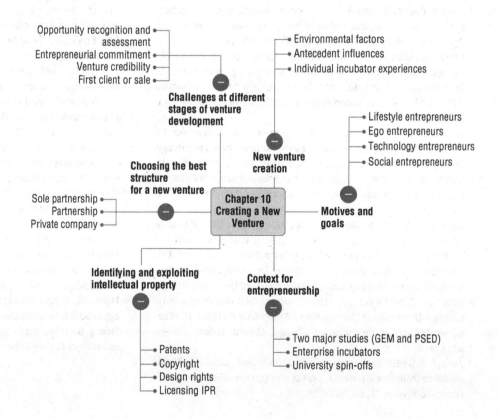

10.0 | New Venture Creation

Creating a new venture is the result of the interaction of individual skills and disposition along with the contextual factors that may create opportunities, provide support, or, conversely, hinder entrepreneurship and the creation of new ventures (**Figure 10.1**). The extent to which an individual is motivated to attempt the launch of a venture depends upon three related factors – antecedent influences, the incubator organization, and environmental factors:

- *Antecedent influences,* often called the "characteristics" of the entrepreneur, including genetic factors, family influences, educational choices, and previous career experiences, all contribute to the entrepreneur's decision to start a venture.
- *Individual incubator experiences* immediately prior to start-up include the nature of the physical location, the type of skills and knowledge acquired, contact with possible fellow founders, the type of new venture, and small business experience gained.
- *Environmental factors* include economic conditions, availability of venture capital, entrepreneurial role models, and the availability of support services. People create new ventures for many different reasons, and it is critical to understand the different motives and mechanisms of entrepreneurship.

Let's begin by identifying the different individual motivations and goals for creating a new venture, and then examine the contextual factors which can enable or hinder this.

10.1 | Motives and Goals

Most entrepreneurs share a need for autonomy and control, but beyond these characteristics there are many different motivations and goals for creating a new venture. Although personality traits and contextual factors influence entrepreneurial behavior, these are poor predictors of new venture creation. Research shows that entrepreneurial intentions are a much stronger predictor of activity.[1]

It's important to recognize that creating a new venture results from the interaction between entrepreneurial intentions and external entrepreneurial events or triggers. Intentions to start a business derive from perceptions of desirability and feasibility and from a propensity to act upon opportunities. Perceived desirability is the personal attractiveness of starting a

FIGURE 10.1 Factors which influence or hinder the creation of a new venture

business; perceived feasibility is the personal belief to have the ability to start a business; and propensity to act on an opportunity depends on the desire to gain control by taking action. Perceived behavioral control or perceived self-efficacy predicts opportunity recognition and self-employment intentions.

There are numerous ways of categorizing the different types of new venture, based upon personal motivations, goals, and other structural factors. Here, we adopt two established and empirically validated dimensions to distinguish some of the fundamental differences between enterprises (**Figure 10.2**). The first dimension is the degree of novelty of the enterprise, ranging from imitative through incremental to radical.[2] The second dimension captures the ambition or scale of the enterprise, ranging from local niches to global mass markets.[3]

- *Lifestyle entrepreneurs* – those who seek independence, through choice or necessity, and wish to earn a living based around their personal circumstances and values, for example, individual professional consulting practices or home-based craft businesses. Statistically speaking, these are the most common type of new venture and are an important source of self-employment in almost all economies. Contrary to popular belief, the majority of such small firms are not particularly creative or innovative, and instead are simply exploiting an asset (e.g. a shop) or expertise (e.g. IT consulting). However, despite the political rhetoric, such firms contribute very little to employment or wealth.[4]

- *Ego entrepreneurs* – those who aim to become wealthy and powerful through the creation and aggressive growth of new businesses (plural, as they are often serial entrepreneurs who create a string of new ventures). They are more likely to measure their success in terms of wealth, influence, and reputation. Although we tend to think of people like Bill Gates or Steve Jobs, more typical examples are in relatively conservative, capital-intensive, and well-understood sectors such as retail, property, and commodities. Successful growth entrepreneurs tend to create very large corporations through mergers and acquisitions, which may dominate national markets, and the founders may become very wealthy and influential. For example, at the national level, the incidence of ego, wealth-motivated entrepreneurs is associated with higher export orientation and job growth.[5]

- *Technology entrepreneurs* - These are the high-profile Silicon Valley and Boston Route 128 start-ups. Education and experience are major factors that distinguish the founders of technology ventures from other types of entrepreneur. The median level of education of technology entrepreneurs is a master's degree and thirteen years of work experience, whereas other entrepreneurs typically have much lower levels of education and experience.[6] As a result, a typical technology entrepreneur will be aged between 30 and 40 years when establishing his or her first technology venture. Although teenage app developers attract most press attention, the median age of technology entrepreneurs in the USA is 39.[7]

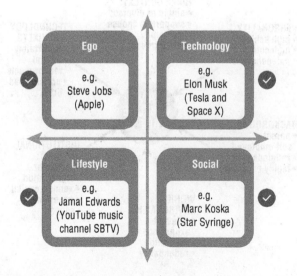

FIGURE 10.2 Different enterprise types by novelty and scale

- *Social entrepreneurs* – individuals who are driven by the desire to create or change something, whether in the private, public, or third sectors. Independence, reputation, and wealth are not the primary goals in such cases, although are often achieved anyway. Rather, the main motivation is to actually change or create something new. Innovative entrepreneurs include technological entrepreneurs and social entrepreneurs, but such ventures are rarely based on inventions, new technology, or scientific breakthroughs. Instead, the entrepreneur has chosen or been forced to create a new venture in order to create or change something.[8]

Entrepreneurship in Action: Elon Musk

Elon Musk is a serial technology entrepreneur and visionary, but contrary to popular belief, he did not create PayPal or Tesla Motors. He was born in South Africa and later obtained Canadian and American citizenship. He earned two bachelor degrees, in Physics and then Economics. After graduation, he started a PhD in Physics at Stanford but dropped out after a few weeks.

At age 24, he co-founded Zip2, an online city guide. He sold the company four years later to Compaq for $341 million, receiving 7% of the sale. He used $10 million of the proceeds to found X.com, an online financial payments service, which a year later merged with Confinity, a money transfer company that included the PayPal service. Musk was rejected as CEO of the new company in 2000 after disagreements over the technology strategy, but he remained on the board and retained 11.7% of the shares. In 2002, PayPal was sold to eBay for $1.5 billion in stock, and Musk received $165 million.

Using $100 million of his windfall, Musk founded Space Exploration Technologies, or SpaceX, in 2002. SpaceX designs, manufactures, and launches rockets, focusing on lower costs and greater re-usability than competing services. It focuses commercial satellite contracts and cargo missions for NASA, but it has longer-term aspirations for space travel and colonization. It has billions of dollars-worth of forward contracts but is a privately-owned company that has yet to declare any profits.

Tesla Motors was founded in 2003, and Musk made investments in the company, joining the board in 2004. However, it wasn't until the company struggled in the financial crisis of 2008 that Musk took a more significant financial and management position, owning 22% of the company and becoming CEO. The company currently offers three electric vehicles, the premium-priced Model S coupe introduced in 2012, the Model X SUV launched in 2015, and the more affordable and mass-market Model 3 sedan, available since 2017. In 2016, Tesla sold around 70,000 cars, worth $4 billion, but has yet to make any profit and made an annual loss of $0.9 billion. The success of the company will depend upon the sales and profitability of the more mass-market Model 3. In an effort to develop the market and infrastructure for electric and self-driving cars, Tesla made all its patents freely available. Musk has also funded development of the HyperLoop transportation system, which aims to provide faster-then-airline speeds long-distance travel.

Entrepreneurship in Action: Social Entrepreneur, Marc Koska, and Star Syringe

Marc Koska founded Star Syringe in 1996 to design and develop disposable, single-use syringes, or so-called "auto-disable syringes" (ADS), to help prevent the transmission of diseases like HIV/AIDS. For example, over 23 million infections of HIV and Hepatitis are given to otherwise healthy patients through syringe reuse every year.

Marc had no formal training in engineering but had relevant design experience from previous jobs in modelling and plastics design. He designed the ADS according to the following basic principles:

1. Cheap: the same price as a standard disposable plastic syringe
2. Easy: manufactured on existing machinery to cut setup costs
3. Simple: used as closely as possible to the same way as a standard disposable plastic syringe is used
4. Scalable: licensed to local manufacturers, leveraging resources in a sustainable way

The ADS is not manufactured in-house but by Star licensees based all over the world. The company now licenses the technology to international aid agencies and is recognized by the UNICEF and the World Health Organization (WHO). Star Alliance is the network which connects the numerous manufacturing licensees to the global marketplace. The alliance includes 19 international manufacturing partners and serves markets in over 20 countries. The combined capacity of the alliance licensees is close to 1 billion annual units.

His dedication and persistent drive over the last 20 years have earned him respect from leaders in state health services as well as in the industry: in February 2005, for example, the Federal Minister for Health in Pakistan presented Marc with an award for Outstanding Contribution to Public Health for his work on safer syringes, and in 2006, the company won the UK Queen's Award for Enterprise and International Trade.

Sources: *Star Syringe corporate website*. http://www.starsyringe.com

Entrepreneurship in Action: Technology Entrepreneur, Mike Lynch, and Autonomy

Mike Lynch founded the software company Autonomy in 1994, a spin-off from his first start-up, Neurodynamics. Lynch, a grammar-school graduate, studied information science at Cambridge where he carried out PhD research on probability theory. He rejected a conventional research career as he had found his summer job at GEC Marconi a "boring, tedious place." In 1991 at age 25, he approached the banks to raise money for his first venture, Neurodynamics, but "met a nice chap who laughed a lot and admitted that he was only used to lending money to people to open news agents." He subsequently raised the initial £2,000 from a friend of a friend.

Neurodynamics developed pattern recognition software which it sold to specialist niche users, such as the UK police force for matching fingerprints and identifying disparities in witness statements and to banks to identify signatures on checks.

Autonomy was spun off in 1994 to exploit applications of the technology in Internet, intranet, and media sectors, and it received the financial backing of venture capitalists Apax, Durlacher, and ENIC. Autonomy was floated on the EASDAQ in July 1998, on the NASDAQ in 1999, and in February 2000, was worth $5 billion, making Lynch the first British software billionaire. Autonomy creates software which manages unstructured information, which accounts for 80% of all data. The software applies Bayesian probabilistic techniques to identify patterns of data or text, and compared to crude keyword searches, it can better take into account context and relationships. The software is patented in the USA, but not in Europe as patent law does not allow patent protection of software. The business generates revenues through selling software for cataloguing and searching information direct to clients such as the BBC, Barclays, BT, Eli Lilly, General Motors, Merrill Lynch, News Corporation, Nationwide, Procter & Gamble, and Reuters. In addition, it has more than 50 license agreements with leading software companies to use its technology, including Oracle, Sun, and Sybase. A typical license will include a lump sum of $100,000 plus a royalty on sales of 10–30%. By means of such license deals, Autonomy aims to become an integral part of a range of software and the standard for intelligent recognition and searching. In the financial year ending March 2000, the company reported its first profit of $440,000 on a turnover of $11.7 million. The company employed 120 staff, split between Cambridge in the UK and Silicon Valley, and spent 17% of its revenues on R&D. In 2004, sales reached around $60 million, with an average license costing $360,000 and high gross margins of 95%. Repeat customers accounted for 30% of sales. In 2011, the company was sold to HP for US $10.3 billion, and in May 2012, Mike Lynch left the company he created and grew.

10.2 Context for Entrepreneurship

Two long-running international studies of entrepreneurship have influenced policy and practice: the Global Entrepreneurship Monitor (GEM) and Panel Study of Entrepreneurial Dynamics (PSED). GEM focuses on economic and institutional factors, whereas PSED emphasizes demographic and cognitive influences. GEM has become more dominant and was established in 1999 by Babson College in the USA and the London Business School in the UK. The GEM model attempts to identify how national policy, financial institutions, and social and cultural characteristics influence new business formation, and ultimately economic growth. It compares data from seventy different countries. More recently the study has also surveyed entrepreneurial attitudes, entrepreneurial activity, and entrepreneurial aspirations.

Nonetheless, the GEM empirical work focuses mainly on macro-factors, such as social conditions (45% of studies), economic conditions (20%), institutional factors (14%), entrepreneurship financial and non-financial support (9%), and government policy (8%), and only 3% of GEM research has examined entrepreneurial skills.[9] Also, although GEM surveys are conducted regularly, the methodology is a cross-sectional survey, so it provides limited insights into the entrepreneurial practices and process. In contrast, the PSED study uses longitudinal panel data from new ventures, so it can provide more realistic accounts of the creation, development, and performance of new ventures across time.[10] Finally, the GEM focus on all new business creation may be misplaced, as research confirms that only fast-growing new firms contribute to economic growth and employment, not all new firms.[11] We explore the challenge of growing a new venture in Chapter 11.

Enterprise Incubators

The experience of a potential entrepreneur prior to creating a new venture will provide valuable resources, but will also influence the type and direction of a new venture. Many enterprises originate from a parent or "incubator" organization, typically either a university, research center, or large established firm.

TABLE 10.1 Examples of Venture Capital- Funded University Spin-Offs, 2011-2014

University	Number of VC-Funded University Entrepreneurs	Number of VC-Funded New Ventures
Stanford, USA	378	309
UC Berkeley, USA	336	284
MIT, USA	300	250
Indian Institute of Technology	264	205
Harvard, USA	253	229
Tel Aviv, Israel	169	141
Waterloo, Canada	122	96
Technion, Israel	119	98
McGill, Canada	74	72
Toronto, Canada	71	66
London, U.K.	71	67

Source: Derived from Pitchbook. (2014). *Venture Capital Monthly August/September 2014 Report*. http://www.pitchbook.com

However, much of what we know about innovative new ventures is based on the experience of start-up firms in the USA, in particular the growth of high-technology firms in biotechnology, semiconductor, and software sectors. Examples of university incubators include Stanford, which spawned much of Silicon Valley; the Massachusetts Institute of Technology (MIT), which spawned Route 128 in Boston; and Imperial and Cambridge in the UK. In particular, MIT has become the archetype academic incubator, and in addition to the creation of Route 128, its alumni have established some 200 new ventures in northern California, which account for more than a fifth of employment in Silicon Valley. This model has been adopted worldwide but with limited success.

In practice, successful spin-outs are highly concentrated in a small number of universities (**Table 10.1**). This is due in part to significant structural differences in location, scale, policy, and technical disciplines taught and researched. Historically, a rare combination of research excellence and critical mass is required to succeed in the commercialization of research and technology. Larger, older, and more prestigious universities typically attract more and better researchers and higher funding; and other commercial investors use the prestige or reputation of the institution as a signal or indicator of quality. Nonetheless, changes in technological opportunity have reduced some of the barriers, for example, software and service innovations present new opportunities, which require less resource to commercialize than prior technologies, such as semiconductors and biosciences.

Entrepreneurship in Action: Boston's Route 128

The cluster of universities in Boston and Cambridge in the USA, which includes the Massachusetts Institute of Technology (MIT), Harvard, Boston University, and 70 other colleges and universities, has a long tradition of spawning spin-off firms.

The success of the region can be traced back to the defense-related investments in computing and software which helped to create incubator firms, such as Compaq, Digital, Data General, Lucent, Lotus, Raytheon, and Wang in the 1970s, and more recently the creation of many life sciences-based ventures in biotechnology and medical devices.

For several decades now, the venture capital industry has consistently funded the creation or growth of around 200 to 300 new firms each year with annual funding of around $2 billion. (This more than quadrupled during the Internet Boom/Bubble of 1998/2000.) To date, MIT alone has helped to create 4,000 new firms worldwide with total revenues of $232 billion, with more than a thousand of these firms still based in Massachusetts.

Source: Wonglimpiyarat, J. (2006). The Boston Route 128 model of high-tech industry development. *International Journal of Innovation Management*, 10(1), pp. 47–64.

Entrepreneurship in Action: Spin-off Companies from Xerox's PARC Labs

Xerox established its Palo Alto Research Center (PARC) in California in 1970. PARC was responsible for a large number of technological innovations in the semiconductor lasers, laser printing, Ethernet networking technology, and web indexing and searching technologies, but it is generally acknowledged that many of its most significant innovations were the result of individuals who left the company and firms that spun-off from PARC, rather than those developed via Xerox itself. For example, many of the user-interface developments at Apple originated at Xerox, as did the basis of Microsoft's Word package. By 1998, Xerox PARC had spun-out 24 firms, including ten which went public, such as 3Com, Adobe, Documentum, and SynOptics. By 2001, the value of the spin-off companies was more than twice that of Xerox itself.

A debate continues to the reasons for this, most attributing the failure to retain the technologies in-house to corporate ignorance and internal politics. However, most of the technologies did not simply "leak out," but instead were granted permission by Xerox, which often provided non-exclusive licenses and an equity stake in the spin-off firms. This suggests that Xerox's research and business managers saw little potential for exploiting these technologies in its own businesses. One of the reasons for the failure to commercialize these technologies in-house was that Xerox had been highly successful with its integrated product-focused strategy, which made it more difficult to recognize and exploit potential new businesses.

Source: Chesbrough, H. (2003). *Open Innovation: The new imperative for creating and profiting from technology*. Boston: Harvard Business School Press.

The creation and sharing of intellectual property is a core role of a university, but managing it for commercial gain is a different challenge. National and regional differences exist, but most universities now attempt to support new venture creation by staff and students.

Changes in funding and law have encouraged many more universities to establish commercialization and technology transfer departments. However, measured in terms of the number of patents held or exploited, or by income from patent and software licenses, commercialization of technology is highly concentrated in a small number of elite universities that were highly active prior to changes to funding policy and law; the top 20 US universities account for 70% of the patent activity. Moreover, at each of these elite universities a very small number of key patents account for most of the licensing income; the five most successful patents typically account for 70–90% of total income.[12]

University spin-outs are an alternative to the use of patents and licensing, involving the creation of an entirely new venture based upon research or intellectual property developed within the university. A spin-out company may be preferable to licensing technology to an established company where:

- No existing company is ready or able to take on the project on a licensing basis
- The invention consists of a portfolio of products or is an "enabling technology" capable of application in a number of fields
- The inventors have a strong preference for forming a company and are prepared to invest their time, effort, and money in a start-up

University policy of taking an equity stake in new start-ups in return for paying initial patenting and licensing expenses seems to result in a higher number of start-ups, whereas granting generous royalties to academic entrepreneurs appears to encourage licensing activity and tends to significantly suppress the number of start-up companies.[13] Moreover, badly targeted and poorly monitored financial support may encourage "entrepreneurial academics" rather than academic entrepreneurs – scientists in the public sector who are not really committed to creating start-ups, but rather are seeking alternative support for their own research agendas.[14] This can result in start-ups with little or no growth prospects, remaining in incubators for many years. Simply encouraging commercially oriented or industry-funded research also appears to have no effect on the number of start-ups, whereas a university's intellectual eminence has a very strong positive effect.[15]

Formal policies to encourage and support entrepreneurship may send a signal to staff and students, but the effect on individual behavior depends very much on whether these policies are reinforced by behavioral expectations. Individual characteristics and local norms appear to be equally effective predictors of entrepreneurial activity. Local norms evolve through self-selection during recruitment, resulting in staff with similar personal values and behavior, and are reinforced by peer pressure or behavioral socialization, resulting in a convergence of personal values and behavior. Where successful, this can create a virtuous circle, the demonstration effect of a successful spin-out, encouraging others to try. This leads to clusters of spin-outs in space and time, rather than isolated entrepreneurial academics.

10.3 Choosing the Best Structure for a New Venture

One of the early decisions an entrepreneur will have to make is the type of business structure to use. When deciding what type of company to form, you need to consider:

1. How much capital is needed to start the business?
2. How much control and ownership do you want?
3. How much risk are you willing to take on in the case of failure?
4. How large could the business become, and how fast?
5. What are the registration, reporting, and tax implications of different structures?
6. What are the proposed harvest strategies or exit routes?
7. Who might become the beneficiary of the business?

The choice of governance and legal structure has a significant influence on the subsequent success of a new venture, due to the access to external resources and ability to grow.[16] The basic options are:

Sole Proprietorship

The advantages are the relatively light regulation and reporting, autonomy of decision-making and total control, direct personal incentive to succeed, and easy to exit. However, this exposes the owner to unlimited personal liability, provides only limited access to external capital and development, and relies on the skills and talent of only one person.

Partnership

The advantages are: easy to establish; larger pool of expertise and capital; partners share all profits; and the flexibility to extend partnerships as the business develops. However, there is potential for personality and decision-making conflicts, buying out partners who wish to leave, and joint unlimited liability of partners. In the UK, a hybrid partnership-company structure is popular, the LLP – Limited Liability Partnership.

Private Company

Easy and cheap to establish, better access to capital for growth, and exposes owners to only a limited liability. The disadvantages are the reporting requirements, rules of operations, different shareholder interests, and restrictions on the sale and transfer of assets.

There is no single best structure for a new venture, but research suggests that some form of partnership is superior at the early stages due to the diversity and depth of expertise and resources, but at later stages a company structure more easily allows the raising of capital.[17]

Entrepreneurship in Action: License or Spin-out? The Lambert Review of Business – University Collaboration in the UK

In the UK, the Lambert Review of Business – University Collaboration reported in December 2003. It reviewed the commercialization of intellectual property by universities in the UK, and also made international comparisons of policy and performance. The UK has a similar pattern of concentration of activity as the USA: in 2002, 80% of UK universities made no patent applications, whereas 5% filed 20 or more patents; similarly, 60% of universities issued no new licenses, but 5% issued more than 30. However, in the UK there has been a bias toward spin-outs rather than licensing, which the Lambert Report criticizes. It argues that spin-outs are often too complex and unsustainable, and of low quality – a third in the UK are fully funded by the parent university and attract no external private funding. In 2002, universities in the UK created over 150 new spin-out firms, compared to almost 500 by universities in the USA; the respective figures for new licenses that year were 648 and 4,058. As a proportion of R&D expenditure, this suggests that British universities place greater emphasis on spin-outs and less on licensing than their North American counterparts. Lambert argues that universities in the UK may place too high a price on their intellectual property and that contracts often lack clarity of ownership. Both of these problems discourage businesses from licensing intellectual property from universities, and may encourage universities to commercialize their technologies through wholly owned spin-outs.

10.4 Identifying and Exploiting Intellectual Property

New ventures are about ideas to value, and there is a real risk is that someone can simply copy your idea. So how can we capture and preserve value from ideas? How do we appropriate the gains?

In some cases, knowledge, in particular in its more explicit or codified forms, can be commercialized by licensing or selling the intellectual property rights (IPR), rather than the more difficult and uncertain route of developing new processes, products, or businesses. For example, in the USA the total royalty income of industry from licensing is around $100 billion; much of this is from payments for licenses to use software, music, or films.

But this raises the question of how to protect intellectual property (IP). There are several routes to doing this; key options include patents, copyright, design rights, and registration. However, such rights are useless unless they can be effectively enforced, and once in the public domain, imitation or illegal use is very likely. For these reasons, secrecy is often a more effective alternative to seeking IPR.

DEEPER DIVE: Creating Value from Knowledge

Read the Deeper Dive_Creating Value from Knowledge document in the ebook or from the book companion site.

Patents

All developed countries have some form of patent legislation, aiming to encourage innovation by allowing a limited monopoly, usually for 20 years. More recently, many developing and emerging economies have been encouraged to sign up to the TRIPS (Trade Related Intellectual Property System). Legal regimes differ in the detail, but in most countries, the issue of a patent requires certain legal tests to be satisfied*:

- *Novelty* – no part of "prior art," including publications, written, oral, or anticipation. In most countries, the first to file the patent is granted the rights, but in the USA, it is the first to invent. The American approach may have the moral advantage, but results in many legal challenges to patents and requires detailed documentation during R&D.

*Also see Invention and Patents: http://www.wipo.int/multimedia-video/en/sme/multimedia/flash/03/ (World Intellectual Property Organization)

- *Inventive step* – "not obvious to a person skilled in the art." This is a relative test, as the assumed level of skill is higher in some fields than others. For example, Genentech was granted a patent for the plasminogen activator t-PA, which helps to reduce blood clots, but despite its novelty, a Court of Appeal revoked the patent on the grounds that it did not represent an inventive step because its development was deemed to be obvious to researchers in field.

- *Industrial application* – utility test requires the invention to be capable of being applied to a machine, product, or process. In practice, a patent must specify an application for the technology, and additional patents must be sought for any additional application. For example, Unilever developed Ceramides and patented their use in a wide range of applications. However, it did not apply for a patent for application of the technology to shampoos, which was subsequently granted to a competitor.

- *Patentable subject* – for example, discoveries and formula cannot be patented, and in Europe neither can software (the subject of copyright) nor new organisms, although both these are patentable in the USA. For example, contrast of the mapping of the human genome in the USA and Europe: in the USA the research is being conducted by a commercial laboratory which is patenting the outcomes, and in Europe by a group of public laboratories which is publishing the outcomes on the internet.

- *Clear and complete disclosure* – a patent provides only certain legal property rights, and in the case of infringement, the patent holder needs to take the appropriate legal action. In some cases, secrecy may be a preferable strategy. Conversely, national patent databases represent a large and detailed reservoir of technological innovations which can be interrogated for ideas.

VIDEO: Invention and Patents

The World Intellectual Property Organization discusses invention and patents at http://www.wipo.int/multimedia-video/en/sme/multimedia/flash/03.

Apart from the more obvious use of patents as IPR, they can be used to search for potential innovations and to help identify potential partners and assess competitors.

For example, the TRIZ system, developed by Genrich Altshuller, identifies standard solutions to common technical problems distilled from an analysis of 1.5 million patents and applies these in different contexts. Many leading companies use the system, including 3M, Rolls-Royce, and Motorola.

Copyright

Copyright is concerned with the expression of ideas and not the ideas themselves. Therefore, the copyright exists only if the idea is made concrete, for example, in a book or recording. There is no requirement for registration, and the test of originality is low compared to patent law, requiring only that "the author of the work must have used his own skill and effort to create the work." Like patents, copyright provides limited legal rights for certain types of material for a specific term. For literary, dramatic, musical, and artistic works, copyright is normally for 70 years after the death of the author in the UK (50 in the USA) and for recordings, film, broadcast, and cable programs, 50 years from their creation. Typographical works have 25 years copyright. The type of materials covered by copyright include:

- "Original" literary, dramatic, musical, and artistic works, including software and, in some cases, databases
- Recordings, films, broadcasts, and cable programs
- Typographical arrangement or layout of a published edition

VIDEO: Copyright and Related Rights

The World Intellectual Property Organization discusses copyright and related rights at http://www.wipo.int/multimedia-video/en/sme/multimedia/flash/05.

Design Rights

Design rights are similar to copyright protection, but mainly apply to three-dimensional articles, covering any aspect of the "shape" or "configuration," internal or external, whole or in part, but specifically excludes integral and functional features, such as spare parts. Design rights exist for 15 years, or 10 years if commercially exploited. Design registration is a cross between patent and copyright protection, is cheaper and easier than patent protection, but more limited in scope. It provides protection for up to 25 years, but covers only visual appearance—shape, configuration, pattern and ornament. It is used for designs that have aesthetic appeal, for example, consumer electronics and toys. For example, the knobs on top of Lego bricks are functional and would therefore not qualify for design registration, but were also considered to have "eye appeal," and therefore granted design rights.

Innovation in Action: Open Source Software

Proprietary software usually restricts imitation by retaining the source code and by enforcing intellectual property rights, such as patents (mainly the USA) or copyright (elsewhere). However, Open Source Software has many characteristics of a public good, including non-excludability and non-rivalry, and developers and users of OSS have a joint interest in making OSS free and publicly available. The open software movement has grown since the 1980s when the programmer, Richard Stallman, founded the Free Software Foundation, and the General Public License (GPL) is now widely used to promote the use and adaptation of open source software. The GPL forms the legal basis of three-quarters of all OSS, including Linux.

Therefore, firms active in the field of Open Source Software have to create value and appropriate private benefits in different ways. The ineffectiveness of traditional intellectual property rights in such cases means that firms are more likely to rely on alternative ways of appropriating the benefits of innovation, such as being first to the market or by using externalities to create value. More generic strategies include product and service approaches:

- *Products* – adding a proprietary part to the open code and licensing this, or black-boxing by combining several pieces of OSS into a solution package
- *Services* – consultancy, training, or support for OSS

Linux is a good example of a successful OSS which firms have developed products and services around. It has been largely developed by a network of voluntary programmers, often referred to as the "Linux community." Linus Torvalds first suggested the development of a free operating system to compete with the DOS/Windows monopoly in 1991, and quickly attracted the support of a group of volunteer programmers. "Having those 100 part-time users was really great for all the feedback I got. They found bugs that I hadn't because I hadn't been using it the way they were. . . after a while they started sending me fixes or improvements. . . this wasn't planned, it just happened." Thus, Linux grew from 10,000 lines of code in 1991 to 1.5 million lines by 1998. Its development coincided with and fully exploited the growth of internet and later web forms of collaborative working. The provision of the source code to all potential developers promotes continuous incremental innovation, and the close and sometimes indistinguishable developer and user groups promotes concurrent development and debugging. The weaknesses are potential lack of support for users and new hardware, availability of compatible software, and forking in development.

By 1998, there were estimated to be more than 7.5 million users and almost 300 user groups across 40 countries. Linux has achieved a 25% share of the market for server operating systems, although its share of the PC operating system market was much lower, and Apache, a Linux application web server program, accounted for half the market. Although Linux is available free of charge, a number of businesses have been spawned by its development. These range from branding and distribution of Linux, development of complementary software, and user support and consultancy services. For example, although Linux can be downloaded free of charge, RedHat Software provides an easier installation program and better documentation for around $50, and in 1998, achieved annual revenues of more than $10 million. Red

Hat was floated in 1999. In China, the lack of legacy systems, low costs, and government support have made Linux-based systems popular on servers and desktop applications. In 2004, Linux began to enter consumer markets when Hewlett-Packard launched its first Linux-based notebook computer, which helped to reduce the units cost by $60.

Source: Dahlander, L. (2005). Appropriation and appropriability in open source software. *International Journal of Innovation Management*, 9(3), pp. 259–286.

Licensing IPR

Once you have acquired some form of formal legal IPR, you can allow others to use it in return for some payment (a license), or sell the IPR outright (or assign it). Licensing IPR can have a number of benefits:

- Reduce or eliminate production and distribution costs and risks
- Reach a larger market
- Exploit in other applications
- Establish standards
- Gain access to complementary technology
- Block competing developments
- Convert competitor into defender

Considerations when drafting a licensing agreement include degree of exclusivity, territory and type of end use, period of license, and type and level of payments—royalty, lump sum or cross-license. Pricing a license is as much an art as a science and depends on a number of factors, such as the balance of power and negotiating skills. Common methods of pricing licenses are:

- Going market rate – based on industry norms, e.g. 6% of sales in electronics and mechanical engineering
- 25% rule – based on licensee's gross profit earned through use of the technology
- Return on investment – based on licensor's costs
- Profit-sharing – based on relative investment and risk. First, estimate total life-cycle profit. Next, calculate relative investment and weight according to share of risk. Finally, compare results to alternatives, e.g return to licensee, imitation, litigation

There is no "best" licensing strategy, as it depends on the strategy of the organization and the nature of the technology and markets. For example, Celltech licensed its asthma treatment to Merck for a single payment of $50 million, based on sales projections. This isolated Celltech from the risk of clinical trials and commercialization, and provided a much-needed cash injection. Toshiba, Sony, and Matsushita license DVD technology for royalties of only 1.5% to encourage its adoption as the industry standard. Until the recent legal proceedings, Microsoft applied a "per processor" royalty to its OEM (original equipment manufacturer) customers for Windows to discourage its customers from using competing operating systems.

VIDEO: Technology Licensing in a Strategic Partnership

The World Intellectual Property Organization discusses technology licensing in a strategic partnership at at http://www.wipo.int/multimedia-video/en/sme/multimedia/flash/07.

However, the successful exploitation of IPR also incurs costs and risks:

- Cost of search, registration, and renewal
- Need to register in various national markets
- Full and public disclosure of your idea
- Need to be able to enforce

DEEPER DIVE: The rise of intellectual property in China and India

Read the Deeper Dive_The rise of intellectual property in China and India document in the ebook or from the book companion site.

Advice for Entrepreneurs: To Disclose or not?

When you need to contact a potential financial backer, manufacturer, or other partner, or need to share your ideas with someone about a new product, process, or business, you should consider a confidentiality or non-disclosure agreement (NDA) of some kind.

Such confidential ideas, or "trade-secrets," cannot be patented but can be an equally important commercially. Also, outside the USA (which has a "first to invent" system, rather than the more common "first to file" patent system), if you tell anyone about your invention before a patent application has been filed, then this will invalidate the application.

A Non-Disclosure Agreement (NDA) is a legally-binding document that records the terms under which you exchange secret information. This does not mean that a duty of confidence does not arise in the absence of a NDA, but a written agreement gives added legal weight. Also, having a signed NDA means you will be able to share more with a potential partner, and are therefore more likely to secure their support.

However, some professional advisers and organizations will be unable or unwilling to sign a NDA. This is often because they do not want to receive any confidential information which might prejudice or conflict with projects they may already be working on. In such cases, it is best to describe and discuss a potential innovation in more general terms of its business benefits, rather than in more detailed technical features and functions.

If you do decide to apply for a patent, the process in most countries is relatively simple, but can be time-consuming and will require the involvement (and payment!) of professional advisers, including the services of a registered patent agent. The basic process is as follows:

1. First prepare a **patent specification**, including drawings if these are useful in describing the invention. The specification should contain a full description of your invention, and it is important that this is as complete description as possible since you cannot make any changes to your specification once you have filed your application.

2. Complete a **formal application** form, with two copies of your patent specification, and with the appropriate fees, request a search. This must be done by a given date, usually within a year of your filing date, to avoid the application being terminated.

3. The Patent Office conducts a **preliminary examination** to make sure your application meets certain formal requirements and search through published patents to assess whether or not the invention is new and inventive. This can take time, typically many months, and in some countries, the back log is years.

4. If you satisfy the formal requirements, you pay another fee and the Patent Office **publishes your patent application** around 18 months from your filing date (or sooner if you have requested a priority date).

5. Finally, you complete and file an **examination form**, together with the appropriate fee, within six months of publication of the application. The Patent Office then examines your application and advises you of any necessary revisions. If your application meets all the requirements of the relevant Patents Acts, they will grant your patent, publish your application in its final form, and send you a certificate. So, from start to finish the process will take two or more years.

For further advice in the UK, see www.patent.gov.uk, or the relevant patent office in your country.

10.5 Challenges at Different Stages of Venture Development

A new venture will face different management challenges at different stages in order to make a successful transition to the next stage, so-called "critical junctures":[18]

Opportunity Recognition and Assessment

At the interface of the research and opportunity framing phases. This requires the ability to connect a specific technology or know-how to a commercial application and is based on a rather rare combination of skill, experience, aptitude, insight, and circumstances. A key issue here is the ability to synthesize scientific knowledge and market insights, which increases with the entrepreneur's social capital – linkages, partnerships, and other network interactions. Research confirms that the ability to recognize and assess opportunities is a critical determinant of new venture success.[19]

Entrepreneurial Commitment

Acts and sustained persistence that bind the venture champion to the emerging business venture. This often demands difficult personal decisions to be made, for example, whether or not to remain employed, as well as evidence of direct financial investments to the venture.[20]

Venture Credibility

This is critical for the entrepreneur to gain the resources necessary to acquire the finance and other resources for the business to function. Credibility is a function of the venture team, key customers, and other social capital and relationships. This requires close relationships with sponsors, financial and other, to build and maintain awareness and credibility. Lack of business experience and failure to recognize their own limitations are a key problem here. One solution is to hire the services of an experienced "surrogate entrepreneur," who may be a successful entrepreneur or angel investor, or have knowledge and experience of the target market.[21]

First Client or Sale

In the early stages, many new ventures rely too much on a few major customers for sales and are, therefore, very vulnerable commercially. As an extreme example, around half of technology ventures rely on a single customer for more than half of their first-year sales. This over-dependence on a small number of customers has three major drawbacks:[22]

1. Vulnerability to changes in the strategy and health of the dominant customer
2. A loss of negotiating power, which may reduce profit margins
3. Little incentive to develop marketing and sales functions, which may limit future growth

Some Final Advice for Entrepreneurs[23]

When you need to contact a potential financial backer, manufacturer, or other partner, or need to share your ideas with someone about a new product, process or business, you should consider a confidentiality or non-disclosure agreement (NDA) of some kind.

Such confidential ideas, or "trade-secrets," cannot be patented, but can be an equally important commercially. Also, if you tell anyone about your invention before a patent application has been filed, then this will invalidate the application.

A Non-Disclosure Agreement (NDA) is a legally-binding document that records the terms under which you exchange secret information. This does not mean that a duty of confidence does not arise in the absence of a NDA, but a written agreement gives added legal weight. Also, having a signed NDA means you will be able to share more with a potential partner and are therefore more likely to secure their support.

However, some professional advisers and organizations will be unable or unwilling to sign a NDA. This is often because they do not want to receive any confidential information which might prejudice or conflict with projects they may already be working on. In such cases, it is best to describe and discuss a potential innovation in more general terms of its business benefits, rather than in more detailed technical features and functions.

If you do decide to apply for a patent, the process in most countries is relatively simple, but can be time-consuming and will require the involvement (and payment!) of professional advisers, including the services of a registered patent agent. The basic process is as follows:

1. First prepare a **patent specification**, including drawings if these are useful in describing the invention. The specification should contain a full description of your invention, and it is important that this is a complete description as possible since you cannot make any changes to your specification once you have filed your application.

2. Complete a **formal application** form, with two copies of your patent specification, and with the appropriate fees, request a search. This must be done by a given date, usually within a year of your filing date, to avoid the application being terminated.

3. The Patent Office conducts a **preliminary examination** to make sure your application meets certain formal requirements and search through published patents to assess whether or not the invention is new and inventive. This can take time, typically many months, and in some countries, the back log is years.

4. If you satisfy the formal requirements, you pay another fee and the Patent Office **publishes your patent application** around 18 months from your filing date (or sooner if you have requested a priority date).

5. Finally, you complete and file an **examination form**, together with the appropriate fee, within six months of publication of the application. The Patent Office then examines your application and advises you of any necessary revisions. If your application meets all the requirements of the relevant Patents Acts, they will grant your patent, publish your application in its final form and send you a certificate. So, from start to finish the process will take two or more years.

For further advice in the UK, see www.patent.gov.uk or the relevant patent office in your country.

Chapter Summary

In this chapter, we have explored the rationale, characteristics, and management of innovative new ventures. Typically, an innovative entrepreneur will establish a venture primarily to create something new or to change something, rather than a means to achieve independence or wealth, although both of these may follow as a consequence. A range of factors influences the creation of innovative new ventures, some contextual, such as institutional support, availability of capital, and culture; others more personal, such as personality, background, relevant skills, and experience. Therefore, entrepreneurship is not just simply an individual act driven by psychology, but also a profoundly social process. The process of creating an innovative new venture requires careful business planning and the systematic assessment and acceptance of opportunities and risks. Innovative entrepreneurs need to be able to identify and exploit a broader range of external resources and sources of knowledge than their more conventional counterparts, including diverse networks of those in the private, public, and third sectors.

Key Terms

Copyright   A form of intellectual property right, which covers a broad range of potential assets, such as artistic outputs. However, it only protects expression of ideas and not the ideas themselves. Therefore, the copyright exists only if the idea is made concrete, for example, in a book or recording.

Global Entrepreneurship Monitor (GEM)   A survey that focuses on economic and institutional factors. The GEM model attempts to identify how national policy, financial institutions, and social and cultural characteristics influence new business formation, and ultimately economic growth. It compares data from seventy different countries. More recently the study has also surveyed entrepreneurial attitudes, entrepreneurial activity, and entrepreneurial aspirations.

Incubator organization   a private firm, university, or public organization which provides resources and support for the generation of spin-out firms.

License   A legal contract to agree the limited use of intellectual property in return for some consideration, usually financial such as a royalty on sales and/or a lump-sum payment. Typically such agreements specify the market scope of the right.

Patent   A form of intellectual property right, which covers a very specific type of innovation, essentially inventions and technologies. There are various legal tests which need to be satisfied for a patent to be granted.

References

1 Krueger Jr., N.F., Reilly, M.D., and Carsrud, A.L. (2000). Competing models of entrepreneurial intentions. *Journal of Business Venturing*, 15, pp. 411–432

2 Bessant, J. and Tidd, J. (2015). *Innovation and Entrepreneurship*. 3rd ed. Chichester: John Wiley & Sons, Ltd.; Eiriz, V., Faria, A., and Barbosa, N. (2013). Firm growth and innovation: towards a typology of innovation strategy. *Innovation: Management, policy & practice*, 15(1), pp. 97–111; Mills, C. and Pawson, K. (2011). Integrating motivation, risk-taking and self-identity: a typology of ICT enterprise development narratives. *International Small Business Journal*, 30(5), pp. 584–606.

3 Tanev, S., Rasmussen, E.S., Zijdemans, E., Lemminger, R., and Svedsen, L.L. (2015). Lean and global start-ups: linking the two research themes. *International Journal of Innovation Management*, 19(3), DOI 1540008; Muñoz-Bullón, F., Sánchez-Bueno. M.J., and Vos-Saz, A. (2015). Nascent entrepreneurs' personality attributes and the international dimension of new ventures. *International Entrepreneurial Management Journal*, 11, pp. 473–492; Douglas, E.J. (2013). Reconstructing entrepreneurial intentions to identify predisposition for growth. *Journal of Business Venturing*, 28, pp. 633–651; Baum, M., Schwens, C., and Kabst, R. (2011). A typology of international new ventures: empirical evidence from high-technology industries. *Journal of Small Business*, 49(3), pp. 305–330.

4 Hessels, J., van Gelderen, M., and Thurik, R. (2008). Entrepreneurial aspirations, motivations, and their drivers. *Small Business Economics*, 31, pp. 323–339; Wong, P.K., Ho, Y.P., and Autio, E. (2005). Entrepreneurship, innovation and economic growth: evidence from GEM data. *Small Business Economics*, 24, pp. 335–350.

5 Nightingale, P., and Coad, A. (2014). Muppets and gazelles: political and methodological biases in entrepreneurship research. *Industrial and Corporate Change*, 23(1), pp. 113–143.

6 Wonglimpiyarat, J. (2006). The Boston Route 128 model of high-tech industry development. *International Journal of Innovation Management*, 10(1), pp. 47–64; Kenny, M. (2000). *Understanding Silicon Valley: Anatomy of an entrepreneurial region*. Redwood City, CA: Stanford University Press; Roberts, E. (1991). *Entrepreneurs in High Technology: Lessons from MIT and beyond*. Oxford: Oxford University Press.

7 Wadhwa, V., Freeman, R.B., and Rissing, B.A. (2008). *Education and technology entrepreneurship*. Social Science Research Network, working paper 1127248.

8 Mair, J., Robinson, J., and Hockets, K. (2006). *Social Entrepreneurship*. Basingstoke: Palgrave Macmillan.

9 Lvarez, C.A., Urbano, D., and Amoros, J.E. (2014). GEM research: achievements and challenges. *Small Business Economics*, 42, pp. 445–465.

10 Ramos-Rodríguez, A.R., Martínez-Fierro, S., Medina-Garrido, J.A., and Ruiz-Navarro, J. (2015). Global entrepreneurship monitor versus panel study of entrepreneurial dynamics: comparing their intellectual structures. *International Entrepreneurial Management Journal*, 11, pp. 571–597.

11 Wong, P.K., Ho, Y.P., and Autio, E. (2005). Entrepreneurship, innovation and economic growth: evidence from GEM data. *Small Business Economics*, 24, pp. 335–350.

12 Shane, S. and Cable, D. (2002). Network ties, reputation and the financing of new ventures. *Management Science*, 48(3), pp. 364–381; Mowery, D.C., Nelson, R.R., Sampat, B.N., and Ziedonis, A.A. (2001). The growth of patenting and licensing by U.S. universities: an assessment of the effects of the Bayh–Dole Act of 1980. *Research Policy*, 30; Henderson, R., Jaffe, A.B., and Trajtenberg, M. (1998). Universities as a source of commercial technology: a detailed analysis of university patenting 1965–1988. *The Review of Economics and Statistics*, 80(1), pp. 119–127.

13 Astebro, T., Bazzazian, N., and Braguinsky, S. (2012). Startups by recent university graduates and their faculty: implications for university entrepreneurship policy. *Research Policy*, 41(4), pp. 663–677; Lee, Y. S. (1996). Technology transfer and the research university: a search for the boundaries of university-industry collaboration. *Research Policy*, 25, pp. 843–863.

14 Meyer, M. (2004). Academic entrepreneurs or entrepreneurial academics? Research-based ventures and public support mechanisms. *R&D Management*, 33(2), pp. 107–115; Butler, S. and Birley, S.

(1999). Scientists and their attitudes to industry links. *International Journal of Innovation Management*, 2(1), pp. 79–106.

15 Di Gregorio, D. and Shane, S. (2003). Why do some universities generate more start-ups than others? *Research Policy*, 32, pp. 209–227; Bray, M.J. and Lee, J.N. (2000). University revenues from technology transfer: licensing fees versus equity positions. *Journal of Business Venturing*, 15, pp. 385–392.

16 Gao, Li, Cheng and Shi (2010). Impact of initial conditions on new venture success. *International Journal of Innovation Management*, 14(1), pp. 41–56.

17 Astebro, T. and Serrano, C.J. (2015). Business partners: complementary assets, financing, and invention commercialization. *Journal of Economics and Management Strategy*, 24(2), pp. 228–252; Coad, A. and Timmermans, B. (2014). Two's company: composition, structure and performance of entrepreneurial pairs *European Management Review*, 11(2), pp. 117–138.

18 Vohora, A., Wright, M., and Lockett, A. (2004). Critical junctures in the development of university high-tech spinout companies. *Research Policy*, 33(1), pp. 147–175.

19 Niammuad, D., Napompech, K., and Suwanmaneepong, S. (2014). The mediating effect of opportunity recognition on incubated entrepreneurial innovation. *International Journal of Innovation Management*, 18(3), DOI: 1440005.

20 Simon, M., Houghton, S.M., and Aquino, K. (2000). Cognitive, biases, risk perception and venture formation: how individuals decide to start companies. *Journal of Business Venturing*, 15(2), pp. 113–134.

21 Zott, C. and Huy, Q.N. (2007). How entrepreneurs use symbolic management to acquire resources. *Administrative Science Quarterly*, 52(1), pp. 70–105.

22 Calori, R. (1990). Effective strategies in emerging industries. In Loveridge, R. and Pitt, M. (eds.). *The Strategic Management of Technological Innovation*, Chichester: John Wiley & Sons, Ltd. pp. 21–38; Walsh, V., Niosi, J., and Mustar, P. (1995). Small firms formation in biotechnology: a comparison of France, Britain and Canada. *Technovation*, 15(5), pp. 303–328; Westhead, P., Storey, D., and Cowling, M. (1995). An exploratory analysis of the factors associated with survival of independent high technology firms in Great Britain. In Chittenden, F., Robertson, M. and Marshall, I. (eds). *Small Firms: Partnership for Growth in Small Firms*. London: Paul Chapman. Pp. 63–99

23 Paasi, J., Valkokari, K., Hytönen, H., Huhtilainen, L., and Nystén-Haarala, S. (2013). *Workbook for Opening Innovation: Bridging Networked Business, Intellectual Property and Contracting*. London: Imperial College Press.

CHAPTER 11

Growing the Enterprise

LEARNING OBJECTIVES

When you have completed this chapter you will be able to:

1. Identify the initial conditions at start-up which contribute to the success and growth of a new venture.

2. Manage the factors which entrepreneurs can influence to promote success and growth, including innovation.

3. Exploit the external factors which influence the opportunities for growth and value creation.

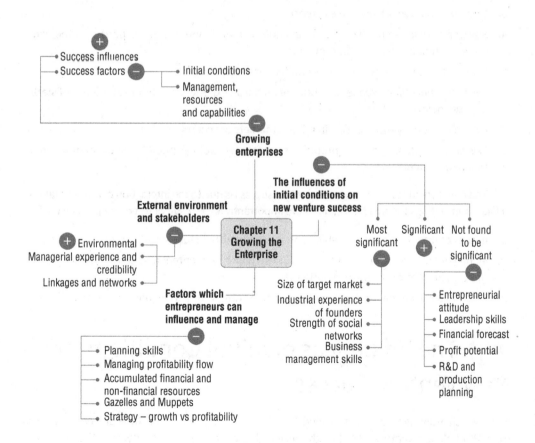

11.0 | Growing Enterprises

In this chapter, we identify the factors which contribute to the success and growth of new ventures, and we try to differentiate the factors which entrepreneurs can influence from those which are more contextual.

Entrepreneurs' motivation, intention, or ambition to grow a venture varies significantly, with some studies suggesting 40–60% of entrepreneurs have no desire to change or grow their business. We referred to these as *lifestyle entrepreneurs* in Chapter 10.[1] However, new venture growth makes a significant contribution to survival, employment, and profitability, so it is critically important both economically and socially. In most developed economies, around 10% of the economically active population engage in new venture creation each year – a slightly higher proportion in the USA and Asia (15%) and a little lower in Europe, excluding the UK (6%). But the rate of churn – new ventures closed less those created – is high.

Closure or exit does not necessary indicate failure, as a founder may choose to change or sell the business or to seek alternative employment. Survival rates are quite high, 80% survive in the UK after two years and 54% after four years.[2] In the USA, there are more short-term failures, probably due to the ease of establishing a business there, but similar rates of longer-term survival: 66% survive 2 years, 50% four years, 40% more than six years.[3]

A study of more than 11,000 new ventures in the USA over a period of five years found that 36% survived after four years and 22% after five years. The researchers identified only eight factors that were consistently found to influence success:[4]

1. *Value chain management* – cooperation with suppliers, distribution, agents, and customers
2. *Market scope* – variety of customers, market segments, and geographic reach
3. *Firm age* – number of years in existence
4. *Size of founding team* – likely to bring additional and more diverse expertise to the ventures, including better decision-making
5. *Financial resources* – venture assets and access to funding
6. *Founders' marketing experience* – but not technical experience or prior experience of start-ups (see below)
7. *Founders' industry experience* – in related markets or sectors
8. *Existence of patent rights* – in product or process technology, but R&D investment was not found to be significant

This clearly demonstrates that new venture success is due to the interaction of a combination of factors, including random chance, but more importantly is the result of three groups of factors:

1. Initial conditions at start-up, which entrepreneurs should take into account
2. Management, resources, and capabilities, which entrepreneurs can influence more directly, innovation strategy in particular
3. External environment and stakeholders, which entrepreneurs can only influence indirectly

11.1 | The Influences of Initial Conditions on New Venture Success

Firms which grow significantly, so-called "gazelles", are very rare, typically representing fewer than 4% of all new ventures.[5] Although these high growth ventures are atypical, they account for a disproportionate proportion of new employment, as much as a third of employment in some countries. The founding conditions have a very significant and persistent effect on the subsequent success and growth of a new venture, but it is difficult to separate the effects of business planning, strategy, and context (**Table 11.1**). Most, but not all, studies suggest that formal business planning contributes to success, as we discussed in Chapter 5.[6]

TABLE 11.1   **Initial Conditions Influencing the Success of New Ventures**

Most significant (5% level):
Size of target market
Industrial experience of founders
Strength of social networks
Business management skills
Significant (10% level):
Product attractiveness to target market
Ownership structure and governance
Not found to be significant:
Profit potential
Entrepreneurial attitude
Leadership skills
R&D and production planning
Financial forecast

Based on 95 new ventures, 1999-2007.

Source: Adapted from Gao, Li, Cheng and Shi. (2010). Impact of initial conditions on new venture success. *International Journal of Innovation Management*, 14(1), pp. 41–56.

Question:

From Table 11.1, what do you believe the most important lessons are for creating a successful new venture?

    Answer: This, and other research, shows that success of a new venture is due to the interaction of a small cluster of internal capabilities and external opportunities: internally, founder's business skills, industry experience, strength of social networks, and governance structure of the venture; and externally, social networks, and the size and attractiveness (e.g. high growth, low competition and regulation) of the target market. Financial and profit forecasts appear to be less influential, reflecting uncertainty.

Entrepreneurship in Action: Gazelles, Unicorns, and Muppets

Most focus in management and policy for entrepreneurship is on the performance and contribution of the high-growth, so-called "gazelle," companies. There is a predilection for animal terms, such as the even rarer billion-dollar "unicorns" (see European Internet Unicorns, below). However, our colleagues Paul Nightingale and Alex Coad argue that we need to have a much finer distinction to disaggregate small firms, in particular the 96% no-growth firms.

    They develop the term "muppets" (all rights reserved) to describe the more typical, economical "Marginal, Under-sized, Poor Performance Enterprises." They argue that the performance and contribution of small firms has been exaggerated significantly, and by most measures, such firms are less productive and innovative than larger firms and contribute less to wealth and employment creation.

Source: Derived from Nightingale, P. and Coad, A. (2014). Muppets and gazelles: political and methodological biases in entrepreneurship research. *Industrial and Corporate Change*, 23(1). pp. 113–143.

    Studies consistently find that the age, educational level, number of founders, and starting capital all have a positive effect on venture success. The effects of age on the success and growth of a new venture are probably the best understood, and they are shown to be significant in almost every research study. The consensus is that the most common age of successful founders is between 35–50 years old, the median age being 39.[7] The explanation for this clustering is that younger founders tend to lack the experience, resources, and credibility, whereas older founders may lack the drive and have too much to lose. Of course, there are many examples of successful entrepreneurs younger or older than this age range, but the association between age of founders and success is very significant.

To understand the influence of education, one study tracked 118,070 new start-up firms over 10 years and found that human capital at foundation, measured by university degree, had a strong and persistent positive effect on subsequent success. In addition, four structural factors at the time of foundation were predictors of success: firm size at foundation (positive), rate of firm entry into the same sector (negative), concentration of the sector (positive), and GDP growth (positive).[8] Other research examined 622 young or new small firms over five years, and found human and financial capital available at start-up was a strong predictor of survival and growth, specifically the founder's education (bachelor's degree or above) and access to bank finance.[9] As with age, there are many examples of successful entrepreneurs who chose not to go to college or dropped out early, but the research does consistently demonstrate a strong association between level of education and venture success and growth, especially in more knowledge- or technology-intensive businesses.

These founder effects are even stronger for technology-based firms. This is partly because of the human capital necessary, especially the high education of founders:[10]

- 85% have a degree, almost half have a PhD
- 12 or more years of experience in large private-sector firm
- Founders' ages cluster mid-30s, two-thirds aged 30–50

One of the challenges of developing a new venture is developing or gaining access to complementary assets, resources and capabilities.[11] For example, a start-up might have the technical know-how or intellectual property but not be able to reach or support potential customers, or conversely, an entrepreneur might identify a market opportunity but not be able to provide the product or service to satisfy this. This is one reason why firms created by pairs or small groups of founders are significantly more likely to be successful than those formed by individual entrepreneurs.[12]

Access to sufficient capital is another widely cited founding condition for success and growth. However, the evidence is more mixed than for the effects of age and education. Some studies suggest that access to external capital is associated with higher growth, especially in the case of more high technology ventures,[13] but others find no such effect or even the exact opposite relationship – that higher growth is associated with maintaining internal funding and ownership.[14] The conflicting evidence and advice may be due to methodological differences, such as definition of high growth, time period studied, etc., but may also reflect the influence of more fundamental moderating factors, for example, the type of venture and market or the roles and control needs of founders.

Entrepreneurship in Action: European Internet Unicorns

Most of the attention is attracted to the Internet giants that originated in the USA, such as Google and Facebook. However, Europe has created its own Internet superstars. Since 2000, 30 European internet ventures have grown to be worth more than $1 billion each. This compares favorably with the USA, with 39 billion-dollar new ventures over the same period.

These are often referred to as "unicorns" because they are so rare. The UK leads Europe with 11, for example, the property website, Zoopla, and food delivery site, Just Eat. Russia is next most successful with five unicorns, third is Sweden with four cases, (including Spotify), France and Finland each have two, but Germany, Spain, Italy, Ireland, Luxembourg, and Israel have only one each. The Anglo-Swedish group, King, developer of the smartphone game Candy Crush, completes the European unicorns.

As in the USA, most the unicorns were formed by pairs or teams of 2-3 entrepreneurs with an average age of 33 at foundation. Only half of European unicorns have reached a trade sale or an IPO, compared with two-thirds in the USA.

Source: Derived from GP Bullhound. (2014). *Can Europe Create Billion Dollar Tech Companies?* http://www.gpbullhound.com/en/research/

Question:

Is it necessary for a new venture to be first to market with a novel product or service to achieve high-growth?

Answer: The First-Mover, or so-called Blue Ocean Strategy, focuses on the creation of new markets through significant product and service differentiation in order to promote growth and minimize competition.

However, Buisson and Silberzahn (2010) examined 24 cases and found that this strategy was not inherently superior. Instead, they argue that market domination is achieved by using four kinds of breakthroughs, separately or simultaneously:

- Technological breakthrough: a new technology that ends up dominating the incumbent technology
- Business model breakthrough: a new way to create value through the exploitation of business opportunities
- Design breakthrough: a new way to design a product without changing it profoundly; this related to the interface between the product and the customer, which is an important factor of adoption
- Process breakthrough: a new way to do things (manufacturing, logistics, value chain, etc.)

Further support for this work is provided by a study of high-growth firms, or "gazelles." Lindiča *et al* (2012) analyzed 500 firms, less than 2% of which were classified as high-growth gazelles, and found that Blue Ocean strategies are not associated with higher growth. Instead, the key to high growth is not necessarily to create a new market, but to be the first to develop and exploit that market. Amazon.com and Apple are good examples, neither of which were the first in the market but were the first to truly develop and exploit it. Moreover, they also found that technological innovation was not sufficient for high growth, and that value or business model innovation was a more significant factor.

Sources: Buisson, B. and Silberzahn, P. (2010). Blue Ocean or fast second innovation? *International Journal of Innovation Management*, 14(3), pp. 359–378; Lindiča, J., Bavdaža, M., and Kovačič, H. (2012). Higher growth through the Blue Ocean strategy: implications for economic policy. *Research Policy*, 41(5), pp. 928–938.

11.2 Factors which Entrepreneurs can Influence and Manage

A study of more than 6,000 start-ups tracked over six years found that survival was strongly associated with initial conditions, such as the size of the firm at start-up and its early growth, but was also a function of the accumulated resources of the firm, financial and non-financial, over time.[15] The growth of a new venture in terms of sales and employment depends upon planning skills and profitability flows.[16]

Another study of 409 SMEs examined the differences between the highest growing, the gazelles, and the lowest growing companies over a four-year period to identify how innovation contributed to the growth. It found that the highest growing companies had higher profitability, increased number of employees, and significantly higher market shares locally, nationally, and internationally, than the lowest growing companies. Several traits were found to contribute to this:[17]

- The "high growers" had significantly younger CEOs than the "low growers," but the average age of 47 years for the "high growers" clearly indicates that several of their CEOs were over 50 years of age

- The "high growers" prioritized growth rather than profitability, market share rather than profitability, and on reinvesting rather than showing profit

- The "high growers" perceived themselves as better than their competitors at understanding customer needs, offering better products, being agile, and at keeping costs low

- The "high growers" had a significantly higher portion of new products as part of the turnover

Innovation, broadly defined, is three times more important to growth than founder attributes or any other factor.[18] Another study, of Korean technology start-ups, also found that innovativeness, defined as a propensity to engage in new idea generation, experimentation, and R&D, was associated with performance. So was proactivity, defined as the firm's approach to market opportunities through active market research and the introduction of new products and services.[19] The same study also found that what it referred to as sponsorship-based linkages had a positive effect on performance. This included links with venture capital firms, which reinforces the developmental role these can play, as discussed earlier.

VIDEO: Michael Rosemann, Queensland University of Technology

Michael Rosemann, Head of the Information Systems School at the Queensland University of Technology, talks about how to develop disruptive thinking patterns at https://www.ispim-innovation.com/single-post/2015/12/08/Michael-Rosemann-How-to-Develop-Disruptive-Thinking-Patterns. Link included with permission of ISPIM.

New ventures which attempt to compete on price, rather than by differentiation, are much less likely to survive. Innovative firms are more likely to grow, in terms of sales and employment, but are not necessarily more profitable than non-innovators.[20]

Much of the research on innovative small firms has been confined to a small number of high-technology sectors, principally microelectronics and, more recently, biotechnology. A notable exception is the survey of 2,000 SMEs conducted by the Small Business Research Centre in the UK. The survey found that 60% of the sample claimed to have introduced a major new product or service innovation in the previous five years.[21] Whilst this finding demonstrates that the management of innovation is relevant to the majority of small firms, it does not tell us much about the significance of such innovations, in terms of research and investment, or subsequent market or financial performance.

Research over the past decade or so suggests that the innovative activities of SMEs exhibit broadly similar characteristics across sectors:[22]

- Are more likely to involve product innovation than process innovation
- Are focused on products for niche markets, rather than mass markets
- Will be more common amongst producers of final products, rather than producers of components
- Will frequently involve some form of external linkage
- Tend to be associated with growth in output and employment but not necessarily profit

The limitations of a focus on product innovation for niche or intermediate markets were discussed earlier – in particular, problems associated with product planning and marketing, relationships with lead customers, and linkages with external sources of innovation. Where an SME has a close relationship with a small number of customers, it may have little incentive or scope for further innovation and will pay relatively little attention to formal product development or marketing. Therefore, SMEs in such dependent relationships are likely to have limited potential for future growth, and may remain permanent infants or subsequently be acquired by competitors or customers.[23] Moreover, an analysis of their growth suggests that the trend has as much to do with negative factors, such as the downsizing of larger firms, as it does with more positive factors such as start-ups.[24]

Innovative SMEs are likely to have diverse and extensive linkages with a variety of external sources of innovation, and in general there is a positive association between the level of external scientific, technical, and professional inputs and the performance of an SME.[25] The sources of innovation and precise types of relationship vary by sector, but links with contract research organizations, suppliers, customers, and universities are consistently rated as being highly significant, constituting the "social capital" of the firm. However, such relationships are not without cost, and the management and exploitation of these linkages can be difficult for an SME, overwhelming the limited technical and managerial resources of SMEs.[26] As a result, in some cases the cost of collaboration may outweigh the benefits.[27] In the specific case of collaboration between SMEs and universities, there is an inherent mismatch between the short-term, near-market focus of most SMEs and the long-term, basic research interests of universities.[28]

TABLE 11.2   **Degree and Type of Innovation and Small Firm Performance**

Type of innovation	Low Performer	High Performer
Incremental product or service	28	86
Incremental administrative	23	67
Incremental technical process	6	85
Radical	0	48
External networks	33	54

% firms in each category which exhibit factor, N=392 firms, all with less than 50 employees
Source: Derived from Forsman, H. (2015). *Small Firms as Innovators: From innovation to sustainable growth*. London: Imperial College Press.

In terms of innovation, the performance of SMEs is easily exaggerated. Early studies based on innovation counts consistently indicated that when adjusted for size, smaller firms created more new products than the larger counterparts. However, methodological shortcomings appear to undermine this clear message. When the divisions and subsidiaries of larger organizations are removed from such samples,[29] and the innovations are weighted according to their technological merit and commercial value, the relationship between firm size and innovation is reversed; larger firms create proportionally more significant innovations than SMEs.[30] The amount of expenditure by SMEs on design and engineering has a positive effect on the share of exports in sales,[31] but formal R&D by SMEs appears to be only weakly associated with profitability[32] and is not correlated with growth.[33] Similarly, the high growth rates are not explained by R&D effort,[34] and investment in technology does not appear to discriminate between success and failure. Instead, other factors have been found to have a more significant effect on profitability and growth, particularly the contributions of technically qualified owner managers and their scientific and engineering staff, and attention to product planning and marketing (**Table 11.2**).[35] Innovativeness is also associated with internationalization and exporting.[36]

Question:

From Table 11.2, what do you conclude are the most significant differences between the low- and high-performing small firms?

Answer: Overall, the high-performing small firms have higher levels of all types of innovation. However, this is not due (only) to differences in radical innovation, the typical lazy explanation. Instead, it is the result of detailed, continuous incremental innovation, particularly of processes and products. Internal and external organizational differences appear to be less important.

Different challenges and conditions will demand variations in innovation strategy. For example, a study of 116 software start-ups identified five factors that affected success: level of R&D expenditure; how radical new products were; the intensity of product upgrades; use of external technology; and management of intellectual property.[37] In contrast, a study of 94 biotechnology start-ups found that three factors were associated with success: location within a significant concentration of similar firms; quality of scientific staff (measured by citations); and the commercial experience of the founder.[38]

The number of alliances had no significant effect on success, and the number of scientific staff in the top management team had a negative association, suggesting that the scientists are best kept in the laboratory. Other studies of biotechnology start-ups confirm this pattern and suggest that maintaining close links with universities reduces the level of R&D expenditure needed, increases the number of patents produced, and moderately increases the number of new products under development. However, as with more general alliances, the *number* of university links has no effect on the success or performance of biotechnology start-ups, but the *quality* of such relationships does.[39]

However, new ventures are diverse, and the type of technology will also have an influence of the trajectory of growth (**Figure 11.1**).

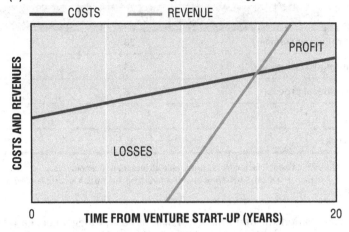

(a) Research-based venture e.g. biotechnology

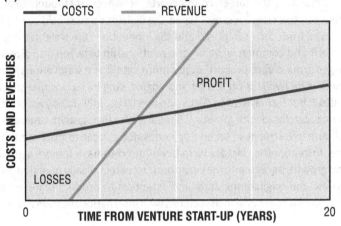

(b) Development-based venture e.g. electronics

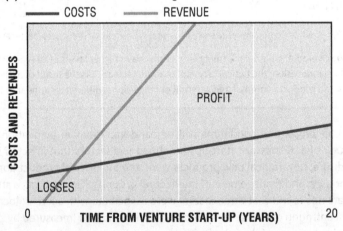

(c) Production-based venture e.g. software

FIGURE 11.1 Influence of technology on the profitability and cash-flow profile of a new venture

Losses: Total cash used = rate of cash-burn X time. It is critical to have sufficient working capital, from savings, loans or equity, to reach positive cash-flow from sales.

Profit: Total cash generated = rate of sales X time. Accounting profit is not as important as maintaining positive cash-flow, so real income is the goal, not just sales.

Funding by venture capital has no effect on the innovativeness of a start-up but does have a positive influence on profitability, perhaps reflecting the priorities of such investors.[40] Financial constraints only effect the likelihood of survival of a new venture in the first few years, but they continue to constrain profitability and growth for a decade after foundation.[41]

Entrepreneurship in Action: Intelligent Energy

The company was founded by a group of academics at Loughborough University in 2001 but can be traced back to Advanced Power Sources Ltd, formed in 1995 by Paul Adcock, Phillip Mitchell, Jon Moore, and Anthony Newbold. The company was based on research since 1988 in the departments of Chemistry, Aeronautical, and Automotive engineering. Intelligent Energy Ltd acquired APS Ltd in 2001, and a private fund-raising also allowed the new company to acquire an irrevocable, worldwide license to exploit all fuel cell know-how which had been developed at Loughborough University.

The company develops compact, air-cooled fuel cells. It uses a technology licensing model, similar to ARM, and licenses its 500+ patent portfolio to a number of automotive firms, including Nissan, Toyota, Suzuki, Vauxhall, Daimler, Ricardo, Hyundai, and Tata (Jaguar Land Rover), consumer electronics companies, and distributed power projects. The company employs 350 people and has offices in Japan, India, and the US.

The company has been highly-effective in promoting itself through high-profile projects and partnerships, such as the World's First Fuel Cell Motorbike in 2005, first manned fuel cell power flight in a EU venture with Boeing in 2008, and collaborated with Manganese Bronze to develop and operate a fleet of 15 zero-emission black cabs for the 2012 London Olympic Games. Intelligent Energy awarded the 2013 Barclays Social Innovation Award by The Sunday Times Hiscox Tech Track 100.

Through a second fund-raising in 2003, the company expanded through the acquisition of Element One Enterprises, based in California. The company raised further funding of £22 million in 2012 and $51 million in 2013. It was floated in London in July 2014, raising a further £40 million and valuing the company at more than £600 million. Singaporean sovereign wealth fund GIC owns about 10% of the company, and Philip Mitchell, one of the founders, owned around £4 million.

VIDEO: Paul Hyland, QUT Business School

Paul Hyland, QUT Business School, speaks about bridging the innovation chasm at https://www.ispim-innovation.com/single-post/2015/12/08/Paul-Hyland-Bridging-the-Innovation-Chasm. Link included with permission of ISPIM.

DEEPER DIVE: Growth of New Ventures

Read the Deeper Dive_Growth of new ventures document in the ebook or from the book companion site.

11.3 External Environment and Stakeholders

The most appropriate strategy for new venture development will be facilitated and constrained by a range of external factors and stakeholders, such as choice of partners, level of competition, availability of venture capital, and opportunities to create value and harvest investments. There are many ways that a new venture can grow and create additional value:

- Organic growth through additional sales and diversification
- Acquisition of or merger with another company
- Sale of the business to another company or private equity firm
- An initial public offering (IPO) on a stock exchange

For example, a venture may have a choice of whether to use its intellectual assets by translating its technology into product and services for the market, or alternatively, it may exploit these assets through a larger, more established firm through licensing, sale of IPR, or by collaboration. The venture needs to specifically consider these environmental factors:[42]

- *Excludability* – to what extent the venture can prevent or limit competition from incumbents who develop similar technology?
- *Complementary assets* – to what extent do the complementary assets – production, distribution, reputation, support, etc. – contribute to the value proposition of the technology?

Combining these two dimensions creates four strategy options:

1. *Attacker's advantage* – where the incumbent's complementary assets contribute little or no value, and the start-up cannot preclude development by the incumbent (e.g. where formal intellectual property is irrelevant or enforcement is poor), the venture will have an opportunity to disrupt established positions, but technology leadership is likely to be temporary as other new ventures and incumbents respond, resulting in fragmented niche markets in the longer term; This pattern is common in computer components businesses.

2. *Ideas factory* – in contrast, where incumbents control the necessary complementary assets, but the venture can preclude effective development of the technology by incumbents, cooperation is essential. The new venture is likely to focus on technological leadership and research, with strong partnerships downstream for commercialization. This pattern tends to reinforce the dominance of incumbents, with the ventures failing to develop or control the necessary complementary assets. This pattern is common in biotechnology.

3. *Reputation-based* – where incumbents control the complementary assets, but the venture cannot prevent competing technology development by the incumbents, ventures face a serious problem of disclosure and other contracting hazards from incumbents. In such cases, a venture will need to seek established partners with caution and attempt to identify partners with a reputation for fairness in such transactions. Cisco and Intel have both developed such a reputation and are frequently approached by ventures seeking to exploit their technology. This pattern is common in capital-intensive sectors, such as aerospace and automobiles. However, these sectors have a lower "equilibrium," as established firms have a reputation for expropriation, therefore discouraging start-ups.

4. *Greenfield* – where incumbents' assets are unimportant and the venture can preclude effective imitation, there is the potential for the venture to dominate an emerging business. Competition or cooperation with incumbents are both viable strategies, depending upon how controllable the technology is – for example, through establishing standards or platforms, and where value is created in the value chain.

VIDEO: Tim Jones, of Innovation Leaders & Future Agenda

Tim Jones discusses the links between innovation, firm growth, and value creation at https://www.youtube.com/watch?v=hQJqSGtGb4U. Link included with permission of ISPIM.

A lack of managerial experience and credibility of founders can also be a major barrier to funding and growing new ventures. A significant challenge for a new venture is to build credibility for a new venture, what our colleague Sue Birley refers to as the "credibility carousel": factors which help to recruit and convince other stakeholders of the viability of a venture.[43] This can be a slow, painful process, but it is essential in order attract the necessary talent, resources, and initial customers.

In the early stage, developing relationships with potential customers and suppliers are the most critical, but as the venture grows, the relationship and role of partners in the network of a new venture will change. The location of a venture also has an effect on performance. Geographic closeness increases the likelihood of informal linkages and encourages the mobility of skilled labor across firms. However, the probability of a start-up benefiting from such local knowledge exchanges appears to decrease as the venture grows.[44]

DEEPER DIVE: The role of external stakeholders

Read the Deeper Dive_The role of external stakeholders document in the ebook or from the book companion site.

This growing inability to exploit informal linkages is a function of organizational size, not the age of the venture, and suggests that as ventures grow and become more complex, they begin to suffer many of the barriers to innovation; therefore, the explicit processes and tools to help overcome these become more relevant. Larger SMEs are associated with a greater spatial reach of innovation-related linkages and the introduction of more novel product or process innovations for international markets. In contrast, smaller SMEs are more embedded in local networks and are more likely to be engaged in incremental innovations for the domestic market.[45] It is always difficult to untangle cause and effect relationships from such associations, but it is plausible that as the more innovative start-ups begin to outgrow the resources of their local networks, they actively replace and extend their networks, which both creates the opportunity and demand for higher levels of innovation. Conversely, the less innovative start-ups fail to move beyond their local networks and are less likely to have either the opportunity or need for more radical innovation.

As a venture seeks to expand, external sources of funding need to be cultivated, which can result in changes of ownership, the dissolution of some of the initial relationships, and substitution for more mature partners in more stable networks. Over time, the roles of different actors in the venture network become more specialized and professional.[46] Individual skills are essential in building and developing such relationships and networks. These skills include:[47]

- Social and interpersonal communication to build credibility and promote knowledge sharing
- Negotiating and balancing skills to balance cooperation and competition, and to develop awareness, trust, and commitment
- Influencing and visioning skills to establish roles, shares of responsibilities, and rewards

Therefore, the challenge is to simultaneously manage the more mature firm and its relations but to maintain the early focus on innovation. To conclude, new venture growth is a consequence of the interaction of internal factors, such as the entrepreneurs' personalities and capabilities, and external factors, such as social and physical network connections (**Figure 11.2**). However, as Figure 11.2 indicates, an entrepreneurial disposition is necessary, but it is not by any means a sufficient condition for innovation or success.

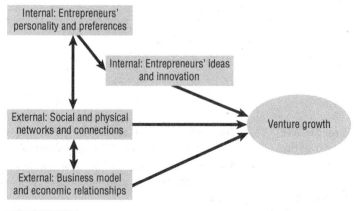

FIGURE 11.2 Internal and external factors influencing new venture growth

Source: Derived from Brink, T. (2014). The impact on growth of outside-in and inside-out innovation. *International Journal of Innovation Management*, 18(4), DOI: 1450023.

Entrepreneurship in Action: Seedcamp

Seedcamp was established in 2007 by Index Ventures partners, Saul Klein and Reshma Sohoni. It provides early-stage mentoring, micro-seed investment, networking, and advice through monthly Seedcamp days and an annual Seedcamp week. Each year, around 2,000 entre-preneurs and businesses compete for seed funding of up to €50,000, but only 20 or so are successful. Seedcamp offers a standard investment of €50,000 in return for an 8–10% stake in the business, but one of the main benefits is the access to an extensive network of mentors, includ-ing entrepreneurs, business angels, and professional services. The main business areas supported are in relatively low-capital technology ventures in internet, mobile, gaming, software, and media.

Source: *Seedcamp corporate website.* http://www.seedcamp.com/

Entrepreneurship in Action: The role of venture capital in innovation

I was recently asked by a friend who works in the R&D group at a large corporation to summarize the role of venture capital in innovation. Trying to make it relevant to his own experience, I explained that we simply provide the R&D budget for companies that would not ordinarily have one! I explained further that the companies we back are, on the whole, small self-contained R&D organizations generating intellectual property and ultimately new products that threaten the incumbents in any particular industry. Venture capitalists believe that to "create value," a small firm should follow a strategy that means it will be needed by or become a threat to global corporations. That way, such cor-porations may be forced to bid against each other to acquire the small firm and obtain the new innovations (or remove the threat), thus providing the venture capitalist with a high-value exit from its investment.

This goes to the very heart of the venture capital business model. Venture capitalists are professional fund managers who invest cash in early-stage, high-risk ventures in return for shares, with the aim of selling those shares at a later date through some form of exit event. The golden rule of investment "buy low, sell high" is modified in the realm of venture capital to "buy very low, sell very high" to account for the extreme risk profile of the early-stage ventures they back.

The follow-up question to what venture capitalists do is usually whether they provide value to early-stage ventures beyond pure finan-cial investment. The question usually provokes a debate, sometimes heated, about the pros and cons of having venture capitalists involved in running a business. In my view, the answer is simple – and is based around a philosophy within the venture capital industry to kill failure early. By allocating their capital only to companies that continue to demonstrate success, venture capitalists deprive underperforming ventures of cash and usually bring about its rapid demise. This is often not the case within the R&D groups of large corporations where un-derperforming or low potential projects can struggle on for years, protected by managers' indecision and political sensitivity. Thus, venture capitalists provide a rigorous and ongoing selection process for the innovation process, holding the companies they back to strict targets and tight deadlines – there is no hiding place.

Thus, venture capital investment provides the cash to drive innovation forward within small companies at a faster rate than would ordi-narily be possible, and it provides a rigorous and ongoing monitoring process that responds by killing failure early. Ultimately, this is under-pinned by the very simplest of selection criteria: will this investment make a significant financial return within 3–5 years' time? Answering that question clarifies even the most difficult of investment decisions.

Simon Barnes is managing partner of Tate & Lyle Ventures LP, an independent venture capital fund backed by Tate & Lyle, a global food ingredients manufacturer.

Chapter Summary

- A new venture represents an opportunity to develop and deliver new technology, products, or services. However, the majority of new ventures fail after a few years, and very few continue to grow.

- The mythology of the lone, risk-taking entrepreneur is unfounded. Internal and external factors contribute to the success and growth of a new venture.

- Internal factors include the education, experience, and capabil-ities of founders, and a focus on innovation and planning.

- External factors include access to complementary resources, social, and business networks, and the regional and national context.

- The availability of financial resources is a significant constraint, not so much at the initial stages, but for subsequent development and growth.

- However, innovation promotes the development and growth of a new venture, and this demands access to complementary resources and capabilities within the new venture and throughout its external networks.

Key Terms

Complementary assets the mixture of diverse experience, expertise, and resources that ventures need to grow, partly achieved through multiple founders and partly through external networks.

Gazelles extremely fast-growing firms, typically double-digit in terms of sales and employment over a prolonged period. Rare, most estimate fewer than 5% of all firms.

Unicorns ventures that have grown to be worth more than $1 billion, even rarer than gazelles!

Muppets (Marginal, Under-sized, Poor Performance Enterprises) more typical, and by most measures, such firms are less productive and innovative than larger firms and contribute less to wealth and employment creation.

References

1 Mahdjour, S. (2015). Set up for growth? – an exploratory analysis of the relationship of growth intention and business models. *International Journal of Innovation Management*, 19(6); Delmar, F., McKelvie, A., and Wennberg, K. (2013). Untangling the relationships among growth, profitability and survival in new firms. *Technovation*, 33, pp. 276–291.

2 Storey, D. and Greene, F. (2010). *Small Business & Entrepreneurship*. Upper Saddle River, NJ: Prentice Hall; Coad, A. (2009). *The Growth of Firms: A Survey of Theories and Empirical Evidence*. Cheltenham: Edward Elgar.

3 Head, B. (2003). Redefining business success: distinguishing between closure and failure. *Small Business Economics*, 21(1), pp. 51–59.

4 Song, M., Podoynitsyna, K., van der Bij, H., and Halman, J.I.M. (2008). Success factors in new ventures: a meta-analysis. *Journal of Product Innovation Management*, 25, pp. 7–27.

5 Storey, D. and Green, F. (2010). *Small Business and Entrepreneurship*. Upper Saddle River, NJ: Prentice Hall; Storey, D. (1994). *Understanding the Small Business Sector*. Belmont, CA: Thomson Learning; Mason, G., Bishop, K., and Robinson, C. (2009). *Business Growth and Innovation*. London: NESTA.

6 Barr, S.H., Baker, T., Markham, S.K., and Kingon, A.I. (2009). Bridging the valley of death: lessons learned from 14 years of commercialization of technology education. *Academy of Management Learning and Education*, 8(3), pp. 370–388; Beaver, G. (2007). The strategy payoff for smaller enterprises. *The Journal of Business Strategy*, 28(1), pp. 9–23; Lyles, M.A., Baird, I.S., Orris, B., and Kuratko, K. (1993). Formalised planning in business: increasing strategic choice. *Journal of Small Business Management*, 31(2), pp. 38–51.

7 Coad, A. (2009). *The Growth of Firms: A Survey of Theories and Empirical Evidence*. Cheltenham: Edward Elgar; Capelleras, J.L. and Greene, F.J. (2008). The determinants and growth implications of venture creation speed. *Entrepreneurship and Regional Development*, 20(4), pp. 317–343; Koeller, C.T. and Lechler, T.G. (2006). Employment growth in high-tech new ventures. *Journal of Labor Research*, 27(2), pp. 135–147; Persson, H. (2004). The survival and growth of new establishments in Sweden. *Small Business Economics*, 23(5), pp. 423–440.

8 Geroski, P.A., Mata, J., and Portugal, P. (2010). Founding conditions and the survival of new firms. *Strategic Management Journal*, 31, pp. 510–529; Gao, J., Li, J., Cheng, Y., and Shi, S. (2010). Impact of initial conditions on New Venture Success. *International Journal of Innovation Management*, 14(1), pp. 41–56; Wadhwa, V., Freeman, R.B., and Rissing, B.A. (2008). Education and technology entrepreneurship. *Social Science Research Network*, working paper: 1127248.

9 Saridakis, G., Mole, K., and Storey, D.J. (2008). New small firm survival in England. *Empirica*, 35, pp. 25–39.

10 Storey, D. and Tether, B. (1998). New technology-based firms in the European Union. *Research Policy* 26, pp. 933–946; Tether, B. and Storey, D. (1998). Smaller firms and Europe's high technology sectors: a framework for analysis and some statistical evidence. *Research Policy*, 26(9), pp. 947–971.

11 Agarwal, R. and Shah, S.K. (2014). Knowledge sources of entrepreneurship: firm formation by academic, user and employee innovators. *Research Policy*, 43(7), pp. 1109–1133.

12 Astebro, T. and Serrano, C.J. (2015). Business partners: complementary assets, financing, and invention commercialization. *Journal of Economics and Management Strategy*, 24(2), pp. 228–252; Coad, A. and Timmermans, B. (2014). Two's company: composition, structure and performance of entrepreneurial pairs. *European Management Review*, 11(2), pp. 117–138; Tidd, J. (2014). Conjoint innovation: building a bridge between innovation and entrepreneurship. *International Journal of Innovation Management*, 18(1), pp. 1–20; Tidd, J. (2012). It takes two to tango: how multiple entrepreneurs interact to innovate. *European Business Review*, 24(4), pp. 58–61.

13 Birley, S. and Westhead, P. (1994). A taxonomy of business start-up reasons and their impact on firm growth and size. *Journal of Business Venturing*, 9(1), pp. 7–31; Davila, A., Foster, G., and Gupta, M. (2003). Venture capital financing and the growth of start-up firms. *Journal of Business Venturing*, 18(6), pp. 689–708.

14 Cosh, A., Hughes, A., Bullock, A., and Milner, I. (2009). *SME Finance and Innovation in the Current Economic Crisis*. Cambridge: Centre for Business Research, University of Cambridge.

15 Coad, A., Frankish, J., Roberts, R.G., and Storey, D.J. (2013). Growth paths and survival chances: an application of Gambler's ruin theory. *Journal of Business Venturing*, 28, pp. 615–632.

16 Koellinger, P. (2008). The relationship between technology, innovation, and firm performance: empirical evidence from e-business in Europe. *Research Policy*, 37(8), pp. 1317–1328.

17 Grundstrom, C., Sjöström, R., Uddenberg, A., and Öhrwall Rönnbäck, A. (2012). Fast-growing SMEs and the role of innovation. *International Journal of Innovation Management*, 16(3), pp. 1–19.

18 Bruderl, J. and Preisendorfer, P. (2000). Fast-growing businesses. *International Journal of Sociology*, 30, pp. 45–70.

19 Lee, C., Lee, K., and Pennings, J. (2001). Internal capabilities, external networks, and performance: a study of technology-based ventures. *Strategic Management Journal*, 22, pp. 615–640.

20 Mayer-Hauga, K., Read, S., Brinckmann, J., Dew, N., and Grichnik, D. (2013). Entrepreneurial talent and venture performance: a meta-analytic investigation of SMEs. *Research Policy*, 42(6), pp. 1251–1273; Delmar, F. and Shane, S. (2003). Does business planning facilitate the development of new ventures? *Strategic Management Journal*, 24, pp. 1165–1185.

21 Oakey, R. (2012). *High-Technology Entrepreneurship*. Oxford: Routledge; Small Business Research Centre. (1992). *The State of British Enterprise: Growth, Innovation and Competitiveness in Small and Medium Sized Firms*. Cambridge: SBRC.

22 Forsman, H. (2015). *Small Firms as Innovators: From innovation to sustainable growth*. London: Imperial College Press; Hoffman, K., Parejo, M., Bessant, J., and Perren, L. (1998). Small firms, R&D, technology and innovation in the UK: a literature review. *Technovation*, 18(1), pp. 39–55.

23 Calori, R. (1990). Effective strategies in emerging industries. In Loveridge, R. and Pitt, M. (eds) *The Strategic Management of Technological Innovation*, Chichester: John Wiley & Sons, Ltd. pp. 21–38; Walsh, V., Niosi, J., and Mustar, P. (1995). Small firms formation in biotechnology: a comparison of France, Britain and Canada. *Technovation*, 15(5), pp. 303–28; Westhead, P., Storey, D., and Cowling, M. (1995). An exploratory analysis of the factors associated with survival of independent high technology firms in Great Britain. In Chittenden, F., Robertson, M., and Marshall, I. (eds) *Small Firms: Partnership for Growth in Small Firms*. London: Paul Chapman. pp. 63–99.

24 Tether, B. and Storey, D. (1998). Smaller firms and Europe's high technology sectors: a framework for analysis and some statistical evidence. *Research Policy*, 26, pp. 947–971.

25 MacPherson, A. (1997). The contribution of external service inputs to the product development efforts of small manufacturing firms. *R&D Management*, 27(2), pp. 127–143.

26 Rothwell, R. and Dodgson, M. (1993). SMEs: their role in industrial and economic change. *International Journal of Technology Management*, Special Issue, pp. 8–22.

27 Moote, B. (1993). *Financial Constraints to the Growth and Development of Small High Technology Firms*. Cambridge: Small Business Research Centre, University of Cambridge; Oakey, R. (1993). Predatory networking: the role of small firms in the development of the British biotechnology industry. *International Small Business Journal*, 11(3), pp. 3–22.

28 Storey, D. (1992). United Kingdom: case study. In OECD. *Small and Medium Sized Enterprises, Technology and Competitiveness*. Paris: OECD; Tang, N. (1995). Technological alliances between HEIs and SMEs: examining the current evidence. In Bennett, D. and Steward, F. (eds) *Proceedings of the European Conference on the Management of Technology: Technological Innovation and Global Challenges*. Birmingham: Aston University.

29 Tether, B. (1998). Small and large firms: sources of unequal innovations? *Research Policy*, 27, pp. 725–745.

30 Tether, B., Smith, J., and Thwaites, A. (1997). Smaller enterprises and innovations in the UK: the SPRU innovations database revisited. *Research Policy*, 26, pp. 19–32.

31 Strerlacchini, A. (1999). Do innovative activities matter to small firms in non-R&D-intensive industries? *Research Policy*, 28, pp. 819–832.

32 Hall, G. (1991). Factors associated with relative performance amongst small firms in the British instrumentation sector. Working Paper No. 213. Manchester: Manchester Business School.

33 Oakey, R. (2012). *High-Technology Entrepreneurship*. Oxford: Routledge.

34 Keeble, D. (1993). *Regional Influences and Policy in New Technology-based Firms: Creation and Growth*. Cambridge: Small Business Research Centre, University of Cambridge.

35 Dickson, K., Coles, A., and Smith, H. (1995). Scientific curiosity as business: an analysis of the scientific entrepreneur. Manchester: 18th National Small Firms Policy and Research Conference; Lee, J. (1993). Small firms' innovation in two technological settings. *Research Policy*, 24, pp. 391–401.

36 Muñoz-Bullón, F., Sánchez-Bueno. M.J., and Vos-Saz, A. (2015). Nascent entrepreneurs' personality attributes and the international dimension of new ventures. *International Entrepreneurial Management Journal*, 11, pp. 473–492.

37 Zahra, S. and Bogner, W. (2000). Technology strategy and software new ventures performance. *Journal of Business Venturing*, 15(2), pp. 135–173.

38 Deeds, D., DeCarolis, D., and Coombs, J. (2000). Dynamic capabilities and new product development in high technology ventures: an empirical analysis of new biotechnology firms. *Journal of Business Venturing*, 15(3), pp. 211–229.

39 George, G., Zahra, S., an Robley Wood, D. (2002). The effects of business-university alliances on innovative output and financial performance: a study of publicly traded biotechnology companies. *Journal of Business Venturing*, 17, pp. 577–609.

40 Arvanitis, S. and Stucki, T. (2014). The impact of venture capital on the persistence of innovation activities of start-ups. *Small Business Economics*, 42(5), 849–870.

41 Stucki, T. (2013). Success of start-up firms: the role of financial constraints, *Industrial and Corporate Change*, 23(1), pp. 25–64.

42 Gans, J. and Stern, S. (2003). The product and the market for "ideas": commercialization strategies for technology entrepreneurs. *Research Policy*, 32, pp. 333–350.

43 Birley, S. (2002). Universities, academics and spin-out companies: lessons from imperial. *International Journal of Entrepreneurship Education*, 1(1), pp. 133–154.

44 Almeida, P., Dokko, G., and Rosenkopf, L. (2003). Startup size and the mechanisms of external learning: increasing opportunity and decreasing ability? *Research Policy*, 32, pp. 301–315.

45 Freel, M. (2003). Sectoral patterns of small firm innovation, networking and proximity. *Research Policy*, 32, pp. 751–770.

46 Oberg, C. and Grundstrom, C. (2009). Challenges and opportunities in innovative firms' network development. *International Journal of Innovation Management*, 13(4), pp. 593–614.

47 Ritala, P., Armila, L., and Blomqvist, K. (2009). Innovation orchestration capability. *International Journal of Innovation Management*, 13(4), pp. 569–591.

CHAPTER 12

Building Resilient Business Models

LEARNING OBJECTIVES

By the end of this chapter you will be able to:

1. Understand the idea of business models as a framework to describe how value is created and captured.

2. Develop the skills to map and build business models and use these to explore value capture.

3. Explore business model innovation – the ways in which entrepreneurs can use new business models to create opportunity by challenging or replacing existing ones.

4. Use this knowledge to develop resilient and sustainable models for long-term value capture.

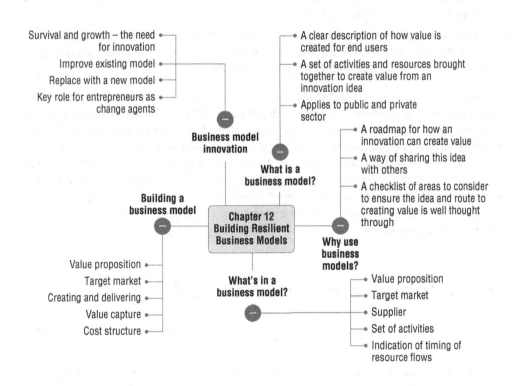

12.0 What is a Business Model?

What makes a good idea special? What's the secret of translating an insight, a flash of inspiration, into something which changes the lives of millions of people? How does a tiny seed become a strong and flourishing tree, bearing fruit for generations? We've tried in this book to answer some of these questions by showing that innovation is a process, not simply a new idea, and that shaping and configuring it is something which effective entrepreneurs do. Whatever the context in which they work, the same message is clear – making innovations which create value is a craft. It's a set of skills which can be learned and practiced, whether in a small start-up or as part of the way a giant corporation renews itself and what it offers the world.

So how do ideas create value? What's the framework or structure which allows this to happen? A helpful answer to these questions is the idea of a business model (BM) – a clear and well-rounded explanation of how value is created for users. It's a set of activities and resources which are brought together in structured fashion and used to create value from a core innovative idea. Here are some examples of business models:

- A theatre uses scripts, actors, scenery, lighting, and music to create a theatrical experience which the audience values
- A car company mobilizes an extensive supply network to bring together components and services and assemble them into a car which the customer values
- A supermarket procures various food and non-food products and makes them available on its shelves so customers can collect them conveniently; they value this and are prepared to pay more than the supermarket paid for the items because they value the service this collection, storage, and display offers them
- An insurance company provides a guarantee of payment to offset the cost of losses due to accidental damage, theft, or other incident; customers value the peace of mind which this brings and are prepared to pay for it
- A smartphone retailer provides a platform across which communications, entertainment, and personalized applications traffic can flow and customers are prepared to pay to own or rent the device because of the functions it offers them

Every organization, public or private sector, offers some kind of "value proposition" – a product or service or some combination which end users value. In commercial markets, this is something they are prepared to pay for, but in other contexts – such as the public sector – services like education, welfare, and healthcare are similarly "valued" by those who consume them.

Innovation – as we have seen – is all about creating new or better ways of delivering such value. So, if we are concerned with capturing value, it makes sense to begin by making explicit the model we are using to create it, checking whether it does the job well, and whether it is sustainable in the long-term or vulnerable to replacement or challenge by someone else – the idea of business model *innovation*.

12.1 Why use Business Models?

It's useful to have a clear representation of where and how value is created for a number of reasons:

- It provides a roadmap for how an innovation can create value – it won't just happen, it needs a framework
- It provides a way of sharing the idea with others – makes the business vision explicit; that can be useful for entrepreneurs trying to pitch their ideas to venture capitalists

or to innovation teams trying to win resources and support for an internal innovation project

- It offers a helpful checklist of areas to consider in making sure the idea and the route to creating value with it is well-thought out

We've already seen examples of business model thinking, for example, Chapter 5 was all about constructing the "business case." This is essentially a document to share with others about what we are trying to achieve, how we will do it, for whom, when, what the costs and rewards will be, etc. It contains the headlines about our underlying innovative idea and how we are going to implement it. And if it doesn't explain clearly how value will be created and delivered, then it is likely to be limited in its impact.

We've been using the idea of the entrepreneur's storyboard as a way of enriching this headline information. As we write the story and retell it, and get others involved to tell it, our story takes shape and becomes a rich narrative. The cast of characters grows as we build our networks. The "scenery" becomes more developed as we pull together key resources. And the plot changes as we rewrite the story to accommodate new ideas and input or to get around unexpected problems and surprise events. What we are producing – the script of our story – is essentially a business model.

Think of any innovation, and you can see it as a story which has meaning for people. Henry Ford's was all about "a car for Everyman at a price everyone could afford." George Eastman's (founder of Kodak) was about moving photography from the world of professionals and putting it in the hands of ordinary families: "You point and shoot and we'll do the rest!" Edwin Land's daughter gave him the idea for his story when he tried to answer her photography question, "Daddy, why can't I see the picture you just took?" He couldn't answer so he worked on the concept which became instant photography based on the Polaroid process. Muhamed Yunis told a "rags to riches" story about "ordinary" people having the discipline and courage to create their own businesses if only they were given a financial chance to get started. His Grameen Bank has grown to one of the world's most important on the back of this business model.

These examples have one thing in common. Their innovations weren't a single idea but a detailed and well-constructed story which gave the idea meaning and direction and helped communicate it to others. At its heart, the story has to identify where the value lies and who will find this important in their lives. But another key part of any entrepreneur's task is sharing this vision with others, to get their support, energy, and commitment to the idea. Each time the story is told, it is refined and improved, embellished with new ideas and shaped by feedback and questions from the audience.

A robust business model, like a good story, doesn't just happen – it is shaped and developed in this process of telling and retelling. The plot emerges, the characters take shape, the scenery moves – and each time we tell it the story is refined and changed. Explaining it to others gives us new insights about what to add or take away. People ask questions or make suggestions which change the way the story unfolds the next time we tell it. They pick up the threads and spread the story, telling it to others so that the idea gradually takes on a life of its own and starts to make sense in other people's lives. And as it does so it becomes stronger and clearer.

Just as in literature there are some common themes which keep coming up, told in slightly different ways, so there are a number of generic "storylines" in business models.

Question:

What kinds of generic business models can you think of, and how do they operate to provide value to their users?

Answer: Table 12.1 gives some examples:

TABLE 12.1 Some Examples of Generic Business Models

Model	Value Proposition
Product or service provider	Offers an end-product or service
Ownership of key assets and renting them out	Rental for temporary period of something valuable– for example, car parks, luggage, and goods storage businesses
Finance provider	Offers access to money and related services
Systems integrator	Pulls together components on behalf of an end customer, for example, building contractors, software service providers, computer builders like Dell
Platform provider	Offers a platform across which others can add value, for example, smartphones and the various apps which run across them, and Intel, whose chipsets enable others to offer computing functions
Network provider	Offers access to various kinds of network service, for example, a mobile phone or broadband company
Skills provider	Sells or rents access to human resources and knowledge, for example, recruitment agencies, professional consultancies, and contract services
Outsourcer	Offers to take over responsibility for management and delivery of key activities, for example, payroll management, IT services, or financial transaction processing

12.2 What's in a Business Model?

Value creation doesn't just happen – it is the result of a structured process which involves:

- A value proposition – what is valued?
- A target market – by whom?
- A supplier – who?
- A set of activities – how?
- A representation of the timing of resource flows – how much?

If our idea is going to work, then the "revenue" from the demand side needs to be greater than the costs on the supply side of doing it. Beyond that, there are important questions about timing – can we ensure the flow of resources out is supported by the flow of revenue in? – and long-term sustainability – how can we protect our model so that others can't instantly copy it, and how can we develop out idea in the long term to counter other competitors coming in to try?

Figure 12.1 illustrates the basic building blocks of the model, and **Table 12.2** gives some examples mapped on to this framework.

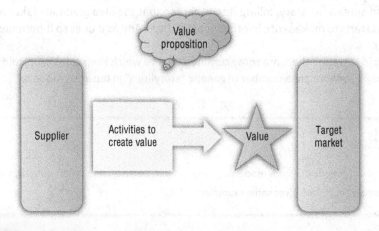

FIGURE 12.1 Outline business model framework

TABLE 12.2   **Examples of Business Models**

Example	Value Proposition?	For Whom?	By Whom – Key Players on Supply Side?	Core Activities to Deliver that Value
Razor blades	Shaving with a fresh sharp blade every time instead of having to sharpen a razor	Men (and later, women)	Manufacturers like Gillette	Design, development, manufacture and distribution of blades, advertising and marketing, etc.
National Health Service (UK)	Healthcare for all; free at the point of delivery	All population (as opposed to healthcare for those who could afford it)	Mobilizes entire medical system of primary and secondary care	Healthcare services
Online banking	24/7 bank opening and ability to operate independent of physical banking offices	Customers unable or unwilling to use "normal" banking hours but who appreciate the convenience; eventually all customers – becomes the dominant model	IT platforms, call center staff, other customer interfaces, back-office systems and providers	Customer service and relationship management
Streaming music services – e.g. Spotify	Rent a huge collection of music and have it available on many mobile devices	Customers keen to access large volume and variety of music and have it available whenever they want it	IT platforms, IP relationship with music providers	Access control, IT distribution and streaming, rights management, rental processing

12.3   Building a Business Model

We can build the model in a simple fashion; first, what is the core value proposition?

Value Proposition

Here, we need to think about the features of the innovation and how it represents something new, which people will value over what they currently have. What differentiates it – what is our "unique selling proposition (USP)?" Why hasn't someone already done this is often a useful question to ask at this stage – we may be reinventing the wheel, or we may be trying to do something which others have found, to their cost, is impossible! But we might also find that things have changed, and we are now able to do something which was previously impossible – for example, the opportunities offered by having GPS positioning in smartphones opens up a whole set of possibilities for location-based services which couldn't have been offered even ten years ago.

Value proposition design is an important first step, and it helps to try and put ourselves in the position of our potential end-user. What does it do for them? A very simple but powerful approach is to ask whether it acts as "pain relief" – in other words, does it make their lives easier in some way? Or does it act as a "delighter" – giving them something they hadn't expected or could never have imagined? In between, there are options around doing something which already exists but is in some way better so that users will prefer it enough to switch.

There are several tools to help with value proposition design, including*:

- Kano method
- Outcome-driven innovation

*Tools available on the book companion website.

- Competitiveness profiling
- Value curves
- Ethnography
- Benchmarking
- Lead user methods

Some examples might help. Typical "pain relief" comes when something is cheaper, faster, easier to use, or solves a problem which they have with an existing product or service. Think about online shopping or banking – it takes away the "pain" of having to go physically to the shop or bank. Importantly, value positions depend on who is valuing them – for many people, the convenience of online shopping makes it a pain relief experience of value. But for some people, the physical activity brings them into contact with others, and there is a sense of shopping as a social activity. They are not likely to value the new idea.

On the "delight" side, think about the smartphone – the idea of a mobile phone was around for a long time, but merging it with all the functionality and design in the early iPhone and its imitators was something which users perceived as so valuable, some of them would queue all night just to get their hands on one.

Target Market

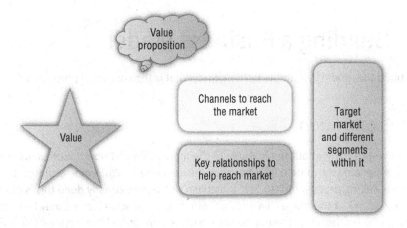

Next, we need to think about the demand side – who is going to value this? It's important here to think about targeting as precisely as we can, for example, not just saying we will offer a bicycle for rent in a big city but specifying for whom – tourists who want to explore, business people who want to avoid congestion of public transport or taxis, etc. And we need to think about how we would reach those people – which channels would we use to find them and make our offer clear to them? Online advertising? Point of sale – advertising stations where the bikes can be found? Newspaper or TV advertising? Then we need to think about how we will interact with them – do we have someone in a stall renting the bikes out personally like a shop, or do we go for an online booking and self-service unlocking model?

In other words, we need to think hard about the specifics of the demand side and how best to make sure the value we are offering in our proposition reaches and is appreciated by the target market.

Creating and Delivering

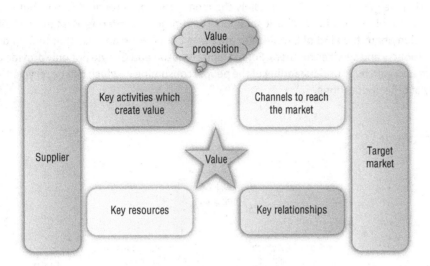

But the offering which we hope they value isn't going to magically appear – we need to create and deliver it. So, we also need to think hard about the supply side – what are the key activities we'd need to do to be able to offer our value proposition? For example, we'd need to purchase or build a fleet of bikes, distribute them around cities, and track them so we know where they are. We'd need to provide for maintaining them and making sure they are available and fit to use – and we'd probably need some kind of emergency response service in case of accidents or breakdowns. We'd certainly need a way of taking money for the bikes! We might not choose to do this all ourselves – we could partner with others – for example, local shops who might offer the bikes and take the money on our behalf, or a local bicycle repair shop who would undertake the maintenance side of things for us. But we'd need to build this network and manage the key relationships in that.

In other words, we need to think equally hard about the specifics of the supply side and how we are going to deliver the best version of our value proposition.

Value Capture

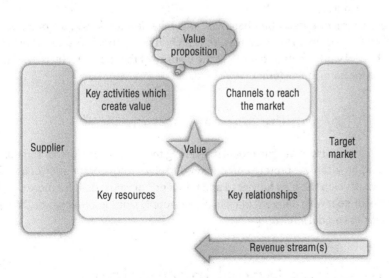

Next, we need to think about how we will capture the value from this – what are the different sources of "revenue" or reward which flow to us from people in our target segment who value what we offer them? This is certainly the money they are prepared to pay, but it might also be information – useful feedback about how to improve our offering. We can also build up information about the kind of people who are using our offering and use that to help design other products and services for them. For example, Amazon and Google not only provide a service but also gain huge understanding of the people consuming it, which can be recycled into a variety of other innovations.

Cost Structure

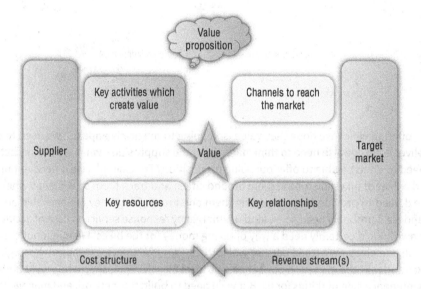

The other side of this equation is, of course, the resources we need to spend – time, energy, money – in creating and delivering our offering. What are these, and how to they break down? How much of them is fixed, and how much varies with the volume of demand? When do these costs kick in – at the start-up stage or through the operation of our model? We also have to think about the timing of these flows and make sure the balance between what we spend and what we get back is positive. We don't want to spend all our resources before we get something back to help refill the tanks!

(The basic structure described here was originally developed as part of an open source project called the Business Model Canvas. You can find more about this, together with videos, cases, and helpful worksheets and tools, at the website of the founders: http://www.business-modelgeneration.com/canvas/bmc).

Sustainability and Resilience

Finally, we need to think about the model in the long term. How easy is it for someone to copy right now, and how can we protect and defend ourselves from competition? Looking ahead, how might we develop the idea further to add new kinds of value, do it for more people on the demand side, or do it with different players on the supply side? In other words, how might we go about business model *innovation*?

12.4 Business Model Innovation

Anyone can have a good idea. What makes successful entrepreneurs stand out is their ability to create a strategic vision – an opportunity and how it can be exploited. In Chapter 4, we looked at a model of "innovation space" and saw that we could explore along a number of dimensions, changing:

- What we offer the world
- How we create and deliver that
- To whom (and the "story'" we tell)

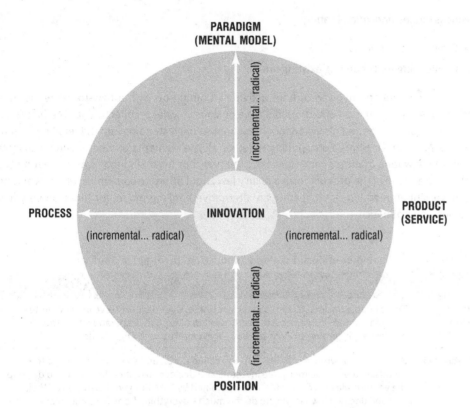

Pulling those elements together into a particular configuration defines what we do – it's our underlying business model. Crucially, we can also *change* this model – replacing, for example, a simple grocer's shop with a supermarket or replacing that with an online service. Or shifting between making or selling a product and renting out the functions which it performs – for example, Rolls Royce no longer selling jet engines but charging customers for the number of useful hours of power which they provide over a thirty-year life. This kind of innovation is our fourth part of the "4Ps" innovation space, essentially changing our mental models about how we create value.

Pivoting the Venture

This process of reviewing and changing business models begins at the very start of any new venture. As we've seen throughout the book, innovation involves uncertainty – we can't predict how our idea will develop and how the story will unfold. Instead, we need to be flexible, adapting and learning as we go through the process. A key concept here is the idea of the pivot – not throwing the idea away at the first sign of trouble but staying with the core principle and moving around that to find a better fit with the context.[1,2]

Successful entrepreneurs learn to pivot by seeing their early steps as experiments, as probes into an uncertain world. They learn and adapt their idea, strengthening it in the light of new information which helps them identify a particular trajectory. For example, YouTube began life as one of many new venture ideas around helping people hook up in relationships. There were plenty of ideas about how to make this happen across an online platform, but when they tested them out, it became clear that one feature in particular – the possibility of sending short video clips of each other – was something the market particularly liked. So, they pivoted around this new information, strengthened that idea, and eventually left the dating application behind to concentrate on what became a huge success. **Table 12.3** gives some other examples of pivoting – changing the business model.

Business Model Sustainability

Business model *innovation* is about:

- Creating new models
- Challenging and changing existing ones

Entrepreneurs are involved in both activities. Coming up with a new-to-the-world idea and making it happen is all about building the business model architecture for the first time. Think about Jeff Bezos and his vision for online bookselling extending into the retailing empire which is Amazon. Or Henry Ford, pulling together all the elements around making a success out of the new idea of motor cars. He wasn't the first, but his main input was in creating the architecture to move the product form a luxury few could afford to something which everyone could. Or Muhammed Yunis, pioneering an alternative banking model for those on very low incomes – microfinance.

TABLE 12.3   **Examples of Business Model Innovation (pivoting) in Start-Ups**

Business	History
Angry Birds	Three people decided to start a games business. Over the next six years they wrote – and abandoned – 51 games and nearly went bankrupt. In desperation, they tried for one last push, writing 10 ideas per day – and came up with Angry Birds.
Instagram	Kevin Systrom wrote a simple HTML app called Burbn and showed a prototype to friends. At a party, he met some investors and decided to quit his job and try to develop the venture. He raised $500,000 and was joined by Mike Krieger; they reviewed their app and decided it was trying to do too much – everything from diary management, hotel, and flight bookings through to photo organizing. They decided to focus on the photo side and prototyped a new app – which people didn't like. So, they went back to Burbn but stripped it down, renamed it Instagram, and eight weeks later, it had attracted 100,000 users and went on to sell for $1 billion two years later.
Air BnB	In 2007, Joe Gebbia and Brian Chesky found themselves in San Francisco unable to pay rent on their apartment. There was a big conference coming to the city and so they decided to rent out three air mattresses on their floor and to offer breakfast to visitors facing the problem of scarce hotel accommodation. They developed a simple website (a blog with maps, called 'Air Bed'n'Breakfast') to help find customers. Two men and a woman turned up, each paying $80 which solved their immediate problem, but it gave them the idea to try and scale this model. They invited a former roommate, Nathan Blecharczyk (a programmer), to join them and set the venture. They hoped to succeed with their model at the 2008 Denver Democratic Convention where there was a similar problem of hotel room shortage – but although they had 800 people listing rooms they didn't make any money.
	To help fund themselves, they ran another business selling breakfast cereal to delegates! Eventually, they raised $20,000 in start-up funding for the room-sharing venture but had learned about the need to modify their original idea – for example, in the area of payments processing. They were earning $200/week and not growing, and they realized part of the problem was the photos of properties they were using were not very attractive. So, they went door-to-door in New York, taking their own pictures and putting them on the website; within a week they had doubled their income. They had another change in direction when that summer, they rented out an entire house instead of just single rooms; the business grew further, and they were able to raise $600,000 in venture funding.
	By 2011, they had further significant investment in their rapidly growing business, and by 2014 it was worth around $10 billion. (Brian and Joe still live in the original apartment which they rented out in 2008.)

But inevitably, once there is a business model out there which seems to be working, other entrepreneurs will look for opportunities around it. They will try to improve upon it, making it cheaper, faster, offering more features, etc.

Think about Michael Dell, who didn't invent the personal computer but found a powerful way of delivering personalized IT solutions at low cost. Or Richard Branson, whose Virgin brand challenged the mainstream world of flying by offering more customer experience. Or Uber, with its challenge to conventional taxi services through applying IT to create what many users see as a more efficient service.

Entrepreneurs may also see a different way of creating and delivering that kind of value – a new business model – which will replace the existing one. (Joseph Schumpeter, the economist who is often seen as the "godfather" of the field of entrepreneurship, uses the phrase "creative destruction" to describe this process.)[3]

Think about Air BnB, which has come to be a dominant player in the accommodation market by using a different business model, based on sharing resources. Or Spotify, which pioneered music streaming as an alternative to purchasing music and allows users to access millions of pieces on a rental basis.

But they may also see a different way of creating and delivering that kind of value – a new business model – which will replace the existing one.

We can see this pattern at the heart of change in any sector. Once a business model is established, there is competition about finding new and modified ways of deploying these – playing with the "4Ps" in terms of streamlining or changing processes, modifying the product/service offering, or changing the positioning in new markets or in the story we tell about our offer.

Entrepreneurship in Action: The Disruptive Business Model of Skype

Skype successfully combined two emerging technologies to create a new service and business model for telecommunications. The two technologies were Voice over Internet Protocol (VoIP) and peer-to-peer (P2P) file sharing. The first allowed the transfer of voice over the Internet, rather than conventional telecommunications networks, and the other exploited the distributed computing power of users' computers to avoid the need for a dedicated centralized server or infrastructure.

Skype was created in 2003 by the Swedish serial entrepreneur, Niklas Zennström. Zennström was previously (in)famous for his pioneering web company Kazaa, which provided a P2P service, mainly used for the (illegal) exchange of MP3 music files. He sold Kazaa to the USA company Sharman Networks to concentrate on the development of Skype. He teamed up with the Dane, Janus Friis, and together they built Skype. Unlike other VoIP firms like Vonage, which charges a subscription for use and is based on proprietary hardware, Skype was available for free download and use for free voice communication between computers. Additional premium pay services were subsequently added, such as Skype-Out to connect to conventional telephones, and Skype-In, to receive conventional calls. The service was made available in 15 different languages covering 165 countries, and partnerships were made with Plantronics (to provide headsets) and Siemens and Motorola (for handsets). Happy users quickly recruited family and friends to the service which grew rapidly.

Given the provision of free software and free calls between computers, the business model had to be innovative. There were several ways in which revenues were generated. The premium services like Skype-In and Skype-Out proved to be very popular with small- and medium-sized firms for business and conference calls, and the licensing of the software to specialist providers and the hardware partnership deals were also lucrative. Later, the large user base also attracted web advertising.

By 2005, there were 70 million users registered, but despite this rapid growth the core model of providing a free service meant that revenues were a more modest $7 million, equivalent to only 10 cents per user. In 2008, Skype had around 310 million registered users – 12 million of which were online at any time. Its revenues were estimated to be $126 million, equivalent to 40 cents per user. This does represent an improvement in financial performance, especially as costs remain low, but the business model remains unproven, except for the founders of Skype. They sold the company to eBay, Inc. in October 2005 for $2.6 billion, with further performance-based bonuses of $1.5 billion by 2009. For eBay, the plan is to use Skype to increase trading turnover by introducing voice bargaining and pay-per-call advertising, and to exploit its previous acquisition PayPal to provide improved billing for Skype customers.

Source: Based on Rao, B., Angelov, B., and Nov, O. (2006). Fusion of disruptive technologies: lessons from the Skype case. *European Management Journal*, 24(2–3), pp. 174–188.

For example, the basic airline business model is that people pay for the service of transportation. Over the years, we have seen competition amongst airlines based on incremental innovations in the service offered – different destinations, different catering, different aircraft, different seating and sleeping options, provisions of lounge accommodation, transportation to/from the terminal, etc.

Process innovations have reduced the costs and improved the flow in areas like check in, reservations, fuel efficiency, terminal turnaround times, etc. Position innovation has segmented the market, first into different classes and experiences and – in recent times – radically opening up the market through low-cost, short-haul flying. And this has led to a paradigm innovation – from being seen as a luxury service for the few, flying has now become the possible mode of travel for the many, rather as Henry Ford changed the earlier transport paradigm with his Model T.

This pattern of innovation involves many different entrepreneurial players. Transatlantic carriers offer flat beds or different customer lounges. Low-cost carriers compete on price, translating their savings through process innovations into lower ticket prices. Niche airlines offer services to remote locations or serving specialist segments – for example, helicopters serving oil platforms.

Entrepreneurship in Action: Business Model Innovation in the Music Industry

Over time, we can see a pattern of occasional breakthroughs in the underlying business model followed by long periods of elaboration – innovation in "doing what we do but better" – around that. For example, the music industry emerged during the early twentieth century when the radio and gramophone made it possible to listen to and own recordings. This dominant model lasted until the late part of the century, where growth in consumer electronics led to the Walkman and other forms of personal music ownership and portability, on a platform of different storage media – cassettes, CDs, etc. The digital revolution and particularly the invention of compression technology around mp3 led to the move into virtual space – and the business model challenge became one of delivering value whilst staying within the bounds of intellectual property rights law! After a period in which various illegal but widely used models proliferated – Napster and beyond – the dominant model became iTunes which orchestrated a very different value network. But that too is being challenged by an alternative business model associated with renting rather than owning music – via online streaming and on-device storage.

CASE STUDY: The Changing Nature of the Music Industry

Read the Case Study_The changing nature of the music industry document in the ebook or from the book companion site.

Sometimes the change comes about by entrepreneurs on the outside looking to challenge, or even disrupt, an existing business model. Sometimes it may involve internal entrepreneurship, changing the organization from within. Think about a pharmaceutical company which spends around 20% of its sales on R&D, funding extensive laboratories and facilities to create new drugs. It pays for testing and approvals, for manufacture and packaging, and for marketing across a global network. People value the health benefits which a drug gives them – and they or the agencies (insurance companies, governments, etc. which represent them) pay for this. The flow of revenue funds the direct costs and also generates a surplus which can be reinvested.

They can invest in refining the business model, adding improvements to make it work better. But they can also change the fundamental approach – as is now beginning to happen in that industry. A combination of rising costs and problems with tight regulatory frameworks have slowed down innovation and reduced the chances of finding blockbuster drugs successfully to market; instead, the model is shifting to one where research is increasingly being carried out by small entrepreneurial labs working in rapidly changing technological fields like genetics and biotechnology.

Once again, we can see the pattern of an established business model being improved and adapted, but at a certain point, a new, competing model comes on the scene to change the whole game. Alan Lafley was the Chief Executive of Procter and Gamble in the late 1990s and oversaw a fundamental shift in their business model. From a well-established company whose strengths had been built on strong emphasis on internal R&D backed up by excellent market research, they shifted to a model called "Connect and Develop" which saw them trying to source 50% of their future innovations from outside the company. Significantly, Lafley called the book he wrote describing the journey "The Game-changer"! [4]

There are plenty of examples of such shifts – for example, companies like Rolls-Royce and Caterpillar moving their business models from selling capital equipment to novel ways of offering the functions as part of a service package, which many of their clients prefer to rent from them. And Amancio Ortega working in a part of Spain with little tradition of textile-making took on the fashion retail industry with his design-led business model of "fast fashion" – the engine behind the success of his company, Inditex, which owns global brands like Zara.

And it's not just in the commercial world that we see this happening. In the human-itarian sector, one of the major challenges has been providing food to people affected by natural and man-made disasters. For a long time, the dominant model was one of collecting, shipping, and distributing food, but recent years have seen a disruptive shift towards giving money to affected people in order for them to procure their own solutions. The process of change has been led by entrepreneurs experimenting with alternative business models.

CASE STUDY: Cash Based Programming in the Food Assistance Sector

Read the Case Study_Cash Based Programming in the Food Assistance Sector document in the ebook or from the book companion site.

Question:

The internet has provided a powerful platform enabling a great deal of business model innovation. Which examples can you think of where an entrepreneur has changed the game through using this platform?

Answer: Table 12.4 gives some examples of business model innovation enabled by entrepreneurs working with the tools of the internet.

TABLE 12.4   **Examples of the Internet as a Route to Business Model Innovation**

Old Model	Internet-Enabled Alternative
Airline and travel booking	Disintermediation – DIY or else via online aggregators
Encyclopedia – expert driven	Wikipedia and open source options
Printing and publishing – physical networks and specialist	Online coordination, self-publishing, long tail, print-on-demand
Retailing – physical presence via shops, distribution centers, etc.	Amazon and online, long-tail effect, database mining, etc.

The Problem of Letting Go

One of the challenges for established organizations – and one of the opportunities for external start-up entrepreneurs – is that business model innovation involves letting go of the past. That's hard to do, especially for companies which have a long history of success based on an established business model.

Entrepreneurship in Action: Problems at Polaroid

Polaroid was a pioneer in the development of instant photography. It developed the first instant camera in 1948, the first instant color camera in 1963, and introduced sonar automatic focusing in 1978. In addition to its competencies in silver halide chemistry, it had technological competencies in optics and electronics, and mass manufacturing, marketing, and distribution expertise. The company was technology-driven from its foundation in 1937, and the founder Edwin Land had 500 personal patents.

When Kodak entered the instant photography market in 1976, Polaroid sued the company for patent infringement and was awarded $924.5 million in damages. Polaroid consistently and successfully pursued a strategy of introducing new cameras, but made almost all its profits from the sale of the film (the so-called razor-blade marketing strategy also used by Gillette), and between 1948 and 1978, the average annual sales growth was 23% and profit growth 17% per year.

Polaroid established an electronic imaging group as early as 1981, as it recognized the potential of the technology. However, digital technology was perceived as a potential technological shift, rather than as a market or business disruption. By 1986, the group had an annual research budget of $10 million, and by 1989, 42% of the R&D budget was devoted to digital imaging technologies. By 1990, 28% of the firm's patents related to digital technologies. Polaroid was therefore well-positioned at that time to develop a digital camera business.

However, it failed to translate prototypes into a commercial digital camera until 1996, by which time there were 40 other companies in the market, including many strong Japanese camera and electronics firms. Part of the problem was adapting the product development and marketing channels to the new product needs. However, other more fundamental problems related to long-held cognitions: a continued commitment to the razor-blade business model and pursuit of image quality. Profits from the new market for digital cameras were derived from the cameras rather than the consumables (film). Ironically, Polaroid had rejected the development of inkjet printers, which rely on consumables for profits, because of the relatively low quality of their (early) outputs. Polaroid had a long tradition of improving its print quality to compete with conventional 35mm film.

Source: Tripsas, M. and Gavetti, G. (2000). Capabilities, cognition, and inertia: evidence from digital imaging. *Strategic Management Journal*, 21, pp. 1147–1161.

Here are some examples of business model innovation strategies – routes along which there might be rich opportunities for entrepreneurs to rewrite the rules of the game.

- User-driven instead of supplier-led, in which the role of active and informed users is re-shaping the trajectory of innovation
- "Servitization," in which manufacturing operations are increasingly being reframed as service offerings – the aircraft engine maker, Rolls-Royce, redefined its business model as "power by the hour" recognizing that what its customers actually valued was the provision of power, not the engines themselves; they now charge users for usable hours of power. Chemical companies are increasingly looking to provide rental models in which they offer services to support the effective use of their products rather than simply delivering bulk chemicals
- Rent not own, in which the value proposition moves to making the functionality available rather than the asset; for example, people are beginning to move to renting music via streaming services like Spotify rather than needing to buy record collections, whilst in city centers the idea of bicycle and even car rental is displacing the need for ownership

Entrepreneurship in Action: Business Model Innovation

For many years, Costas Markides at London Business School has been researching the links between strategy, innovation, and firm performance. In recent work, he argues for the need to make a clearer distinction between the technological and market aspects of disruptive innovations and to pay greater attention to business model innovation.

By definition, business model innovation enlarges the existing value of a market, either by attracting new customers or by encouraging existing customers to consume more. Business model innovation does not require the discovery of new products, services, or technology, but rather the redefinition of existing products and services and how these are used to create value.

For example, Amazon did not invent book selling, and low-cost airlines such as Southwest and easyJet are not pioneers of air travel. Such innovators tend to offer different product or service attributes to existing firms which emphasize different value propositions. As a result, business model innovation typically requires different and often conflicting systems, structures, processes, and value chains to existing offerings.

However, unlike the claims made for disruptive innovations, new business models can coexist with more mainstream approaches. For example, internet banking and low-cost airlines have not displaced the more mainstream approaches, but have captured around 20% of the total demand for these services. Also, while many business model innovations are introduced by new entrants, which have none of the legacy systems and products of incumbent firms, the more mainstream firms may simply choose not to adopt the new business models as they make little sense for them. Alternatively, they may make other innovations to create or recapture customers.

Sources: Markides, C. (2006). Disruptive innovation: in need of a better theory. *Journal of Product Innovation Management*, 23, pp. 19–25; Markides, C. (2004). *Fast Second: How Smart Companies Bypass Radical Innovation to Enter and Dominate New Markets*. San Francisco: Jossey-Bass.

Chapter Summary

- Innovation is about using change to create value, and business models provide a way of articulating and mapping the ways in which this process happens

- A robust business model should set out the value proposition, the target market, the supply side, and the cost and revenue aspects; building the model will be the focus of much discussion, but this helps ensure that innovation proposals are robust and well thought out

- Business cases represent the stories which can be told based on a clear business model about the need for and likely benefits of innovation

- We can map the benefits from changes in products/service offerings, process changes, or position innovations on a business model framework

- But changing the business model itself is also a powerful source of innovation, especially since it often involves changing the underlying system/architecture rather than just the components

- Business model *innovation* is about:
  - Creating new models
  - Challenging and changing existing ones

  Entrepreneurs are involved in both activities.

Key Terms

Business case   a framework for summarizing the core innovation idea and how it will be developed

Business model   an explanation of how value is created for customers

Business model innovation   creating new models or changing existing ones

Cost structure   a list of the various elements of costs which will be incurred in delivering the value proposition

Revenue stream   a list of all the possible sources and mechanisms through which resources flow back into the venture

Servitization   an example of business model innovation in which manufacturing organizations increasingly shift their approach to providing services wrapped around their core product offering

Value proposition   a statement of what the end user/customer will value and which differentiates your offer from others

References

[1] Ries, E. (2011). *The Lean Startup: How Today's Entrepreneurs Use Continuous Innovation to Create Radically Successful Businesses.* New York: Crown.

[2] Blank, S. (2013). Why the lean start-up changes everything. *Harvard Business Review*, 91(5), pp. 63–72.

[3] Schumpeter, J. (2006). *Capitalism, Socialism and Democracy.* 6th ed. London: Routledge.

[4] Lafley, A. and Charan, R. (2008). *The Game-changer.* New York: Profile.

CHAPTER 13

Learning to Manage Entrepreneurship

LEARNING OBJECTIVES

By the end of this chapter you will have:

1. Reviewed and consolidated the key themes in the book.

2. Explored the importance of managing "intelligent" failure.

3. Looked at learning as a process of reflection and concept-building.

4. Practiced using an "audit" approach to guide learning and capability building around entrepreneurship skills.

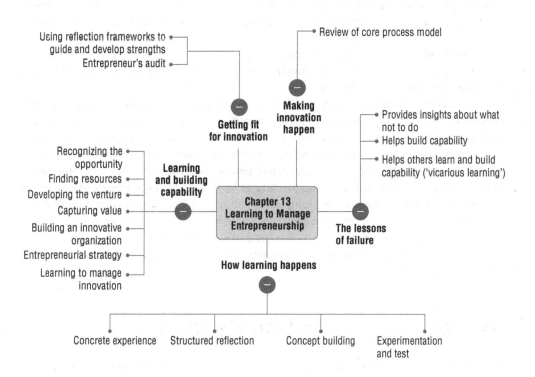

13.0   Introduction

Innovation matters. Unless established organizations are prepared and able to change themselves and what they offer the world, there is a clear risk that they won't survive or grow. Creating new ventures is now recognized as an increasingly important source of economic and employment growth and a powerful engine for social change. But innovation doesn't just happen – it's not simply flash of inspiration or a "Eureka!" moment. Creating value from ideas takes time and effort channeled across a process, a journey from initial idea to its successful implementation and diffusion.

The energy and passion which drives through the process is *entrepreneurship* – the seeing of opportunities and making them real. It is clearly involved in a start-up where a new business requires individuals/a small group to channel their creative energy and drive to make something new. But it's also needed in an established company where renewal comes through stimulating and enabling the same drive and creativity to deliver both a stream of improvement innovations and the occasional inspired leap, which helps reinvent the business. And increasingly, such drive, energy, and enthusiasm is being harnessed to more than economic growth – in start-ups and established organizations where the challenges of sustainability are being picked up. Social entrepreneurship is literally about changing the world – but it uses the same basic engine.

This process works all across the economy – whether we are talking about cars, clothes, or silicon chips. It isn't confined to manufacturing – it works just as powerfully for the services that make up the majority of most economies – banks, insurance companies, shops, and airlines all have to look hard and often at the innovation challenge if they are to stay ahead.

For public services and in social enterprises, the same is true – but we begin to see that it isn't always money which drives the entrepreneurial wheels. Here, innovation is targeted at improving education, saving lives, making people more secure, and addressing other basic needs. And whilst some innovation is about taking costs and waste out of established service delivery processes, much is about coming up with new and better ways of improving the quality of human life. Whether in a start-up or across a large public-sector department, there is a strong thread of social entrepreneurship running throughout, driven less by a desire for profits than literally wanting to change the world.

Innovation is about uncertainty – but it isn't unmanageable. Experience suggests that it is possible to repeat the trick, to capture lessons about how to make the journey, and use those to help guide the next one. "Serial entrepreneurs" are not born lucky but have held on to the hard-won lessons of experience and used that knowledge in their next ventures. Organizations delivering a regular stream of new products and services do so because they have embedded the same lessons in their structures and procedures for innovation. Experience is often a harsh teacher – many of the lessons come through failure, through understanding what doesn't work. But "intelligent failure" – the ability to capture the essence of what went wrong and use that to design better approaches for the future – is a key part of building entrepreneurial skills.

So how might we use these lessons to review and strengthen our capability? That's the purpose of this final chapter.

13.1   Making Innovation Happen

It's worth reminding ourselves again of the core process model which we have been using – our roadmap for the entrepreneurial journey (See **Figure 13.1**). By now, you'll appreciate that this is a very simple sketch describing a complex process, but at least it helps us remember the key stages involved.

We know that this process is influenced along the way by several things which can help or hinder it – for example, having a clear sense of direction (an innovation strategy) or working within a creative network of players. We looked particularly at some of the levers we could use as architects and managers of the process. For example, how can an entrepreneur channel his or her energy, passion, and idea in such a way that it motivates others and gets them to "buy into" the vision? How can we construct innovative organizations which allow creative ideas to

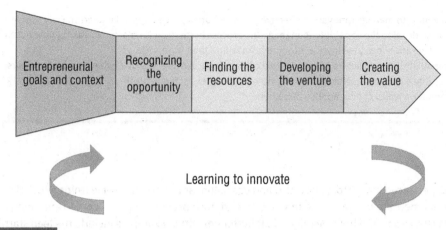

FIGURE 13.1   A model of the entrepreneurial process

come through, let people build on and share knowledge, and feel motivated and rewarded for doing so? How can we harness the power of networks, making rich and extensive connections, to deliver a stream of innovations?

Anyone can get lucky once – but if we are going to be able to repeat the trick, then we need to acquire and practice the skills of entrepreneurship. Nobody starts with a perfect set of these. We learn and adapt our approach, building capability through a process of trial and error, gradually improving our skills as we find what works for us.

We need to recognize the importance of failure in this. Innovation is all about trying new things out, and they may not always work. Experimentation, testing, prototyping, and pivoting are all part and parcel of the innovation story, and it is through this process that we gradually build capability.

13.2   The Lessons of Failure

Most smart innovators recognize that failure comes with the innovation territory. *"You can't make an omelette without breaking eggs"* is as good a motto as any to describe a process which by its very nature involves experimentation and learning.

It's impossible to predict how a market will react, how technologies will behave, and how new business models will gain acceptance, so the approach is one of experimentation around a core idea. Feedback from carefully designed experiments allows the venture to pivot, to move around the core focus to get closer to the viable idea which will work.

The problem is not with failure – innovations will often fail since they are experiments, steps into the unknown. It's with failing to *learn* from those experiences.

The Value of Failure

Read The value of failure document in the ebook or from the book companion site.

Question:

Why might failure be an important and valuable thing in innovation?

Answer: Failure is important in at least three ways in innovation:

- It provides insights about what not to do. In a world where you are trying to pioneer something new, there are no clear paths, and instead, you have to cut and hack your own way through the jungle of uncertainty. Inevitably, there is a risk that the direction you chose was wrong, but that kind of "failure" helps identify where not to work – and this focusing process is an important feature in innovation.

- Failure helps build capability – learning how to manage innovation effectively comes from a process of trial and error. Only through this kind of reflection and revision can we develop the capability to manage the process better next time around. Taking time out to review projects is a key factor in this – if we are honest, we learn a lot more from failure than from success.
- Failure helps others learn and build capability. Sharing failure stories – a kind of "vicarious learning" – provides a road map for others, and in the field of capability-building, that's important. Not for nothing do most business schools teach using the case method – stories of this kind carry valuable information which can be applied elsewhere.

Experienced innovators know this and use failure as a rich source of learning. Most of what we've learned about managing innovation and entrepreneurship has come from analyzing what went wrong and how we might do it better next time. Examples include the lean start-up approach, Robert Cooper's work on stage gates, NASA's development of project management tools, Toyota's understanding of the minute trial-and-error learning loops which their *kaizen* system depends upon, and which have made it the world's most productive car-maker.[1,2] Google's philosophy is all about "*perpetual beta*" – not aiming for perfection but allowing for learning from its innovation. And IDEO, the successful design consultancy, has a slogan which underlines the key role that learning through prototyping plays in their projects – "*fail often, to succeed sooner!*"

Rather than seeing failure as a problem, we should see it as an important resource – as long as we learn from it. So, it might be helpful to pause for a moment and think about how individuals and organizations learn?

13.3 How Learning Happens

The psychologist David Kolb developed a simple model of learning which is worth bringing in here – he used it to talk about how adults learn, but we can adapt it to think of entrepreneurs and organizations.[3] **Figure 13.2** gives a simple illustration.

The model suggests that learning is not simply about acquiring new knowledge – it is a cycle with a number of stages. It doesn't matter where we enter, but only when the whole cycle is complete does learning take place. So, to enable effective learning about how to manage innovation better we need to:

- Capture and reflect on our experiences, trying to distill patterns from them about what works and doesn't work
- Create models of how the world works (concepts) and link these to those we already have
- Using our revised models engage again in innovation, trying new things out

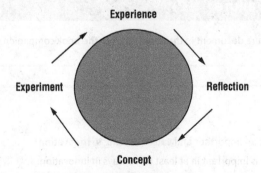

FIGURE 13.2 Simple model of David Kolb's learning cycle

Source: Adapted from Kolb, D.A. (1984). *Experiential Learning: Experience as the Source of Learning and Development.* Upper Saddle River, NJ: Prentice Hall.

There are many ways we can help this process, for example:

- Rather than simply stepping back for a reflective pause, we could employ some structured question frameworks; we could ask others to help us in the process, acting as critical and challenging partners to help us learn
- We can develop our own concepts, but we can also use, adapt, and try out new ideas developed elsewhere; the "theory" of innovation and entrepreneurship has emerged from many experiences codified into a rich body of knowledge, and this is available to draw upon – we don't have to reinvent the wheel
- Similarly, we don't have to make all the mistakes ourselves – we can learn from other's experiences

There is growing interest in planned experimentation and learning as a key framework for developing entrepreneurial ventures. Concepts like "agile software development" and "lean start-up" essentially build on the idea of setting up high frequency versions of the above learning cycle so that organizations can quickly learn and adapt their ideas, enhancing the chances of succeeding in innovation. Rather than a master plan, they seek to develop the capability for fast learning.[4]

13.4 Learning and Building Capability

Let's go back to our core process model and try to frame some useful reflective questions for individual and organizational entrepreneurs.

We can ask ourselves some key reflection questions around each stage – and we explore some examples in the following section:

Recognizing the Opportunity

How well do we:

- Explore the technology space – finding opportunities but also check who else is doing it?
- Explore market space – finding out if there is a market and how big, how fast it's growing, etc. How do we find out about competitors real and potential and about barriers to entry?
- Explore what others are doing – who else is or could be playing, and could we learn from them?
- Explore future space – do we look ahead at how threats and opportunities might develop and affect both technical and market space?
- Explore with others – do we bring different stakeholders into the process, using their perspectives and ideas to enrich the variety and generate new directions?

Finding the Resources

How well do we:

- Know which resources we will need to take our opportunity forward
- Plan ahead to identify the resources which we will need – and work out where and how we will get those we don't have
- Identify who else we will need to help us take things forward
- Find partners and build rich networks to enable us to access wider resources
- Build contingency plans – what if we can't get access to these key resources? What other routes can we take to exploit this opportunity?
- Learn from how others have obtained resources

Developing the Venture

How well have we thought through:

- How we will manage the project from our initial idea to full-scale launch?
- Who will we need to involve, and how will their involvement be timed?
- Is there a clear project plan with a timeline and plans for resources – especially cash flow – throughout the life of the project?
- Do we have criteria for stopping the project if it is going seriously off-track?
- How will we know how well we are doing in terms of project progress? When and how will we review?
- Do we have contingency plans – what if something goes unexpectedly wrong or happens late?

Capturing Value

Have we thought about how to:

- Capture and appropriate the benefits from our venture
- Protect our intellectual property
- Spread, diffuse, and scale our idea
- Develop our business model further to ensure it remains sustainable
- Ensure long-term viability of the venture – next stages of growth or exit
- Capture learning from the experience

Entrepreneurial Strategy – Having a Clear Sense of Direction

Innovation requires a clear sense of direction, otherwise our journey is going to take us nowhere. Having a clear innovation strategy is essential for success. How far have we thought about questions like these:

- Do we have a clear and concise "story" which we can share with others about our idea?
- Where will we be in a year's time, and how will we know whether or not we have succeeded?
- What comes next if things go well, and what will we do to grow or develop the venture further?
- Can we "paint a picture," make our idea come alive for others to see and share what excites us about what we are trying to do?
- Is there a clear road map for how we will get from our idea and exciting vision today to making that dream a reality next year?

Building an Innovative Organization

We've seen throughout the book that innovation isn't a solo act but a multi-player game. So, we also need to think hard about the kind of organization we build to help take our venture forward, and in particular:

- Have we got the key skills and resources which we need to make the venture succeed?
- Have we identified the key people who will help us achieve our vision?

- How will we motivate them – how will we get them to "buy in" to what we are trying to do?
- How will we handle conflicts and disagreements?
- How will we take decisions and make sure everyone sticks to what is decided even if they don't agree?
- How will we communicate and keep everyone in the loop?
- How will we make sure teams perform as greater than the sum of the individual parts rather than less?

Learning to Manage Innovation

Looking back on the project (whether it succeeded or failed):

- What could we do more of (because it helped)?
- What could we do less of or even stop doing (because it didn't work, slowed things down, or in some other way blocked the project)?
- What new/different things might we try?
- What advice would we give to someone else about to start a new venture, based on what we have learned?
- What three key "do's" and three key "don'ts" would we take away from this venture and apply to our next one?
- What have we learned?

13.5 | Getting Fit for Innovation

Learning isn't easy – individuals and organizations are usually too busy getting on with building and running their ventures to find time to stop and think about how they might do things better. But assuming they did manage to get offline and reflect on how they might improve, then the kind of questions we've been looking at would provide a useful starting point.

We can use the idea of comparing against what we've learned about good practice to develop simple "audit" frameworks which could be used for diagnosis. How well do we do things compared to what the "good practice" is? Where are our strengths? Where would we want to focus our efforts to improve the organization? This kind of audit and review process doesn't carry any prizes, but it can help with making the organization more effective in the ways it deals with the innovation challenge. And that might lead to some pretty important outcomes – like survival or growth!*

We can develop many different reflection frameworks dealing with different aspects of innovation and entrepreneurship.[†] Some of these look at the whole process in general terms, and some look at individual skills and capabilities. Some focus on capabilities to manage the more radical end of innovation, and some deal with sector differences, like how to manage innovation in services. There are those which focus on aspects of the organization – like how well it is able to engage its whole workforce in the innovation process.

The purpose of using them is the same – to help us focus the learning process and develop our skills and capabilities. It's not the audit frameworks so much as using them in the *process* of questioning and developing our capability which matters. As the quality guru, W. Edwards Deming, pointed out, "If you don't measure it you can't improve it!"

---

*Additional examples of frameworks are available via the book companion website
[†]Related activities can be found in the print workbook.

13.6 Managing Entrepreneurship

Success isn't about luck – but there is probably some truth to the old saying attributed to various famous sportsmen and women: "The more I practice, the luckier I get!" Entrepreneurship is about managing a structured and focused process, engaging and deploying creativity throughout but also balancing this with an appropriate degree of control. No organization or individual starts out with this – it's essentially something they learn and develop over time. This learning can come through trial and error, but it can also come through learning from others and building on their hard-won experience. It can come through using tools and models to help understand and engage with managing innovation more effectively. We hope that the lessons we've tried to capture in the book provide some helpful input to this process.

Chapter Summary

- Wherever innovation happens – big firm, small firm, start-up business, social enterprise – one thing is clear. Successful innovation won't happen simply by wishing for it. This complex and risky process of transforming ideas into something which makes a mark needs organizing and managing in strategic fashion.

- Entrepreneurship provides the drive, the motive power behind innovation. But force alone won't make effective change, and many entrepreneurs fail. Those who succeed – and especially those who do so repeatedly – understand that innovation is a process to be understood and managed.

- It's a generic process, running through four core stages – recognizing opportunities, finding resources, developing the venture, and capturing the value.

- We know that this process is influenced along the way by several things which can help or hinder it. Is there clear strategic leadership and direction? How can we construct innovative organizations which allow creative ideas to come through, let people build on and share knowledge, and feel motivated and rewarded for doing so? How can we harness the power of networks, making rich and extensive connections to deliver a stream of innovations?

- A wide range of structures, tools, and techniques exist for helping think about and manage these elements of the innovation process. The challenge is to adapt and use them in a particular context – essentially, a learning process.

- Developing innovative capability needs to begin with an audit of where we are now, and there are many ways of asking and exploring the core questions:

  ○ Do we have a clear process for making innovation happen and effective enabling mechanisms to support it?

  ○ Do we have a clear sense of shared strategic purpose, and do we use this to guide our innovative activities?

  ○ Do we have a supportive organization whose structures and systems enable people to be creative and share and build on each other's creative ideas?

  ○ Do we build and extend our networks for innovation into a rich open innovation system?

Key Terms

Agile innovation approach which stresses progress through a series of short learning cycles rather than a single "master" plan for innovation

Innovation audit structured review of innovation capability across an organization

Innovation strategy statement of how innovation is going to take the business forward and why

Innovation strategy deployment communicating and enabling people to use the framework, sharing the vision

Lean start-up approach originally developed around software innovation which involves developing a venture through a series of short, fast-learning cycles of experimentation and review

Learning cycle a model of how organizations and individuals learn

References

[1] Cooper, R. (2001). *Winning at New Products*. 3rd ed. London: Kogan Page.

[2] Monden, Y. (1983). *The Toyota Production System*. Cambridge, MA: Productivity Press.

[3] Kolb, D. and Fry, R. (1975). Towards a theory of applied experiential learning. In Cooper, C. (ed). *Theories of Group Processes*. Chichester: John Wiley & Sons, Ltd.

[4] Morris, L., Ma, M., and Wu, P. (2014). *Agile Innovation: The Revolutionary Approach to Accelerate Success, Inspire Engagement, and Ignite Creativity*. New York: John Wiley & Sons, Ltd.

Index